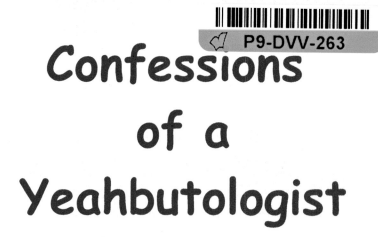

Confessions of a Yeahbutologist

A Memoir of
Dealing With Faith Quandaries

Dave R. Garwick

This book is a work of personal memory, to the best of the author's recollection.

For information contact the author at loonkk11@gmail.com

Book and Cover design by Mike Foley

ISBN: 9781727788891

First Edition: October 2019

9781727788891

TABLE OF CONTENTS

PART II MAKING A YEAHBUTOLOGIST

PART III THE WAY I THINK

PART V   WHEN I DON'T HAVE A CLUE

PART VI THE REASON I FOLLOW CHRIST

First Off

DEFINITIONS

"YEAHBUTOLOGIST" Noun. A person who invariably responds with, "Yeah, but …" As in, "Yeah, but … what about this question?" Always used as a response. Sometimes used with the adverbial phrase "what if." As in, "Yeah, but …. what if …?" or "Yeah, but …. how come?" Etymology: the syntactic conflation of "yeah" and "but" with the "ologist" suffix intended to lend intellectual credibility to a concept coined by the author of this volume and used by no other self-respecting writer before the date of this publication. Or, probably, after. Especially in the hereafter.

APOLOGIES

May the reader forgive the author for ignoring the advice of one medieval Rabbi Menachem Mendel Morgensztern who also apparently ignored his own advice when he said,

All that is thought should not be said,
All that is said should not be written,
All that is written should not be published,
And all that is published should not be read.

DEDICATION

This book is dedicated to our grandsons Oliver and Charlie who are the reason I write this book, my humble effort in this seductive culture to guard their Christian faith and our hope of joyous eternal life together.

ACKNOWLEDGMENTS

The first thanks goes to my long-suffering companion in all things. My wife, Ann, patiently and graciously listens night after night after night to my latest musings and then oh-ever-so-gently offers bite-sized morsels of editorial medicine. And forgiveness.

And what man could be so blessed as to have both of his sons-in-law contribute to his hobby? Michael Childe was an eagle-eyed proof reader and Karl Oberjohn was the one who on the back cover photographed the author talking yet another person to death.

Throughout this project, as they always have been, my daughters Kirsten Childe and Karen Oberjohn always have been the cheerleaders of this father. Even as they sometimes roll their eyes at the things that come out of his mouth. Or keypad.

I owe a special debt of gratitude to my brother-in-law Mike Foley who developed the cover art.

I have also been blessed with the honest feedback of many friends:
Rick Shenk
Nina Olsen
Ron Wipf
Greg Donnelly
Becky KenKnight
Meg Newswanger
Linda Boyadjis
Marge Hanson

Introduction

 FOOLS WALK WHERE ANGELS
FEAR TO TREAD

I FLATTER MYSELF INTO THINKING that I see some of myself in
my young grandsons.

In a moment, I'll introduce you to the nine-year-old. But it's
the six-year-old who, like his grandpa, is sometimes known to
live dangerously. My daughter and son-in-law looked as if six-
year-old Charlie had just smacked them in the face with a
pancake. Nine-year-old big brother had a tentative smile that
kind of said, "Oh boy. Now what?" He may have been looking
for the nearest door.

Not Charlie, the only one at the table with no observable reaction. He still wasn't looking up from the serious work of coloring his placemat at the pancake house. All the serving staff and most of the customers were wearing their Minnesota Vikings jerseys. That's because the Vikings were playing on this day. And it's not just that they were playing, but they were taking on the Green Bay Packers. In Minnesota and Wisconsin, that is legendary, big-time stuff. Our kids' household is a stronghold of fanatic Vikings loyalty. They all have Vikings jerseys. At the table, I was commenting on the loyal fanaticism of Minnesota Vikings fans.

Without taking his eyes off his coloring placemat, Charlie simply adds, "Not me. I'm a Packers fan."

One more comment without looking up: "I don't like the Vikings."

I have never seen coffee turn so cold, so fast.

A week later, cousin Nina asked Charlie if we should get him his own Packers jersey. Again, matter-of-factly, he drives one more nail into the family tree. "Yeah, Packers are best. But any team is OK. Just not the Vikings." Where does he come up with this stuff?! Days that will live in infamy. Like the olde saying, "Fools walk where angels fear to tread." Except that Charlie is no fool: when he pokes a tiger in the eye with a stick, he knows exactly what he's doing.

That's more than can be said about what his grandfather did the first time that I offered a commentary on a Vikings-Packer game. This would be the second-closest time I ever came to getting my glasses busted as a pastor. As I did every year, I had been visiting our congregation's college students throughout the five-state area. I was returning home from a whole week on the road. That will be my excuse for what happened next. I pulled off the highway to gas up at the end of an afternoon – an afternoon when the Minnesota Vikings had just beaten the

Green Bay Packers. It's important to mention that this particular gas station happened to be in Wisconsin.

I didn't realize that during football season, everyone in Wisconsin thinks they're from Green Bay. So when I went in to pay for the gas, I noticed all the Packer merchandise. I might have been road-weary and perhaps a little punchy, but I just couldn't resist. To lighten up the defeated looking cashier, I think I said something like, "You can still sell this stuff?" I might not have actually said "stuff." But I was smiling, friendly like.

I can't repeat his end of the conversation, other than to say that he clearly invited me to exit the store before he did something to my teeth. When I explained that I hadn't yet paid for the gas, he kind of repeated what he had just said. This time, he added other parts of my body to his plans. He actually leaned over the counter to get my attention. He got it. And I got a free tank of gas. There must have been a decent bone in his body, after all, because he didn't call the Wisconsin State Patrol to report a Minnesota driver skipping off without paying for the gas. So, long before Charlie, I too had walked where angels fear to tread. I like to think that maybe he gets some of that from me.

There is a part of me which feels that writing a book like this might be another exercise of a fool walking where angels fear to tread. How is it even possible for a pastor, of all people, to even BE a yeahbutologist? But I stand in the same line that includes Jesus' hand-picked apostle, Thomas. And way up ahead of me is John the Baptist whom God hand-picked to prepare the way for the arrival of Jesus.

ALBERT AND I

WITH APOLOGIES TO THE GREAT MAN, I have always identified a little bit with Albert Einstein. A very little bit.

To those who are familiar with my apparent I.Q. on some things, my comparison here may come as a bit of a surprise. To those who have had to duck some of my offhand remarks, maybe not so much of a surprise. The great scientist also had a way of surprising people by some of the things he said. Like E=mc2. Or this one: "Do not worry about YOUR difficulties in mathematics. I can assure you mine are still greater." That particular remark took me off-guard until I recognized the same thing about myself. It is what I study most deeply that leads to my yeahbutology.

I suspect that in any field, the most profound questions often come from those who are deepest into the subject. The toughest faith questions can come from those who are theologically trained. By virtue of my professional training and role, it has been my business to know the challenges and alternatives to just about every notion of faith. I have been blessed with the ability to seek and often see the other point of view. So I can usually appreciate how just about anything can make sense.

But those same blessings have sometimes also fed the curse of quandary. Sometimes, from a purely human rational perspective, the challenges can make as much or more sense to me than the official line of thinking which I have promised to uphold. This is nothing new to me, anymore than it was to Einstein himself. Or maybe to some of you who also struggle with some seriously disturbing challenge about something or someone you know a lot about which also means the world to you.

MY VERY OWN PRIVATE FLAT EARTH SOCIETY

BY THE TIME I WAS ELEVEN YEARS OLD, I had a lot of experience with smoke screens.

That's part of why I had squeezed myself up onto the back shelf of my folks' black and white 1957 Ford Fairlane. I'd been doing that sort of thing for most of my life. Well, at least as long as I could remember. Which at that age hadn't been all that long. Half a lifetime earlier, when I had been a lot smaller, we had lived in San Francisco. I had gotten into the habit of tucking myself up on to the back shelf behind the back seat. I would lie on my back, totally surrounded by blue sky and glass, and look straight up at the massive tubular spans arching to the skies as we crossed the Golden Gate Bridge every week or so.

Those were the years of living dangerously, before child safety laws and even seat belts. It turns out that what was most dangerous in that car was the blue haze of my parents' second-hand cigarette smoke which was always burning my little lungs. That's what I was always trying to get away from on the back shelf of that rolling gas chamber. Actually, though, my folks may well have done me a health favor in the long run since their noxious second-hand smoke was the reason I myself was never interested in taking up the habit.

The smoke got worse when we moved to the frigid Midwest where it seemed the car windows were rolled up tight much of the year. By this time, my shelf-life had expired because I had outgrown the tight space. I had long since given up the futility of thinking that I could ever escape the smoke. So I simply imagined that I was breathing fresh air by looking up to the sky through the back window.

On this particular occasion, there was another reason for my back window rubber-necking. According to the historical records, it must have been about 8:30 in the morning on May 5, 1961. I have no idea why I wasn't in school at that hour because that was a Friday.

Like all other people in the United States, we were listening to the radio during the launch of America's very first astronaut into orbit. He was my first real-life super hero and his name was Alan Shepard. All listeners across the nation were holding their breaths as the famous radio broadcaster Walter Cronkite narrated the whole event live. Everyone was excited to know what our guy would be seeing up there for the first time.

They kept saying that: "first time." This was the first time this, the first time that, the first time something else. Then it hit me. As I listened to the blast-off, it occurred to me that if this was the first guy to go beyond this planet, then that must mean that no one had ever actually seen the Earth. So, as I watched the stationary clouds above the trees that were whizzing past us, I got to thinking: YEAH, BUT what if the Earth turns out to be flat, after all?

Actually, like every other space thing in those early days of yesteryear, the Soviet Union had beaten us to that punch. Just a few months earlier, it had sent the really, really first man into orbit. Obviously, nothing had been said about that cosmonaut seeing a flat Earth. On the other hand, nobody ever believed what the Commies said, anyway. Even we kids knew that our government always told the truth and Russia only did propaganda.

For example, when Russia blasted Yuri Gagarin into orbit, it was God that grabbed the headlines of what he saw. Nikita

Khrushchev, the dictator of the atheist state, said that when Gagarin looked out the window of his space capsule, what he did not see was God. (Gagarin's closest friends later claimed that no such comment had been made by the Russian Orthodox cosmonaut. In fact, Gagarin had had his daughter baptized the day before his space flight).

Long before I was eleven years old, I had learned the hard way that grown-ups didn't always get everything right. What if the experts had gotten this all wrong? I, like everyone else, had been taught kitchen wisdom like, "the proof is in the pudding" and "seeing is believing." No one had ever actually seen the Earth, and now an American was seeing it for the first time. So, I thought, what if he does not actually see what everyone expects him to see? Would that mean that everything else would have to be wrong as well – all that math and science? Apparently, that car trip must have taken a little while for us to get where we were going.

 WHAT GOES AROUND ....

NOW FOR MY NINE-YEAR-OLD GRANDSON, OLIVER. Fifty-seven years after that orbit, early on a summer morning, I am on Thursday duty with the privilege of taking care of my six-year-old and nine-year-old grandsons. I'm making their favorite breakfast of french toast glazed doughnuts drizzled with melted milk chocolate, each garnished with two little sausages, beside bottles of strawberry skim milk. They were happily playing a board game in the living room. I had just been disinvited with the caution that, "It's a pretty complicated game, grandpa. Lots of rules. Maybe after you watch us play for an hour, you can play."

That's why I was in the kitchen. I know my place. I thought my timing was perfect. I was just putting on the finishing culinary touches when I heard their giggles begin to unravel into increasingly angry charges and counter-charges of cheating. Right on schedule. When I walked into the battle zone, six-year-old Charlie was poised with a small, light-weight mesh trash basket held like a weapon over his head. Older brother Ollie was yelling threats. Trying to interrupt the escalation with a little lightness, I said, "Before you kill each other, your french toast doughnuts are ready!"

Charlie stopped in mid-motion with a grin and Ollie screamed, "He's trying to kill me!"

I tried to blow it off with a wave of the hand, "C'mon, you guys are both horsing around and he's not going to kill you. Breakfast is ready!"

Charlie hopped right to the table and Ollie stormed past it and right to his room, slamming the door. Three times. Just to make sure his hearing-aided grandpa could hear. Charlie did not look up while he quietly enjoyed his breakfast.

Behind the doors of his self-imposed exile, Ollie continued to rage at the injustices of life about which nobody, especially his grandpa, seemed to care. I decided to let the volcano blow itself out. When I did not respond, he eventually ventured out of his room for a more direct, face-to-face confrontation.

He took his place in front of his cold breakfast and sobbed through spasms of air-gulping, "And now I'm probably going to starve to death because I'm too upset to eat, and last night I only ate a little bit of supper and before that I hardly had anything to eat for lunch, and I think I have a cut or something inside my nose and it really hurts."

"Well," I said, "that's probably good news there since you don't have to eat through your nose."

He stopped sobbing and gave that a moment of thought. "Well, yeah, but I won't be able to breathe and I'll probably suffocate while I'm eating!" The new threat to his survival started the tears again.

"Except for one thing," I said. "Nobody can breathe while they're eating. Otherwise, you'd choke on food going down your wind-pipe. You're OK."

Once again, this interrupted the spasms of sadness as he sought another angle of apocalypse. He held up the pointer finger of discovery and said, "But I haven't eaten hardly anything for fifteen days."

In my mother's worst moments of frustration, she used to curse me with the wish that someday I would be blessed with offspring who would do to me what I did to her. She dubbed me The Crepe Hanger, the doom-slinger who specialized in draping the black crepe paper of pessimism over everything that went wrong. Even though she was now long gone, her curse was coming round. I have to admit that even though I am not a Buddhist, thoughts of karma were dancing in my head. On more than one level here, I think God must have a sense of humor.

So I thought this would be a good time to bring God into the discussion. "Again, you're fortunate," I said, "because when Jesus was in the wilderness, he didn't eat for forty days and HE survived. Let's see, forty minus fifteen means you've got at least, what, thirty days yet before you've got to worry about starving to death."

Again, the sobbing paused while he checked the math on his fingers. "Yeah," said Ollie, "but he was God. He could do anything." This boy was definitely bone of my bone and flesh of my flesh. He had inherited not only my genes for the dramatic but also my genes for the philosophical.

Game on. "Yeah," I said, "but they say that even though he was totally God, he was also totally human. Did you know that he even got so upset that he cried and once he even got mad at God for letting him get hurt on the cross?" Check.

And mate. "Yeah, but grandpa," he wailed, "your job is to keep Charlie from killing me!"

Had I just seen the first tender sprout of a yeahbutologist?

PART I

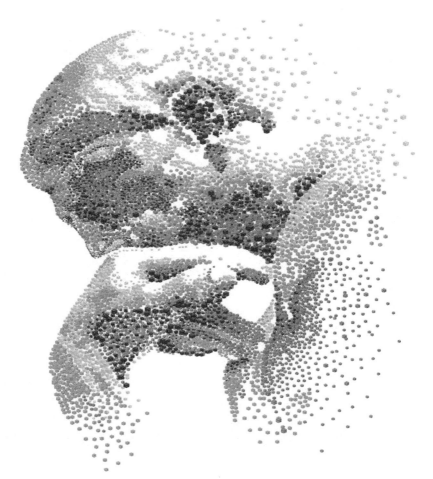

READ BEFORE YOU READ

Chapter One

Maybe You Should Not Read This Book Right Now

My Patient's Last Words

MY FIRST CAREER WAS AS A speech and language pathologist. I spent a fair amount of time working in hospitals, usually with patients who had brain problems like strokes and tumors and injuries of one sort or another. There was one particular case that, in retrospect, seems like a bridge between my first clinical career, and my later pastoral one.

On one occasion, I was asked to do my part of the examination at the patient's bedside. His frightened wife was in denial about the extent of his stroke and she was having a hard time adjusting to his needs. If she could observe the bedside evaluation, the hope was that she might begin to come to terms with the extent of his challenges.

Her sixty-year-old husband had suffered a major stroke that almost totally wiped out his ability to understand or meaningfully express thoughts in any way at all. Yet he was totally alert, could hear fairly well and could seem fairly conversational as he nodded and chuckled and gestured ..... and babbled total gibberish.

His wife seemed to be gazing off into the distance as I held up a pencil in front her husband. "Bud, what is this thing called?"

He smiled and nodded his head. "Yagadumpfsishmigadalum." Or something like that.

I looked across the bed to his wife to make sure she was following as I motioned the pencil toward Bud. "Show me what you do with this."

He just looked at me with that affable smile. "Ahidonantishmo."

His wife tried to help me understand that Bud wasn't wearing his hearing aids. "Maybe you should go over to the other side of the bed and talk in his better ear." I switched sides.

This time I offered the pencil to him. "Can you show me what you do with one of these?"

He took the pencil and simply held on to it as he smiled at me.

"You need to get closer to him and speak a little louder," said his wife.

I followed her directions and repeated the same procedure with a comb and got the same friendly gibberish. He put the comb in his mouth, tasted it, took it out again and gave the expression of a poor taste review. This time I noticed his wife's reddening eyes.

Next, I picked up a styrofoam coffee cup and again asked what it was called.

He slowly shook his head and chuckled as if he were sharing a joke. "Gobedindovahshigolambe."

I handed him the coffee cup and asked him to show me what we do with something like that. He took the cup, turned it over, double-popped his eyebrows and said, "Hell if I know, but it runneth over." He gave a sly grin which seemed to say, "What d'ya think of THAT?"

His wife was overjoyed. Clinically, this sort of thing would be seen in patients from time to time. We called it a "shutter effect" where the mind would inexplicably peek open for a fleeting second that usually would never be seen again. These were the last words Bud ever spoke. But I remember those words probably better than anyone remembers my own sermons on the Twenty-Third Psalm.

That was about as dramatic as my work would ever get in a hospital. Television writers would probably never do a hospital series called "Therapists On the Line." Medical shows almost always focus on emergency departments, where I would someday spend a fair amount of time as a pastor. Therapists like myself would usually come into the picture much further down the line, days after a patient's life functions were stabilized in Emergency, days after the patient was off things like breathing machines and was at least somewhat alert. People like I were the long-distance runners of the team. Therapy was not something that was done during the life and death phase of a crisis.

The same with this book. Faith questions for Christians often happen at moments of disaster, which may not always be the best time to read a book like this. Case in point – more accurately, twelve cases in point. Even if some of Jesus' apostles had been able to read, they would probably not have been much in a reading mood when a ruthless squall suddenly came upon their roofless boat on the open sea. Jesus was apparently sound asleep and the seasoned fishermen were out of their minds with terror when they screamed at him about sleeping on the job (Matthew 8:23-27). He awakens, tells them that they don't seem to have a lot of faith and then miraculously calms the storm. Only afterwards did the apostles start reflecting on what that was all about.

We see the same thing when Jesus himself was approaching his crucifixion. Hours before his arrest, "... being in agony he prayed more earnestly; and his sweat became like great drops of blood falling down to the ground (Luke 22:44)." These words were penned by a physician and he was describing an actual medical condition. Specialists these days call it "hematidrosis." Under the most extreme emotional stress, blood that feeds the sweat glands can actually leak through skin pores.

The next day, when he was hanging on the cross, "at about the ninth hour, Jesus cried out with a loud voice, saying, 'Eli, Eli, lema sabachthani?' That is, 'My God, my God, why have you forsaken me (Matthew 27:46) ?'" These were emergency room cries from the same one who had repeatedly explained to his followers exactly why he was voluntarily going to endure this ordeal.

Sometimes, when people hear a sufferer ask, "Why did God do that?" they mistakenly think that this is a request for information or an answer. More likely, what they are hearing is someone screaming in pain. My experience is that moments of major personal crises are times of emotional bleeding, not intellectual chess. The emergency room phase of any crisis in life has more to do with the realms of emotion and crying, terror, pain, screaming, confusion, non-alertness, anger, striking out, bleeding and .... well, you get the picture.

Over the years, I have spent a fair amount of time with my own extreme pain in emergency rooms. Let me assure you that most of what comes out of such a person's mouth, including words, is about trying to relieve pain. Theological discussions and books like what you have in your hand are not always particularly helpful at that moment. Nevertheless, in these pages I will be looking for truth wherever it leads, whether or not it makes one feel better. That is why this book may be more helpful during calmer times when a person is trying to sort things out, rather than in the emergency room phase of a life crisis.

Charlie The Tuna

Television and I kind of grew up together. Technically, it was born before me, but it really didn't start to breathe much until about the time I did. It looks like maybe we'll also be passing away about the same time. My childhood memories are bookmarked by television shows and commercials. I know about what year something happened because of what commercials and songs were playing then. "See the USA in your Chevrolet! America is asking you to call …" I can sing the whole thing. That commercial brings to mind tomato soup, grilled cheese sandwiches, and the TV western, "Bonanza," on Sunday night, right after "Walt Disney's Wonderful World of Color" (as opposed to black and white television from which the show was liberating us).

A little later there was a series of television cartoon commercials by Starkist Tuna. The main character was a tuna named Charlie who was always dejected because he never got chosen by Starkist. Each commercial involved another stunt where Charlie tried to make himself out to be a real classy tuna in order to appeal to Starkist. Alas, each time his friend would break the news, saying, "But Charlie, Starkist ain't exactly looking for tuna wid good taste. Starkist wants tunas dat taste good."

Well, this memoir is not published by Starkist. I am not fishing for ideas about God that necessarily "taste good." When the Bible says that God desires this, requires that, forbids something else, I often hear people say, "I wouldn't worship a god like that." Remarks like that have always made as much sense to me as someone saying they won't breathe air because they don't like the way it smells. When I have told people that the book of Revelation talks about the saints in Heaven spending all their time singing the praises of God, more than one person has said how boring that all sounds to him. I hear fishermen say that they expect to spend all their time in Heaven fishing. Hunters imagine themselves hunting, baseball players imagine an eternity of baseball, and book lovers look forward to endless reading in some magnificent library. C.S. Lewis wrote a small fantasy called *The Great Divorce* which tells the story about people on a city bus which disturbingly levitates off the street and takes them all to Heaven. The long and short of the story is that only one of the passengers even wants to stay in Heaven. The rest voluntarily leave because Heaven is different from what they had imagined it would be. It does not cater to them. The first one to leave was the pastor who was needed elsewhere to lead a Bible study.

My yeahbutology is driven to understand what is true about God, regardless of whether or not I happen to like it. In fact, a lot of my yeahbutology kicks in when God's ways just do not seem to line up the way I would like.

Chapter Two

In The Interests Of Full Disclosure

I Want To Be Up-Front

THOUGH I WILL CONSTANTLY TALK about my faith challenges, I do hold a quite traditional Christian faith in Jesus Christ. Specifically, I believe he is unique and necessary for all human beings to live in eternal wellness. I trust the face value of the careful reading of the Bible. For me, careful means that each passage is understood in the context of all other passages. It also means that each passage is informed by the best understanding of the historical context in which it was recorded.

I'm (NOT) Going to Make You Love Me

In the first years of competing for the heart of the girl who would someday become my wife, one of the biggest hit songs was by Diana Ross and the Supremes and The Temptations. The title was, "I'm Going to Make You Love Me." It's still one of my favorite nostalgia pieces. That song really played to my teen-aged passions because I was, in fact, doing everything I could think of to make her love me. However, I found out in a dozen ways that I could not make her anything. She would love me or she wouldn't. Her choice, not mine. Furthermore, in the years since, I have learned a thousand times in a thousand ways that I cannot make anyone anything. Especially in matters of faith. Jesus often said that faith had a lot in common with sheep farming. To which I got introduced one night in the Army.

Having been an enlisted man for three years, I was now a brand-new second lieutenant. I wasn't used to being saluted. En route to my first night of duty at a new post outside of Denver, I had picked up a hamburger to eat along the way. I was wearing my Class A dress uniform as I drove up to the guard sentry. Two intimidating guards with automatic rifles and a deadly looking German Shepherd approached my car. They suddenly noticed that I was an officer. Both snapped to attention, saluted, and barked, "Good evening. SIR!"

Just as smartly, I returned the salute. With the same right hand that held the Whopper hamburger. String onions draped off the visor of my saucer cap. I don't remember much of what followed, other than two corporals almost exploding as they fought to keep straight faces. In my rear view mirror, I saw them both double over to the ground in hysterics.

Three hours later, I was driving an Army sedan, with a loaded .45 pistol strapped to my side. I was also armed with a compass, a flashlight, a map and my orders to check on six manned signal outposts somewhere in the vicinity of Pike's Peak. All night long, I drove lost on gravel switch-back roads through parts of the Rocky Mountains. I never did manage to find three of the installations. I doubt that I was missed too much by the guys in those lonely, air conditioned, beer-equipped communication vans. I've always kind of suspected that maybe the new lieutenant wasn't really expected back too soon anyway. If at all.

I was absolutely, totally and hopelessly lost in the night. At one point, I stopped the car, opened the door for a little fresh air, and tried to use the compass, the map and the stars to figure out where I was.

I heard the blood-curdling scream of a woman. It sounded like maybe a hundred meters off across the road, somewhere in the pitch black forest. Another scream. And another one. I can't say that I felt all that heroic. Another scream.

I switched off the car, kept the interior lights and the headlights on, locked the door, switched on my flashlight, chambered a round in my .45, flicked off the safety and moved out into the forest thickets. Another scream.

I looked back to make sure I could still see the car. Another scream whipped my attention around again to find …. a lamb, bleating its head off, just ten feet away. It is absolutely amazing how something can sound so much like so many other things. Especially in pitch darkness, all alone, out in the middle of nowhere. I must not have been too far from a ranch. It was maybe two o'clock in the wee hours of the morning and I was way behind schedule. I was lost, myself, and I figured that the lamb was in better shape than I was. I wished it well.

Jesus said that the only ones who can recognize his voice are the ones who are his sheep to begin with (John 10). But as I learned that night on a dark mountain road, when it comes to lost sheep, I've got to be a little careful to not let my helping hand strike again. I cannot presume whether or not a particular lamb is from Jesus' fold. Even if I did know for sure that someone wasn't a lamb at all, like a wolf in sheep's clothing, I do not have the ability to make one a sheep, no matter how hard I try to persuade him. As far as lambs that belong to other flocks, I don't know anybody who can talk one into joining a different group. This memoir is not a sneaky attempt to make anyone a Christian.

Even if it were within my capabilities, it would not be within my rights, since Jesus himself never made anyone follow him. That is why I try to find the most respectful and appropriate ways to share Jesus with everyone. All sheep need nourishment. Whether or not a lamb accepts it is also beyond my capabilities to understand or my abilities to make it happen. It's not only horses that can be led to water but can't be made to drink.

I suspect that a lot of Jesus' sheep are away from the flock because they are distracted by any number of things within and without. I hope to do better for them than I did for that lamb in the mountains. I'm not at all sure that I have always done so well in that department. This book is my humble attempt to help all sheep hear his voice, so that his distracted ones might recognize it.

Some Christians may be offended at the very idea that a pastor would even have faith questions, much less have the poor taste to hang such dirty laundry in public. The reason I talk about my faith challenges is to affirm the legitimacy of sincere questioning and to show how faith can coexist with and even be strengthened by sincere challenges. My goal is to strengthen Christians who have sincere questions, to reclaim others who have walked away for what they may decide were unnecessary reasons, or just maybe to offer non-Christians a way to respect the validity of accurately understood Christianity.

This book is intended to show that, even though no faith can be proven, Christianity is as eminently reasonable as any other belief system, including scientific endeavor. This book is written as a memoir to show how one person has come to terms with serious challenges to the faith. Others may well find other ways to make sense out of things.

A skeptical reader might be tempted to dismiss this book outright as nothing more than another version of the old Sunday School joke. The teacher asks third grader Billy if he can guess what is grey and has a bushy tail and is furry and climbs trees and eats nuts. He thinks for a moment and answers, "Well, I was going to say a squirrel, but the answer always seems to be Jesus." Likewise, a scoffer might dismiss this book by thinking, "It doesn't matter what the question is because, for this guy, the answer is always the same."

Guilty as charged. This book stands at the bar to answer prosecutors' challenges to the validity of Christianity. Increasingly these days, the default assumption is that all supernatural schools of thought, especially Christianity, are simply uninformed, unthinking, unintelligent, self-fulfilling superstitions. The skeptic essentially says, "Christianity just doesn't make sense." This book attempts to offer ways to answer those charges by showing that, to the contrary, such things, in fact, CAN make sense. My effort here is to see if, indeed, Jesus can be a rational answer to important riddles. My toughest struggles satisfy me that the answer is clearly "yes."

These kinds of challenges are high explosives which can blow someone's faith to smithereens. Killer questions can become faith killers. It is claimed that it was Jesus who said that one's relationship with him determines one's destiny for all eternity. Again, the yeahbutologist thinks, "Maybe. Maybe not." But it seems to me that wherever the stakes in life are high, whether it be relationships, business, career, or life and death matters, especially matters of possible eternity, it does not seem wise to let the questions have the last word.

All my life, especially in my years as a pastor in the pulpit, I have been a card-carrying yeahbutologist. Even so, I have survived such explosions with my faith remaining not only intact, but strengthened, and strengthened specifically because of these truth traumas. But I always carry within me the faith-shrapnel that floats around and which periodically and painfully pokes through to the surface. This memoir is my account of how I have tried to handle these explosions and the lingering shrapnel in a way that is constructive both for me and those around me. I have been surprised to discover that I seem to come to terms with my biggest God questions in the same way that I typically handle most other serious matters in life. In my case, I have come to terms with my faith issues the same way that I and many others have lived with challenges in science, in the military and in parenting.

Even so, I can hear a skeptical voice within me which whispers, "Oh sure. You can find a way to explain anything. That's nothing more than a rationalizing sleep aid for yourself." The truth is that these kinds of questions have only kept me awake. I am not a doubter, per se'. But I have always thought of myself as some kind of faith-descendent of one particular apostle who, thanks to Jesus, has forevermore come to be known as "Doubting" Thomas. Instead of outright dismissing something, I usually try to cover my bases by entertaining alternatives in a more tentative way by saying, "YEAH, BUT ...." As with just about any subject, I never stop turning over the coin. So the questions never do seem to end. But, for me, neither are they THE end. I write this book to offer a way that yeahbutologists need not let the questions have the last word.

Chapter Three

Pastors Have Questions Too

THERE WAS A TIME WHEN I used to feel like a total fraud when I went to church. I had all these questions in my mind. When I looked around, it seemed like I was the only one who wasn't swallowing all this stuff, hook-line-and-sinker. Everyone else around me was sitting so nice and prim and proper. That pastor up there was cranking out phrases that I had heard a thousand times but which never totally made much sense to me. Our sins are "justified by grace, through faith." We were to live "IN Christ." He "died FOR our sins." I didn't have a blessed clue what that meant. More than once, I wondered if the pastors themselves understood what these code phrases meant because, when I asked, I just got more official churchy refrains. Were these just formulas which they memorized in pastor school?

Then one day I saw a bumper sticker by the American Indian Movement which said, "CUSTER died for your sins." I don't know why, but somehow that kind of shook things loose. If I could understand how Custer died for our sins, maybe I could understand what it meant that Jesus died for our sins. Lo and behold, I would come to discover that my naïve little question is THE big issue among the brightest minds in all Christianity! Twenty theologians will have thirty-two opinions, and some of those ideas once got people burned at the stake!

Fast forward a couple decades and now I sometimes felt like I myself was the fraud because the one in the pulpit was ME! I was now in the business of proclaiming. And all the while that I was projecting the surety of what I was proclaiming, there was still a voice inside me saying, "YEAH, BUT how can you really know for sure?" Or, "YEAH, BUT, who do you think YOU are to sound so smart and wise?" Or, "YEAH, BUT how about those six other ways of interpreting that passage? In the interest of full disclosure, shouldn't I also be telling the people about those other ways as well?" Or, "YEAH, BUT how could I say this or that when I knew of so many exceptions to the rule?"

One of my favorite television shows was called "Kung Fu." A young Chinese priest-in-training is mentored by a wise old blind priest who calls the student "grasshopper." When I was training to be a pastor, I too had an old, wise mentor. He too was blind. At eighty-nine years of age he had advanced cancer and was no longer able to get to the front door of his own home. So I had been told to just knock and let myself in. I found him hard at work, with his eyes closed, reclining in his lounger in the living room. He didn't hear me come in. Counting on his fingers, he seemed to be silently rehearsing something. Every now and then he would shake his head and start all over again.

I didn't want to startle him, so I cleared my throat and jangled my keys until he looked up. "Pastor Tollefsrud, it's Dave."

This old retired pastor had been a family friend of ours for twenty years or so. He had always predicted that someday I would enter the ministry. That's the only thing that made me question his wisdom since his prediction always seemed so preposterous to me. I don't know what he thought he saw in me. I was a speech and language pathologist, I loved what I was doing and I had no desire to look for any greener pastor pastures. Besides, when it came to religion, I had nothing but questions and I was just beginning to warm back up to church after a couple rather chilly decades with all God stuff.

"Oh, Dave!" He chuckled, "Forgive me. I didn't mean to ignore you. Between my deafness and my blindness, I can get so lost in my questions that I'm sometimes in a world of my own. Hope you haven't been standing there too long. How rude of me."

"Not at all. I just walked in, but I didn't want to startle you."

He looked my direction, but his eyes didn't really focus too well. "You caught me rehearsing my list. I work on that thing every day."

He said it like I knew what he was talking about. "Your list?" I said.

"Well, with any luck, I think I'll probably be going home before too much longer. You know that, don't you?"

I really didn't know how to answer. "Mmm," was all I could come up with.

"So, I've got a whole list of questions that I don't want to forget when I get to Heaven."

Now I really was lost. What would someone like him be doing with questions for Heaven? I had heard him in the pulpit and I don't remember hearing anything about questions. "Your list?"

"Well, actually, it's more like a number of lists. I've got one list of six questions for John the Baptist when I meet him." He thought that one over and recounted on his fingers. "No, seven. Seven questions for the Baptist. That's the shortest list, I think."

"I've also got twelve questions for Abraham. Twenty-two for Jesus. But that's not the longest list. That one goes to the apostle Paul: thirty-four questions. As of this morning. Wait a minute: thirty-five now. Of course, there's King David. Also, Jesus' stepfather, Joseph, is someone I look forward to meeting."

This was the first time that it had ever occurred to me that questions and profound faith could dwell side-by-side in the same person. It never dawned on me to ask or wonder what those questions were. I simply didn't have a file anywhere in my brain called "questions from pastors." It never occurred to me that there was such a thing.

What I do wonder is whether my friend will even care about these questions, much less remember them, in his new eternal digs (pun intended). How many burning questions of early childhood do any of us recall?

Chapter Four
For Whom This Book Tolls

This Book Is For Me

MY MOMENT BENEATH THE FIRST AMERICAN ORBIT revealed a quirky little thing that has always been part of me: the "YEAH, BUT" component of my brain. No matter what the subject matter, I'm always thinking, "YEAH, BUT what if?" This quite often leads friends and family to respond with, "YEAH, BUT so what?" Or, to treat myself to a taste of my own medicine, "YEAH, BUT what if all of my questions are nothing more than my own weird wiring that has to make a big mystery out of everything?"

My decision to enter the ministry cost me a lot of friendships outside the faith. I fully expect that this confession of being a yeahbutologist will probably cost me a few friendships inside the faith. This may be especially true of some people in my parishes who heard me confidently proclaim the Gospel. These people may have somehow missed my mention of the conundrums that sent me on the quest which formed my sermon in the first place. When a pastor did not deliver a sermon well, I would assume that he didn't really believe what he was saying. When he did deliver it well, I dismissed him as a pretentious know-it-all who was beyond any critical thought and questions of his own. I've since discovered that I am not the only shepherd whose own faith has been most intensely tested during the years of ministry. The pastor is the theologian in the trenches who takes the Bible to the street and tries to connect what should be with what is. The pastor's role is to relate what is unseen with what is seen, whose place is to proclaim the goodness of God to those who just cannot see it through the tears. The pastor's job is to connect the ancient ideas of the Bible with the modern ideas of people who less and less grant authority to the Bible.

Any Christian, and especially a pastor, who lives IN the world but is not OF the world can be the loneliest of targets. At least if Jesus was telling the truth. He promised as much, time and time and time again. He reportedly and repeatedly talked about the reality of an enemy of God. If such a thing is true, it would make all the sense in the world - in both worlds, actually - that the enemy of God would specially target the ones whom God has chosen as the tenants to work his field. To be clear, such targets are not just the church's hired guns but anyone who claims to be a follower of Jesus Christ.

Maybe my problem is just that I stay up way too late. Interesting things can be heard on the airwaves of the night. It was about 1:30 one morning and I was listening to a quite rational sounding person explain how she contacts spirits. She expressed concern that listeners would dismiss her as sounding too "out there" and "flakey." She went on to talk about how departed spirits can choose to communicate or not to communicate with us mortals. She said that if people had been hard to communicate with on Earth, they might continue to be so in the spirit realm. She talked about fine-tuning one's vibrations to be in cosmic harmony with the spirits.

I'm pretty sure that was where I stopped vibrating. My first reaction was to do exactly what she was afraid of: I wrote her off as a flakey charlatan. How does she know all this about spirits? It all sounded so preposterous to me. But, then, how about the Bible passage I had just preached on that very morning? It said and therefore I said that the human Jesus was the same God who was there at the beginning of the universe and that all things were made through him. Would THAT sound any less preposterous to people who were not in the club? Who says all those things about Jesus? The apostle Paul? How did HE know all of this? And we buy into all of it simply because he claims to be telling the truth? Don't they all?

All of the most key assertions about Jesus in traditional Christianity are far more amazing than anything which that lady on the radio could ever come up with. Mediums and the spirit world are pale things compared to God wanting to save a humanity that usually has driven him to the brink of mass annihilation. I'm thinking of a God who came to Earth as a vulnerable human baby. I'm thinking of a God who allowed himself to be tortured and executed as a sacrifice to pay off the sins of the people who drive him nuts. I'm thinking of a God who supposedly came back from the dead in order to cancel the permanence of death, who floated up to Heaven and promised to return to make a whole new Heaven and Earth for those who love him. At least the mystic on the radio claimed to know her claims through her own direct experience. I myself cannot claim that much. Am I less likely to be deluded by ancient assertions of others whom I have never known? Are her claims more incredible than those of Christianity? I would imagine that a lot of the arguments I might give to support the validity of my faith are arguments that she could use to bolster her own.

When my faith is rejected by so many credible people, and when it has such major potential costs like martyrdom and social derision, I need to explain, at least to myself, why it is true, and not just for me. I have long struggled to come up with a reason for my faith that satisfies the grand inquisitor within me which always challenges me with, YEAH, BUT. Quite often, the question takes the form of, "YEAH, BUT what you say about Jesus is no different from what people of all persuasions might say about their own faiths." For example, I might be tempted to say that Christianity carries weight with me because it has survived for over two thousand years. "YEAH, BUT Judaism has survived much longer than that. And so has Buddhism. Islam is only a little younger." Or, I may say that Christianity is the only faith where salvation does not depend on what a person accomplishes. Enter the inquisitor in the back of my head who whispers, "YEAH, BUT do you think it's true simply because you like its system better than other systems?"

As a pastor, I have heard lots of reasons which people have given for why they think they are Christians. One frequent remark is, "I don't know how a person could get through life without Jesus." Or, "I want to have a good marriage and give my kids a foundation that keeps them out of trouble." The trouble is, I know a lot of serious Christians whose families have fallen apart. At the same time, I have known a number of non-Christians who have remarkably healthy families and who are every bit as moral and ethical, if not more so.

I have heard other people say, "I don't know how a person could have any hope approaching death if they didn't believe the promises of Jesus." Here comes that voice again: "YEAH, BUT, there are lots and lots of Jews and Muslims and Buddhists and atheists who are just as serene in their earthly struggles and in their approach to death as any Christian."

Some Christians will say that if you look at the way things are in the world and how it's put together, there is simply no other way than Jesus to make sense of things. The problem is that the vast majority of the most intelligent, most highly educated thinkers these days have all kinds of other explanations that make more sense to them. Some of those ideas have made a lot of sense to me, though I'll deny in a court of law that I ever said anything like that. Or the clincher: "I just have the love of Jesus in my heart and I know in my heart that ...." I am in no position to doubt such a person. In fact, I have some envy there. But except for my family, I honestly can't say that I've ever had that kind of feeling about anything. I think I'm probably in good company, though. I know of only one follower of Jesus in the Bible who ever talked about that burning in his heart for Jesus. This was a guy who didn't even know that he had been walking with Jesus that whole afternoon of the resurrection, on the way to a village called Emmaus (Luke 24).

My yeahbutology is also a little bit like my grandson's breakfast bombast. He could not understand why his grandpa could see the most horribleist thing in the whole world going on and still stand by and do nothing. At the same time, there is no question in my mind about our deep relationship with each other. I'm more than a little bit that way with God. As much as this memoir is about my puzzlements with God, these reflections are at least as much about trying to come to grips with conundrums about myself. From the first moment that I considered the ministry, I have always had the sense that this could be a journey of tremendous sacrifice, not just for myself but for my wife and daughters. For that reason, I was just as clear in my mind that I would never sign on for that kind of sacrifice unless Jesus Christ were unique and necessary for the most important things in existence. But then, why was I willing to do this for someone whose most important things could never be proven or at least explained in a way that didn't leave me with more questions?

This Book Is For Other Questioners

At the time of this writing, fewer and fewer people in America and Europe are active Christians. My sense as a pastor is that the majority of people who call themselves Christians are inactive ones by any definition at all. Others are simply not interested for all kinds of reasons. These first two groups no longer feel the social stigma to pretend otherwise. Others intentionally separate themselves from Christianity, again for all kinds of reasons. There are many whose faith has genuinely run aground on the submerged reefs of serious questions. Sometimes, I suspect that some people seize upon a killer question as a convenient opportunity to avoid having to think harder or do things which they don't want to do.

I have no statistics to back this up, but my years as a pastor lead me to believe that the vast majority of Christians are essentially yeahbutologists. My experience has been that for most Christians, politics or personal desires almost always prevail over the teachings of Jesus. The frequent response almost always begins with, "YEAH, BUT."

If it is said that Jesus told us to endlessly forgive others, the yeahbutologist may think, "YEAH, BUT then the person will never change."

If it is said that God has consistently and without exception prohibited something for thousands of years throughout the entire Bible, the yeahbutologist races in. The person who otherwise accepts the most amazing claims about Jesus, will now instinctively say, "YEAH, BUT, that particular prohibition was meant for less educated people in different times, places and cultures who didn't know any better."

If it is said that Jesus consistently told his followers to give to any who ask, the yeahbutologist may think, "YEAH, BUT isn't that just enabling their irresponsibility?"

If it is said that Jesus told his followers to pray for their enemies, the yeahbutologist may say, "YEAH, BUT you won't stop a terrorist with that."

If it is said that Jesus is the only way to Heaven, the yeahbutologist may say, "YEAH, BUT I have a friend who is not a Christian and he's just as good as anyone else."

If it is said that some things won't be fulfilled until Jesus' second coming, the yeahbutologist may say, "YEAH, BUT what if that is just an excuse to explain why Jesus really wasn't the Messiah in the first place?"

If it is said that the Bible is the only written Word of God, the yeahbutologist thinks, "YEAH, BUT what if the

Bible is really no more than what Christians think about the sacred books of all other faiths?"

If it is said that millions of people have experienced the power of the Christian faith, the yeahbutologist thinks, "YEAH, BUT what if that's no different than what millions of other people say about their own faiths?"

If it is said that it is the nature of God not to be seen or heard, the yeahbutologist thinks, "YEAH, BUT how does that kind of god look any different from no god at all?"

If it is said that we need to listen for God's answer, the yeahbutologist thinks, "YEAH, BUT how do you know that what you think God is saying is not just you talking to yourself?"

Whenever an explanation is offered to explain any mystery of God, the yeahbutologist thinks, "YEAH, BUT how do you know that this isn't just a rationalization that you would never accord to anyone else?"

Hans Christian Anderson wrote a fairy tale about a vain Emperor who got duped into parading around in his imaginary clothes. He had been tricked into believing that the clothing could be seen only by people who were worthy. Anyone who admitted that they couldn't see the clothes was therefore exposing himself as unworthy and an enemy of the Emperor. So, as he paraded in all his naked glory, everyone knew better than to call it like it was. Except for a little boy who asked aloud why the Emperor was naked. For many people these days, the pomp and ceremony of church can seem like a parade of people who wear a certainty of faith that looks more like the Emperor's new clothes. But a lot of others on the sidelines keep their concerns to themselves because, just like the subjects of the fabled Emperor, they don't wish to appear unfit, stupid, or incompetent. When I envisioned the cover for this book, I was tempted to avoid the cost of cover art altogether by packaging the whole thing in a plain brown wrapper.

Unpacking and repacking questions like these can take more time, effort and resources than a person might have. That is what this memoir tries to do.

This Book Is For Those Looking In From The Outside

This book may also be of some interest to those who stand outside the stained glass windows, looking in, maybe even with a rock in their hands.

"So if she's so smart, why did she chose YOU?" A good friend recently teased me with that question when I told him that my wife was at a research conference that week in Washington, D.C. When we were dating in our teenage years, that same question used to drive me nuts when I began to wonder the same thing. I did not like the fact that she could easily have lots of other options besides me.

In our mid-twenties, Ann and I were sitting in the living room of our first house, holding our first child, talking to the first insurance agent. It was evening and he wanted to get the show on the road, so he got right down to business. "Well, I know you kids are busy."

Back in the day, most people got the daily news in several pages of large sheets of thin paper that were called newspapers, as in paper with news. These used to get delivered right to your house every day. In those days, every birth was published: the baby's name, gender, parents and addresses. From there, business people would go to huge paperback books called phone directories and look up your phone number. They would call you to set up an evening visit to offer you some chance-of-a-lifetime opportunity. Life insurance agents preceded realtors who preceded other nice helpers (sarcasm intended). All to welcome your little one into the world. This fifty-something insurance salesman had thinning hair and a mild case of dunlop disease (as in, over his belt). And he started off by calling us "you kids." Strike one.

"So, I'll get right down to business," said he. To just me. Strike two.

"Now that there is a little mouth to feed, what will happen to the little lady here if, God forbid, you should drop dead?"

Hmmm. "Drop dead" said he. If my wife wasn't thinking it, I sure was. I said to him, "Well, 'the little lady' here will probably do even better without my mouth to feed."

He thought I was kidding. "Seriously, though, young man, I'm talking about income. Consider her vulnerabilities. Without your income ..."

I interrupted him. "Actually, she's the main breadwinner in this family. She makes a lot more than I do."

I think this was the first time that he turned to her in the conversation. "So, you work?"

"I teach," was her typically understated answer.

"Well, that's nice," he said. As in, "sweetie." And strike three.

Now was my opportunity to take credit for her. "She's a professor and she writes an academic textbook."

He got the message. And the door. And we eventually got another agent.

She still answers that way even though she is much further along in her career. "I work at the U," is all you'll ever get out of her. Not me. I'm still taking credit for her. She's the most famous I'll ever get.

In the early years of our romance, I thought I would have done anything in my power to keep her from walking away from me. But that's not true. It would have broken my heart if she had. But unless I was willing to be abusive, I certainly would not have stood in her way. Millions of people, probably most people, have suffered the loss of a love. Some people deal with it better than others. But the vast majority do allow their loves to walk away. The ones who make the news are the exceptions precisely because they are the exceptions.

The kind of god who is portrayed throughout the Hebrew Scriptures and the New Testament is a god who seeks relationship with humans. I imagine that he would have been capable of making creatures that had no choice but to love him or obey him. But the entire Bible describes individuals and entire nations walking away from him all the time. In the case of Jesus, these often included his own followers. He never stood in their way. He never said or did an unkind or disrespectful thing to them. Neither did he manipulate them in order to hang on to them. He simply would say that those who do not hear his voice are lambs who cannot recognize his voice because they are not of his flock. I write this book in the same spirit of respecting the people who consider my thoughts and say, "Thanks, but no thanks."

The fact that there are so many alternatives to God may not indicate the absence of God but rather the existence of a certain kind of god. This God will not even eliminate the competition in order to force people to love him. This God desires relationship with those who love him freely.

I have been forever grateful that my wife did not feel compelled to choose me. Therefore, it seems reasonable to me that a relationship type of god would create human beings who have the ability to choose him or reject him. Most have chosen to reject him. But then again, only one woman on Earth has ever chosen me as her companion. That one woman has had every opportunity and more than a few good reasons to walk the other way.

Why would a skeptic or outright rejecter waste any time reading a book like this? Only the person reading this far could answer. Could be intellectual curiosity, along the lines of, "How could any intelligent, educated person in his right mind actually believe this kind of stuff?"

Maybe the skeptic wants to be doubly sure before actually casting the last stone. Maybe a person is actually comfortable in having walked away, but is intellectually vigilant enough to make sure that every last stone is turned over (maybe before throwing it). Maybe this is the astrophysicist I heard at a conference who said that he did not believe in God, but really wished that he did.

I am not above caring what smart people think of me. And lots of my smartest friends are more than a little cool to classical notions of Christianity, especially when Christians don't keep their ideas to themselves. As always, I hear a voice say, "Shouldn't that tell you something, that lots of your smartest friends don't go along with your faith?" But not all of my smartest friends, by a long shot. I rarely come across any idea in any domain that doesn't have well-supported disagreements from extremely brilliant people. History is littered with the debris of intellectual majorities. Nevertheless, it is clear to me that Christianity can never be compelling according to worldly standards. Neither can Christianity make sense according to reasoning that is not interpreted by everything that goes into a faith perspective.

So why would I even bother to write a book that would likely erase any lingering doubt about me actually being a fully certified, intellectual Neanderthal? There are at least two reasons why I dare to walk where angels fear to tread. Because I typically hold to the traditional ideas of Christianity, I believe that Jesus said two things about each person's future. First, I believe that every person will live out eternity in Heaven or in Hell. Secondly, I believe that the only way to get to Heaven is by accepting Jesus Christ as Lord and Savior. How could I believe such things and then not give my best effort for the eternal life of anyone who crosses my path? To not give this my best shot would be simply illogical at the very least and cosmically immoral at the very most.

In trying to imitate Jesus, I am also a big believer that every person has the right to freely accept or reject anything, including God the Father and Jesus Christ himself. It's also my sense that people cannot have a choice about something unless they know the options from which to choose and the freedom to do so. God has not only allowed this choice, but has actually insisted on it throughout every page of the Bible.

There are well-informed people who still give Jesus Christ a well-reasoned thumbs down. Some of these are dear friends who are at least as smart and decent as I like to think I am. I can usually understand how they see things the way they do. Jesus himself is on record saying that he and his message would not score with most people. I myself believe that if people, including church-goers, really heard what Jesus really said, most people would scatter. Love your enemy as yourself? Pray for your enemy? Really? Forgive someone who sins against you seventy times seven times? Give to everyone who begs? Pick up your own cross and suffer like Jesus?

I think that, short of looking through certain spiritual faith lenses, many fundamental tenets of Christianity make absolutely no sense at all, according to the ways of this world to which most people subscribe. Without those lenses (which many would dismiss as "rose colored glasses"), other explanations that exclude any notion of God may be a lot simpler and might make a lot more sense. Since the vast majority of even religious people have never claimed to see or hear God, I can understand why the simplest conclusion could be that there is simply no such Being in the first place.

Spoiler alert again: I do have a possible answer to those questions a little later in the discussion.

At the same time, I think lots of people reject Jesus Christ by mistake and are not giving themselves a fair chance to choose. Some people are pushing back not so much at Jesus as much as what some human organizations and zealots have done with him and in his name. Oftentimes, people attribute to Jesus things which he would have never done. He often winds up paying the bill for other people's manipulative and disrespectful attempts at conversion. Many have choked with severe allergic reactions to the arrogant, self-righteous, judgmental and presumptuous way things are sometimes presented (like the pastor you'll read about who condemned me to Hell).

I do not presume to know how it is for anyone else. Truth is, I am still trying to figure out my own self. This memoir is simply my effort to describe how faith has survived in one genuine, card carrying, honest-to-God yeahbutologist.

Chapter Five
What This Book Is Not About

My Faith Is Not In Institutions

I DO NOT EQUATE JESUS CHRIST WITH ANY INSTITUTION or person who claims his name.

We were camped deep in the woods on what was supposed to be a relaxing church men's fishing trip weekend. But a heavy and blustery rainstorm had dropped the temperatures to the low forties. Even the fanatic fishermen in the group had to concede that their plans were washed out. In front of these fishing fanatics, I knew enough to appear really disappointed. And dry.

This disaster only got worse when we had no choice but to go for a steak supper at the nearby lodge. That was where a big part of my life got rained on. On the front desk of the lodge there was a newly delivered stack of evening newspapers from the nearby city. The headlines

were about something from forty years earlier:
"American Dachau Liberators Massacred Unarmed
Captured German Guards." There were photos. I was
more than shocked. My dad had been one of the
liberators at Dachau. He never played up his role in the
war. He mostly talked about this only with me and only
after I had been in the Army myself. I had always known
about his time in Dachau because he never wanted
people to forget what had happened. My dad was and
has always been my war hero.

But Dad had never told me anything about a massacre
of unarmed enemy prisoners. In fact, of all the books and
media about Dachau that I had followed over the years, I
had never heard this story. Nobody I have told this story
to had ever heard of it. My hope was that this was a
bogus rumor that would not survive scrutiny. I was
wrong. Over the next couple months, I was able to rather
quickly determine that the incidents were well known by
the Army and our government. It was attested to by
Army physicians on the scene. The only point of
contention was how many surrendered German soldiers
had been machine-gunned in cold blood. Authorities
claimed anywhere from a few dozen to hundreds. Most
of the murdered German guards were recent arrivals to
Dachau themselves, having been transferred there to
stand in for the regular cadre who had fled before the
oncoming Americans.

Again, Dad had never said anything about this. He had
recently died, so I was spared having to ask him about it.
But now I had to find some way to deal with this on my
own. Like a crystal keepsake that I had dropped on a
stone cold floor, my thoughts and theories exploded in a
million directions. My fingers trembled a little as I
separated the fragile papers of my dad's war
memorabilia. It was like the feeling I experienced in my

own basic training when we had been taught how to defuse buried landmines. That training exercise was all pretend. What I was doing now really could explode. World War Two munitions were being stumbled upon and defused every week these days all over the world. I carefully compared his personnel file with the hour to hour movements of his infantry company. To my relief, it turns out that his unit entered the concentration camp the day after the initial liberation. So, the good news was that he himself could not have even been present when the atrocity occurred. The bad news was that I also had to surrender the image of my hero storming Dachau (it turns out that there was no military assault at all: the initial troops simply walked in with no resistance).

In the war of my generation, it was the cold-blooded massacre at a place in Vietnam called My Lai (pronounced mee – LIE) where 2nd Lieutenant William Calley ordered his platoon to massacre hundreds of innocent, unarmed men, women and children. Calley was the only one punished. He served only three and a half years under house arrest. Unlike many alleged atrocities, the Dachau and My Lai massacres cannot be dismissed as unsubstantiated rumors or the unfortunate confusions in the fog of war, or cases of panicked self-defense.

Some philosophers say that it is a good thing to live in the tension between opposite pulls. Well, that is definitely me when it comes to my country and my church. For better or worse, I am an American Christian, identified by two institutions which I believe have earned the right to be looked to as the high water mark in so many ways. At the same time, I have never been a person who believes in "my side, right or wrong." I am not a company man. For me, the issue is integrity, which at least means holding myself and "mine" to nothing less than the same standards I would apply to others. In fact,

I hold myself, my country, my church and my family to far higher standards than I apply to others.

Where my nation is concerned, I live in the tension between pride and confession. My ancestors and I have offered our lives to defend America in every war from the American Revolution to Vietnam. The first was a lieutenant who died in the Revolution. The latest one was also a lieutenant who served during, though not in, Vietnam. That was me. In between was a Civil War sergeant fighting for the North who is buried where he fell in Chattanooga. Both of my grandfathers were combat infantrymen in the First World War. When I was a child I watched my father's father slowly die from the mustard gas that fifty years earlier had poisoned him. My father was a combat infantryman who was wounded in the Battle of the Bulge in the Second World War. I'm proud of their service and I'm proud of mine. Dad's medals, including the Bronze Star for valor in the Battle of the Bulge, hang on my wall. Beside that hang my insignia, rank and Honorable Discharge. Though I was nothing even close to being any kind of hero, I, like my fathers before me, am a proud war-time veteran of the United States Army. All four of us, like millions of other men and women, placed our lives in harm's way for noble reasons. We served honorably to stop forces of oppression against helpless people.

That is why I cringe at those times when my country has intentionally betrayed its own high ideals. More troublesome to me than the atrocities of rogue Americans have been some of my country's official policies which have deliberately, repeatedly and needlessly victimized innocent people. Things like the slave industry of America's founding fathers continue to stain this nation to this very day. The more than 15,000 deaths of civilian American Indians on the Trail of Tears in the mid-eighteen hundreds triples the number of Americans who died on the Bataan Death March. The forced internment of 115,000 innocent and uncharged Japanese American citizens cost them their homes and businesses. This was done at the very time that 33,000 of their sons were fighting and eight hundred were giving their lives in World War Two. While my father was fighting fascism in 'the good war', our bombers were intentionally fire-storming hundreds of thousands of civilians, including entire families, in cities like Hamburg and Dresden and Plauen and Tokyo and Hiroshima and Nagasaki. Our people knew at the time that such things were atrocities because even then these tactics were strongly opposed by many senior military planners. Such deliberate mass annihilation of civilians would be unthinkable today, even if conducted by the worst terrorists.

The shame lives on by readers who know these things and whose instinct is to defend or minimize or excuse these atrocities. At some level, this so-called patriotism is more offensive to me than when people deny the Holocaust. Hundreds of thousands of my fellow veterans were slaughtered in 'the good war' in order to end this kind of barbarism and especially the willful complacency of a public that allowed it to happen.

I once preached a sermon about the upcoming celebration of Ash Wednesday which, on that particular year, coincided with Valentine's Day. The last time those two holidays had happened together was in 1945. Of course, being the amateur historian I am, I had to research what had transpired on that particular day. Since Valentine's Day and Ash Wednesday both have to do with personal sacrifice, I told the stories of half a dozen American servicemen who had given their lives on that day. But I also explained how, on that exact day, our bombers deliberately fire-stormed Dresden and turned into ashes upwards of twenty-four thousand civilian men, women and children. These people were not unintended "collateral" damage but intended victims. I did not mention the American fighter planes that afterward strafed fleeing civilians. On that specific morning, those Lutheran and Catholic civilian kinsmen of mine awakened for what would be their last day on Earth, to celebrate, of all things, Ash Wednesday.

Because this pastor was a veteran, I was often asked and expected to speak and preside at Memorial Day services. This always was my hardest day every single year. For me to even dare allude to the fact that Jesus commended dying but never killing for our beliefs was treading on thin ice. I justifiably felt, and still feel, the private shame of hypocrisy because I shied away from sharing that whole message.

Especially troubling to me is the realization that some readers right now are more bothered by my telling of the story than by what we actually did. I consistently see the same blinders among presumably compassionate Christians who are more upset with descriptions of abortion than with the abortions themselves. I consider it a shameful embarrassment to excuse or rationalize or selectively turn a blind eye to our own betrayals of who we claim to be.

Where the institutional Church is concerned, I also live in that tension between feeling good and feeling bad at the same time. I am humbled to have been ordained into that institution which is by far the most important means of preserving and spreading the gospel of Jesus Christ. I am humbled to have even had a small part to play in an institution which unquestionably has accomplished more good on this Earth in every way imaginable, for more people, and for longer than any other group of people which has ever existed. The institutional Church has sacrificed hundreds of thousands of its own faithful for peoples other than themselves in establishing orphanages, hospitals, schools, relief agencies, and advocacy for indigenous peoples. At the same time, it must be said that some of the most heinous crimes of that same institutional Church were played out in many of these very places.

The good that organizations do does not give them a pass when their leaders and members violate the most important things they stand for. It is precisely because it claims the loftiest identity of being the Body of Christ that I writhe whenever large elements of Church organizations, officials and other Christians have violated everything imaginable of Jesus Christ, and have done so in his name. The evil deliberately committed by large elements of the established Church is the most reprehensible of sins that infect every member of the entire human race. I'm thinking of the Crusades, the Inquisition, the conquest of the Americas, the disassembling of American Indian cultures, the institutionalized Church's cooperation in American slavery, its complicity with and protection of Gestapo killers, the active support of abortion by so-called progressive Protestants and the protection of priests who have prayed over and then sexually preyed on its own young. I am less than mollified when the Church ceases such things only when forced.

To someone who has worn the uniforms of both Church and state, these atrocities offend me in the deepest ways. Especially because I am a member of and have been a commissioned leader in these institutions, I am responsible for helping see to it that these things are never, ever forgotten. Even as I write these words, I feel immense pressure to not talk about such shame. I expect these remarks to cost me friendships because many patriotic Christians regard loyalty to "the company" to be more important than what these institutions are supposed to be about. At the same time, it feels absurd to talk about how much these memories haunt me. My psychic discomfort doesn't deserve to even be mentioned alongside the torment suffered by actual victims of "my people."

My struggles with the deliberate disgraces of the institutionalized Church have helped me understand what my faith is and is not about. My faith is only in the Father, Son and Holy Spirit, not in what some refer to as "organized religion", a term that could never have been thought up by anyone who has actually worked in a church. I believe the Church is holy in the sense that, unlike any other organization, it is set apart by God for Jesus Christ's supernatural mission and for supernatural accountability. But because so much good has been commingled with so much evil, I have come to believe that the institutionalized Church and it's representatives do not have divine privileges or divine immunity from evil. Though it works for a Savior of self-sacrifice, it behaves no differently than any other organization of lofty ideals. In fact, I believe that by virtue of its size, power and privileges, the institutionalized Church is especially prone to "absolute power corrupting absolutely." At its worst, the institutionalized Church's reason for existence too often takes a back seat to the first self-serving instinct of all organisms to survive and then grow bigger and stronger. So, when I say that I hold to rather traditional Christian faith, it is not a faith in the institutional church. One of my mentors, Harry Wendt, would say that the Church is what's left over when the building burns down.

At the same time, I would suggest that just as food should not be judged by how some people abuse it, no religion or any other organization should be defined by the worst of its members. More specifically, I do not think it is necessary or fair to walk away from Jesus because of the misdeeds of people who go by his name. For example, Jesus clearly opposed adultery but he never gave anyone, much less his followers, the right to abuse, harm or disrespect anyone who did any of the sins which have always been prohibited in the Bible. To the contrary, he protected them and forgave the ones who repented.

But if it isn't fair to blame Jesus for the bad things that Christians do, I'm still seriously bothered that he allows "his people" to do such things in his name in the first place. This persists as my greatest faith quandary and is the subject of Chapters Twenty-Three and Twenty-Four.

My Faith Is Not In The Effectiveness Of Christianity

My faith is not in humanity or even in the most elevated of teachings. One of the most common accusations is that Christianity is full of hypocrites. Well, it is. I have led entire congregations of US hypocrites. But, it also has to be said that hypocrisy is a charge that can only be leveled at individuals or groups who claim to aspire to good things in the first place. And technically speaking, only preachers can be guilty of not practicing what they preach. Most people reading these words like to think of themselves as basically good people. But we are lying or simply unaware if we do not admit our hypocrisy with which Jesus Christ himself is about to confront us.

I also believe that few people get up in the morning and try to figure out how much evil they can accomplish. When we do not practice what we preach, my experience is that this most often reflects the automatic human default of being self-serving, unthinking, short-sighted, and limited in anticipating unintended consequences. Because I am one of these flawed people, I know first-hand that Americans and Christians are in no way intrinsically better than any other people. No one is exempt from the sinfulness which I believe plagues all mortals and the organizations which magnify our natures.

Ours is a success-oriented, pragmatic culture which goes with what works and what sells. To the contrary, my faith has never been about which notion or religion or philosophy seems to work best, or which appeals to me, or which lines up with my style or personality or politics. At the risk of high-minded arrogance, I like to hope that my quest seeks what is true, whether or not it is my ox that gets gored.

Most philosophies and religions that deal with human problems are primarily concerned with getting people to make themselves better: to make themselves more enlightened, to make themselves more sincere, to make themselves more loving or more compassionate, to make themselves more motivated, to make themselves more inspired, to make themselves more healthy, to make themselves more spiritual, etc. Christian teaching certainly does implore people to do better. Some Christians, with whom I disagree, think that this should be the main focus of Christianity. I am not at all sure that Christianity has done a lot better than any other system in the citizenship department, especially considering the incomparable abuses of the Church in history, pulpit and chamber. I personally know many non-Christians who have it all over many of "us believers." If the goal is to teach and motivate people to be happier or more successful in this life, I would hesitate to point to Jesus Christ or any of his apostles as examples.

To the contrary, what draws me to the Gospel is that it is not another human self-improvement (which usually is to say self-interest) coaching program. Workshops, programs and personal resolutions notwithstanding, even the best within me and among us consistently falls so far short. I am convinced that after all the wonderful coaching in this world that is so helpful, what is finally needed is rescue.

When we were brand-new Tenderfoot Boy Scouts, Tom and I just about got OUR tender feet blown away. The two of us were hiking our way through the woods to learn how to read animal tracks. Being ever so observant, we observed a nasty looking, spring-loaded contraption that was hidden under a bunch of dry leaves. We realized right away that this thing could really hurt some poor animal. After all, this thing had spring-loaded metal jaws. So we sprang it. It was really kind of cool, actually, snapping a big stick into tiny toothpicks. We found a second one and did the same thing, as we also felt compelled to do with a third and a fourth hazard. Someone really wasn't being careful. When we sprang them all, we headed out to the road to begin our trek back home.

We were kind of proud that we'd done a whole lot more than just help some poor old lady cross the street. Who knew, maybe we'd even make into one of those real-life hero stories in the back of the national Scout magazine, *Boys' Life*. That was right about the moment that we almost qualified for something more like Boys' Death. Bullets started cracking past our ears as trappers were discovering our handiwork. We hit the ditch as more bullets dusted up right beside our heads. We learned some brand new words that afternoon as these two trappers yelled warnings before walking away.

A couple years later, our troop was on a camping trip near a big lake about sixty miles from home. We were on the buddy system as Tom and I swam out to the floating dock. We were almost at the dock when I inhaled some water, choked up and started to go down fast. Tom reached out for me and I clung on to him, and somehow didn't drag him under as we both kicked for our lives. Tom saved my life so that fifty years later I would become a pastor in the little village on that very same lake. Three years later, though, Tom moved and we were no longer in the same troop. So I wasn't there to return the favor when he drowned in an overturned Eskimo kayak. He is the first person I knew whose body was donated to the medical school. Still saving lives.

Christianity is fundamentally about somebody else saving my life. Drowning people do not need someone yelling self-help instructions on how to swim better. People in this kind of trouble need to accept rescue BECAUSE we are drowning.

Despite humanity's phenomenal improvements in myriad ways, it was Jesus two thousand years ago who said that the poor will always be among us. He was obviously right. As of this writing, one person dies from hunger every second somewhere in the world, even with all the heroic improvements in world hunger relief. Five or six people just died from hunger alone in the reading of those last two sentences. Much or most of such suffering is directly attributable to human malpractice such as political acts or misconduct such as crime and war. In many ways, crime and war casualties have been trending down. But humanity has never been able to rid itself of the astounding malevolence that is unique to its life form. I find it literally incredible that skeptics of Christianity so often place their hopes in humanity. To the contrary, humanity's poor track record makes the point that we cannot save ourselves and that what we need is to BE saved. Which is what a savior does.

PART II

THE MAKING OF A
YEAHBUTOLOGIST

Chapter Six

How Could A Pastor Be A Yeahbutologist?

AS A LUTHERAN PASTOR, I HAVE STOOD in the tradition of the sixteenth century German priest and theologian who was named Martin Luther (not to be confused with his most famous namesake, Martin Luther King, Jr.). He was known for driving his mentors nearly out of their minds with his never-ending, self-tormenting questions. Luther's mentor was an old, blind priest named Father Staupitz. In the original movie *Martin Luther*, the young priest happens upon the old sage napping in the courtyard, or trying to, wide-rimmed hat trying to give some privacy to his bowed head. The young Luther, totally oblivious to his mentor's need for solitude, rushes up with his latest theological puzzlement. When the old man doesn't stir, the troubled Luther rouses him with the latest question and begs to know what the wise man thinks. After many more seconds of silence, Staupitz looks up and sighs, "I think, young Martin, eat more food, get more sleep, and learn more about God."

I didn't become a pastor until my mid-thirties. Up to then, my vantage point had been from the pew. From that perspective, it always looked to me as if the one who elevated himself in the pulpit thought he had all the answers. I know that later, as a preacher myself, my silver-tongued oratory may well have conveyed that same misimpression to many others. When this book is up for the Pulitzer Prize, I will not be surprised to hear from some who may be shocked in at least a second way. It was specifically when I was in the pulpit that the God-questions were especially active in my mind. In fact, these quandaries have always been the most active part of my theological thinking, preaching, teaching, counseling and writing.

Unlike many of my pastor friends, I did not attend a church college. I did not major in any of the subjects that people typically take who are headed for seminary. I did not come from a family dynasty of pastors. I have often felt like my unofficial patron, St. (Doubting) Thomas, who didn't seem to "get the memo" or who didn't get the assignment when it was passed out in class. He wasn't there when the risen Jesus appeared to all the other apostles. The apostle Paul also came aboard late, weeks or months after all the action. "But," he said, "by the grace of God, I am what I am, and his grace toward me was not in vain (1 Corinthians 15:10)." That's me. Hence my quandary years in the pulpit. Hence, this book.

One of the essential notions of Christianity is that God came down to humanity, where we are, as we are. That was Jesus. He was like us with one significant exception: he did not sin, though a lot of his own people thought he did. He did break a lot of man-made rules about rituals, but he always did the will of God without exception. Pastors, on the other hand, are mortals like every other mortal, especially in the matter of sinfulness and outright cluelessness. From Genesis all through Revelation, God chose women and men who so often were among the most flawed. The greatest of all Jesus' apostles was Paul who could say that he himself was the worst of all sinners (1 Timothy 1:14). Even the chief of the apostles, Peter, went down in holy history as the one who denied that he even knew Jesus. Not once, but three times and at the precise moment when Jesus needed him most. He wasn't alone in that regard. Even when Jesus walked with them, the missteps of his hand-picked apostles sometimes looked more like twelve Donald Ducks on a banana peel.

In the realm of questions, special mention has to go to a couple people who were particularly close to Jesus. In *The Scars That Shaped Me* (2016, Desiring God) Vaneetha Randall Risner talks about Jesus' slightly older second-cousin whom we know as John the Baptist. He was the one who first identified Jesus as the Lamb of God. John is the one who baptized the thirty-year-old Jesus. And yet, when John was in prison, he sent his own followers to ask Jesus if he really was the one who was promised of old. That's because he was rotting in prison, and the ancient prophecy (Isaiah 61:1) said that the Messiah would set the captives free from prison. "Or shall we look for another (Matthew 11:2-3)?" Soon thereafter he was beheaded.

Of course, there was the apostle Thomas who had proclaimed that he himself would die with Jesus. What he is most remembered for took place just hours after Jesus had been crucified. Not that any of the apostles, apart from the apostle John, had even stood by Jesus at the cross. That's because they had all been taking cover in some locked room out of fear. Except for Thomas. He had not been hiding out with them. So, he was not there when the crucified Christ suddenly appeared, fully alive.

When Thomas returned to the room, and everyone told him that Jesus was alive and had appeared to them, he uttered his now infamous response: "Unless I see in his hands the mark of the nails, and place my fingers into the mark of the nails, and place my hand into his side, I will never believe (John 20:25)."

In terms of having questions, yeahbutologists stand in a long and distinguished tradition. After Jesus was crucified and after he had appeared to them two times, the apostles next saw him on a mountain in Galilee. This time it was more than just one of them who doubted (Matthew 28:17)! But the questions did not have the last word with those first yeahbutologists.

Four things about these first questioners stand out for me. First of all, these questions were seen as important enough to be remembered. Secondly, the propensity to question did not disqualify the apostles. Thirdly, in the case of Thomas, the reason for his questioning was so validated that Jesus gave him exactly what he needed to restore his belief. Finally, the apostle Paul said that God chose him specifically because of his particular weakness. It is entirely possible that it was Thomas' questioning which made him particularly useful to the mission of faith. Maybe that's the case with me.

Thomas was called a doubter because it was Jesus himself who called him a doubter. But, what exactly did it mean that he was a doubter? Would anyone seriously suggest that Thomas was actually doubting in the same way as the enemies of Jesus who were sure that he was a fraud? Or, could it be that he was doubting like someone who says that something is simply too amazing to grasp? Maybe Thomas was saying that he doubted not so much Jesus but the hysterical exaggerations of the other apostles. That's what the holed-up apostles thought of the women who first discovered the empty tomb and ran to report to them what the two angels had told them.

Or was his statement a cry of disappointment as it was with a couple others? Two other dejected disciples were kicking stones down the road on their way to the nearby village called Emmaus. They were so downcast that they didn't even realize that it was the risen Jesus who was walking beside them the whole way. Or, maybe Thomas was doubting more like Martha who was the sister of Lazarus who had just died. She was so upset at Jesus for not coming to help until it was too late. He asked her if she didn't believe in the resurrection. What she said was that she did believe that her brother would rise on the last day. Jesus pressed her further to ask if she believed that everyone who believed in him would actually rise from the dead. She answered by saying that she did believe that he was indeed the Messiah. But she did not say anything about believing any specific thing about her brother's rising from the dead then and there.

Almost all Christians today would answer the same way about someone coming back from the dead: eventually, but probably not immediately. (As someone who has spent a lot of time at cemeteries, I don't recall seeing too many people standing vigil by the gravesite, waiting expectantly over four days for a cameo appearance of their dearly departed. The mourners usually clear out immediately after the graveside committal service, even when the weather is pleasant). Martha's response could seem totally faithful. After all, Jesus had repeatedly warned his apostles to not speculate about when Heaven things would happen. Maybe this is all that Thomas was saying.

As with Thomas, with John the Baptist, with Pastor Tollefsrud, with me and probably every other earnest yeahbutologist, there is sincere and serious wondering.

People are on a spectrum of inquiry, just like each person is on a spectrum of just about anything. I would guess that wherever someone is on the spectrum, few would be comfortable actually telling God, "I doubt you." A lot of people with quandaries might not want to go so far as to call themselves an actual skeptic. Maybe the issue is simply a matter of "having questions." But, in one way or another, we are all yeahbutologists.

Chapter Seven
The Growing of a Yeahbutologist

I AM THE ONLY PERSON IN MY IMMEDIATE FAMILY who has a strange middle name. Everyone else has a first name as a middle name, like Elizabeth or Marie or Solveig or Michael or Wesley or Griffith. Mine is Rieker. All my life I have had to explain what a rieker is and why somebody would name their kid something called a rieker. That's my mother's father's name: Dave Rieker. The story goes that in our heritage, it was traditional to name the first-born grandson after the mother's father. I won the lottery. Which is also why my first name was not David but Dave, because his name was Dave. I have had to live with government clerks always asking me, "Are you SURE it isn't David?" Even grandpa's discharge papers had a company clerk forge his signature as "David Rieker." Government clerks, most especially Army clerks, are not always the best ones to get cute with. So the signature stayed. Imagine my surprise when, on a vacation, I took my family to visit my grandparents' graves, only to read his gravestone say "David." When I confronted my mother about this, she shrugged her shoulders and said, "So sue me!" Her response confirmed that we were, in fact, of Yiddish stock.

Dave/David Rieker might also be the reason why I never became a Hollywood child star. Grandpa was a cowboy extra in westerns before there was sound. He talked about how boring he thought it all was. All day long, they rode back and forth and back and forth in some barn that had scenery painted on the wall. He eventually quit and went back to the plains of North Dakota to run grain elevators. He saw no future in these ridiculous things called movies. That's why my people hail from the prairie and not from Tinseltown. This is because Dave Rieker had a trust problem with the movie industry. It's possible that I may have inherited more than his name. Maybe I also inherited a hypersensitive trust gene.

The Growing Of A Yeahbutologist: The Early Years

My best guess is that my early life is what twisted my wiring into that of a yeahbutologist. There is a growing consensus in some neurological research that chronic stress in childhood, and maybe even in adults, can lead to permanent structural changes in the brain that have a big impact on how one sees the world and responds to it.

When that eleven-year-old Flat Earther wondered where no one else in their right mind would have wandered, it obviously was not because I was some child prodigy in metaphysical cosmology. My questioning of the unquestionable was not a precocious game. It was something that I had learned to do as a matter of survival since the days of my first memories. There are times when ferreting out the truth is a matter of life and death. From the time I was a young child, much of my life has been a matter of trying to figure out what is really true, who is telling the truth, on whom I can bank my life and the lives of those I love. That vigilance was necessary to protect my own family and my career well into the years of my ministry.

In my growing up years, we moved twelve times and I attended thirteen schools. Counting all the short moves after Ann and I married, schools, military bases and our own family years, the total comes to something like thirty-nine places where I've lain my head.

"Was your father in the military?" is always the first thing people will ask.

"No," I say with a totally straight face, "he was a fugitive from justice."

A long, awkward silence is typically followed by, "Oh, I'm, I'm uh, I'm sorry."

I usually put the other person out of his misery immediately. "No, I'm just kidding."

A sigh of relief, until I add, "Well, at least, I don't think he was. I mean, I was just a kid. I was always told we were moving because Dad was getting a better job. Every year. For kind of, like, my whole life."

Right.

Without going into details, my guess is that my dad and our family were going through a major case of what people today call PTSD, Post Traumatic Stress Disorder. I was born in the early aftermath of the Second World War. My little sister and I were part of a relatively small subset of the first Baby Boomers whose fathers had survived particularly heavy combat: "survived" as in "the walking wounded."

A public television documentary said that only about six percent of American servicemen experienced heavy combat. Seven out of ten of those became combat casualties. Such was our dad. He had been under fire for most of four hundred consecutive days when his eardrums were blown out in the Battle of the Bulge. A German 88 shell scored a direct hit on his log-covered fox hole. When he came to, his bisected foxhole buddy lay on either side of him. When I was a teenager, Dad and I were watching a television documentary when, all of a sudden, Dad saw himself and that buddy of his on the newsreel. That footage was shot, so to speak, the day before the incident.

That nineteen-year-old soldier went on to be one of the first troops to liberate Dachau. When I was eight years old, Dad received a thank you gift in the mail from a guy whom he had befriended there. That guy had been a thirteen-year-old who had been operating the oven where he had been forced to cremate his parents, his little sister and his grandparents. Dad shared his cigarettes with the chain-smoking kid who used those to calm his nerves. The gift in the mail was a box of cigarettes and a letter.

When the European war ended, Dad immediately began training for the invasion of Japan. He was the first person to tell me that I owed my existence to the atomic bomb. He had been saved from having to be sacrificed on the beaches of Japan. So, I live specifically because upwards of a quarter million others were incinerated. For that matter, I also know that I'm alive only because another young soldier was shot to death, point blank by my father. I wonder if there is a name given to those of us who live specifically because someone else was killed? Dad came home, started college and married my mother. He dropped out of college shortly before I was born. Perhaps this was connected to two subsequent hospitalizations for "nervous" issues.

For several reasons, I don't share the specifics of what happened to me throughout my earliest years. Suffice it to say that parts of my story might well make it into the paper these days. However, I do not have sufficient confidence in the details of my little-boy memory to risk inaccurate defamations of people. Also, I want the images to die with me. Twenty years of total estrangement from both parents' families, Dad's undiagnosed alcoholism and absolutely the worst of everything that goes with it followed us for the rest of our parents' lives, well into my adulthood.

As with so many troubled families, some of the worst things in my childhood family got immeasurably worse around Christmas. That's why my heart has never been all that much into celebrating Christmas during thirty years of leading congregations in joyful Christmases. My mind has never quite been able to close the gap with my heart for that darkest week of the year. But like so many performers, pastors sometimes have to soldier on, even when their hearts are not in it.

It was in the early years of special trauma, when my life depended on needing to know whom and what to trust, that a defective brick was unintentionally mortared into my faith foundation. With all the stressed conflict and stretched finances in our home, Mom and Dad still found a way to ensure that Santa didn't pass us over. Even as a little boy, I dreaded the advancing storm front of my family's Christmas. So, it was that much more important that the days leading to Christmas were filled with hopes that Santa Claus was coming to town to fulfill some pretty desperate wishes. My wish list for Santa never had anything to do with toys. The night before Christmas, Santa Claus was what faith was all about to me. In the morning, we found proof that he was real, that he really had read our letters, that he really knew what was in our hearts, that he had really been there and had delivered. But before long, my "yeah-but-what-if" questions finally forced my parents to admit that it was all make-believe. The price for growing up was that I now was expected to go along with the parent-approved lie for the sake of my little sister.

Oh yeah, there was one other character I heard about at Christmas. I grew up learning about him because no matter where we moved, my parents always found a congregation and saw to it that my sister and I faithfully participated in Sunday School. Especially at Christmas, the same ones who had made promises about Santa kept talking like Jesus was real too. But the little yeahbutologist never saw a single thing that he left behind for us. Especially peace.

Even with all the stops along the way, from San Francisco Bay to the Badlands of North Dakota to points farther east, I decided to call one of those places my "hometown" because we stayed there longer than anywhere else. Our folks found a wonderful congregation that had a Scout troop. This church became my shelter from the storms. My dad became a lay leader in the congregation, a Sunday School teacher and one of the adult leaders in the Scout troop. With tremendous support of both of my parents, I became an Eagle Scout there and also earned a number of other awards. The first one was the religion medal which was called the "God and Country." However, within ten years, I had all but lost faith in both God and country.

Throughout junior high, my best friend and I hung out every day after school at the church helping (aka pestering) the janitor and the Youth Pastor. Strangely, I have lots of holes in my memory about what I did all those hundreds of hours at the church. Why can't I even recall how the building was laid out? I have always found it strange, that everything from those first years has seemed like a distant dream. Even after visiting that town on business many times since as an adult, it took me years to actually walk into that church which felt only vaguely familiar. For some reason I do not understand, I do not want to ever go in there again. The thought terrifies me.

Maybe it's my own version of some kind of PTSD.

The Growing Of A Yeahbutologist: The Teenage Years

In tenth grade, my family suddenly left that church in a fury of anger. In its annual fund drive, which our brand of churches call the stewardship campaign, the church office had suddenly decided to publish how much each family pledged. This congregation was the wealthy church in town and our family was squarely middle-middle class. My parents were utterly humiliated. So much for my shelter from the storms. So much for church. What took the place of that church was the beginning of an allergy to congregational politics that never left me. Those allergies became part of how I later led congregations as a pastor. Among other things, I distinguished myself as a renowned light-weight when it came to fund-raising.

My folks soon relocated us to another church in town. Though we regularly went to church each Sunday, my parents were concerned that I didn't seem to be engaging things there. So the senior pastor offered me the chance to attend an intense one week personal faith retreat that summer at a nearby church college. It changed my life. It ignited a life-long struggle and a life-long love.

I didn't know it at the time, but the particular month I got that invitation also happened to be the same month that American religion started to go up in flames. Of course I didn't know it then, but the *Time* magazine on the newsstand that very month was the first one to ever have a cover with no image. On a solid-black background, the April 1966 issue simply asked, "Is God Dead?" I never read the article, but strangely enough, and totally unrelated, this became the same month when the dormant yeahbutology gene in my soul was activated.

At that faith development retreat, there was a guest speaker who called himself The Weed. The twenty-something provocateur said something like, "They say that you people are the best and brightest in your church youth groups. Well, this week I'm here to help you discover if you really believe all the stuff your mommies and daddies and pastors have been feeding you. Hope you're up for it."

By this time, I was a seasoned state tournament debater (OK, we captured last place) and served on the State Central Committee of one of the major political parties. Long before Clint Eastwood made the phrase famous, I remember The Weed's dare and thinking something like, "Go ahead. Make. My. Day."

Well, he did. In spades. He described himself as an eleventh year (as if that was supposed to be a good thing) graduate psychology student from Greenwich Village in New York. Also, he was a serious Jew. One who did not particularly like Christianity.

Over the next couple days, he explained that Jesus himself was a Jew who never knew a thing about something called the NEW Testament. Jesus only read the OLD Testament which, by the way, was written by Jews, not Christians. Furthermore, he said, how could our pastors keep a straight face and tell us that the Old Testament was really about Jesus? Isn't it strange, he said, that the people who wrote the Old Testament don't believe any of that stuff about Jesus? These experts, he said, study nothing but the Old Testament, they grow up reading the Old Testament in its original language, and they don't see Jesus in those books.

This guy, however, was one Jew who also studied the New Testament. He knew it inside and outside, far better than any of us did. Hour after hour, day after day, he proved to us that the New Testament contradicted itself. And furthermore, since Jesus was such a good guy, he never would have said that he was God, because no Jew would ever have said anything like that. He said that whoever wrote the New Testament put words in Jesus' mouth. And, by the way, even our New Testament experts say that we don't really know for sure who really wrote a lot of the New Testament anyway. How could we trust stuff when we don't even know who wrote it?

To make matters worse, he said, the writer we do know, the apostle Paul, was a flat-out liar because he knew that a lot of the stuff he said about Jews was dead wrong. Et cetera.

There were more than a couple kids who became so rattled that they had to go home. At least one upset teen developed some kind of cardiac problem. Not me. I was made of tougher stuff. At the same time, I was glad that I would never have to debate this guy. He was a theological lawnmower.

We had been told that the first few days were designed to challenge our faith. Other people would help us glue it all back together in the remaining days. (Hopefully before the Last Days). That second part never happened. The gluing job fell to my discussion leader who was a quiet, golden-haired lass who was a year older and was from another town. Her father was a pastor. By the end of the week, my head was spinning and I was beginning to lose my balance. The best part of losing my balance is that I fell for her. I took her on a tandem bike ride, tipped us over, skinned up her knee, kissed her under a cherry tree, and married her (a few years later).

The Weed had landed some pretty solid hits on my faith. More precisely, he had ignited a grass fire that never went out. To this day, everything gets interrogated by the voice of The Weed. In the days, months and years to come, every single idea in church fell apart in my debater's mind. In church one Sunday, the congregation was singing something like "The Old Rugged Cross." While they were singing that, I was silently humming what was becoming my YEAH, BUT theme song. Gershwin's line from *Porgy and Bess* was, "The things that you're libel to read in the Bible, they ain't necessarily so."

The Growing Of A Yeahbutologist: The Young Adult Years

It was not just church that was taking a beating with me, but my faith in anything. God and country did a head-on crash.

Dad was my war hero in an age that glorified the recent World War II victories of our fighting men in the movies, the TV shows, and the toys of boys. I wanted to be a hero like him and both my grandfathers. That was my dream, not his. When I lionized his wartime heroism, he corrected me. His soul would never stop bleeding for what he had had to do and see and hear and smell and remember every day and every night. I never felt any expectation from him that I should become a soldier. In fact, when I left for basic training, I am told that he became depressed.

When I enlisted in the Army during my war, I, like every other serviceman and woman, made a promise to give my life if necessary for my country. That seemed pretty noble to an idealistic nineteen-year-old. Not long before that, I had been a seventh grader who, like everyone else, had narrowly survived a nuclear holocaust of the Cuban Missile Crisis. These were the same Commies who were going to destroy us if not stopped in some place called Vietnam. By the time I was thrusting bayonets into dummies in basic training, it started to dawn on me that I would have to be willing to kill people on purpose and many others by accident. Particularly as a "cannon cocker" and later as a commander of same, I might have to do this in large numbers. Relatively few of my brothers in arms thought about this and many fewer seemed bothered. We were encouraged to think of such things as unavoidable necessities. The military called it collateral damage. You can't make omelets without cracking eggs.

I didn't realize it at the time, but my whole worldview had been colored by my father's horrors from the Battle of the Bulge and the Dachau concentration camp. I'm glad and proud that he did what he did, because that seemed eminently necessary to stop the Holocaust. But even though he had to fight them, Dad always said that most German soldiers were essentially no different from him. He and the first man he killed could easily have been brothers. At the most fundamental level they clearly were.

Long after the Vietnam war, at a military air show, I came across a typewritten poem in a home-made frame. This poem was about something which had happened at about the same time that I was trying to sort out my thoughts about becoming a combat officer. The soldier named J. Vincent Hansen gave me permission to share these words which he wrote:

> I once killed
> a man at Pleiku.
> And when he died
> I died too.
>
> And that is when
> I first knew,
> When soldiers die
> They die in twos.

I saw that in my dad.

I just came across an updated documentary on the Second World War which was titled, *World War II: In*

Color. Watching real-life footage of mass slaughter is about the last thing I would want to see in color. I once asked Dad what color he associated with his war. He didn't even have to think about it. The color was blue.

"That really surprises me," I told him. "I would have figured something more like red or maybe black."

He looked right through me with what they call "the thousand yard stare." Just like I knew whom he was talking about, he said, "That was the color of his eyes."

"Whose eyes?" I asked.

The stare. "His eyes."

I was beginning to wonder if I needed to slap him across the face to bring him back to Earth. But I also could perceive some kind of ghost behind me. Part of me was afraid to ask. "Dad, I have no idea who you're talking about."

Now my father looked me straight in the eye with a long, long pause. I recognized that disgusted look. Louder than words, his look said, "You're going to make me say it, aren't you?"

After several seconds, he looked down and said, "The first German I ever killed." Few actual combat vets ever want to talk about their war in much detail. For many, the most offensive thing you can do is ask them if they ever killed anybody. In my experience, the vets who like to talk about combat are often the ones who did not actually see a whole lot of it.

He killed "his" first German when he and that enemy soldier were each serving as point scouts for their respective patrols deep in a forest. As each of them scrambled up his opposite side of an embankment, they startled each other when they came face to face. Both reflexively fired at point blank range. The other guy missed, which is why you are reading this. My father hit the mark, as he would say, "totally by dumb luck."

Instinctively, he threw himself on top of the dying soldier in the hail of crossfire from their respective patrols. After dad's squad drove off the German unit, he cradled that young man and talked to him as his enemy died in his arms. Before he passed, the soldier fumbled his wallet into my dad's bloody, shaking hands. In his own dying tongue, the German asked Dad to return this to his family. "Zum meine familia, bitte?" Then, Dad gently closed the eyelids over the blue eyes of the first soldier he ever killed.

When my dad later looked inside that wallet, he found a photo of the young man with his parents and his little sister. And he found identification papers. The man he had just killed was the same age and even had the same curly light blond hair as my dad. Each of them had been confirmed in his home Christian church. And they both had blue eyes. Years later, I would stand at Dad's deathbed as his older brother, my Uncle Hank, gently closed my father's blue eyes, minutes after he passed from a brain tumor. Blue eyes to blue eyes, like a favor returned.

Timing may not have always been my greatest skill. It was in my fourth year of service, right in the middle of Officer's Basic Artillery School, that my willingness to buy into the Vietnam War eventually collapsed. I was still twisting in the wind with God's commandment which I had always been taught was, "Thou shalt not kill." I never came across one pastor or chaplain who came up with anything better than to counsel me that it was all a matter of conscience. I couldn't understand why pastors and chaplains were telling me that I had their blessing to break a commandment if my conscience was not bothered. Decades later I came to believe that what God prohibited was not killing and not even war, since he immediately commanded the Hebrews to do both. I think that what God prohibited was the self-authorized act of murder.

Mainly because he saw what hatred could do on all sides of every conflict, Dad refused to ever let me use the word "hate" when I was growing up. Nevertheless, I have no doubt that he would approve me saying that there was, indeed, one thing that he truly, truly hated, with every bone in his body and with every shock in his nightmares. He absolutely hated everything he had to do in his war. My war hero taught me again and again that war should be used only when unquestionably necessary as the absolute last resort to protect the defenseless. I remember Dad expressing his frustration with the inaction of the relatively new United Nations. His bottom line, however, was to say that as long as everyone was still talking, they weren't shooting. Long after my war-time confusions, I learned that the Church had long accepted this kind of notion, called Just War Theory. I have also learned that this theory, like most theories, has often been twisted to justify just about anything. In my barracks, what I myself had been increasingly unable to explain to myself why this war was absolutely, positively, necessary. My misgivings were later affirmed when our military's eventual withdrawal from Vietnam did not, in fact, lead to the feared Domino Effect of all the world falling to Communism. To the contrary, our enemies became forgiving friends and strong market trading partners. The hated Viet Cong, from whom I thought we were protecting the people, disappeared when we did. The motto of the Artillery School was "Mission First, People Always." I calligraphed that motto above the poster of a lone survivor who was standing atop a pile of rubble that used to be Manhattan. It didn't survive long on my wall. Authorities failed to appreciate the irony. I was ordered to take it down. Imagine that.

It no longer worked for me to simply say that I was an American and that my country, right or wrong, was calling me. On the other hand, I didn't come from a pacifist background and my religious tradition did not have pacifist roots. Rightly or wrongly, I believed that especially since I had voluntarily enlisted years earlier and had participated all this time, that I probably wouldn't qualify at this point as a conscientious objector. So, instead, I actually prayed that if I were sent into combat, something would prevent me from having to kill others. I still had three years left in my hitch. My battalion was on combat "Jump Status" as the next artillery unit to go. But from what I could see, the war was beginning to wind down. I figured that, with any luck at all, the party might be over before we got there. In the decades since, I've discovered how many of us played that crap game. I won my bet, but I carry survivor's guilt for those who didn't. To this day, I beat myself up for having placed my naïve faith in my government which willing to trade over a million lives for its lies.

The reason my dad had to do what he did was because of what most German Christians had allowed their own government to do. But I've also had to swallow the fact that American Christians have long perpetrated or knowingly tolerated persecution against African slaves and their descendants, women, Jews, Native Americans, Japanese Americans, and the mentally handicapped. Persecution of the different and defenseless by so many American Christians has continued to morph into present-day violence against the sexually different, the unborn and immigrants.

Similar horrors have been and still are perpetrated by many other nations and religions. But this does not mitigate the scandal of such things done by the people, the nation, and the faith of which I am part. And now the reader may be pardoned for choking when I say that this is one of the reasons that I am a firm believer in the Gospel of Jesus Christ. More on that to come.

My lessons in trust continued to erode after I worked for a candidate who would became the only President in United States history to resign because he lied. T.H. White wrote a book about it called *Breach of Faith*. No kidding. That hit it on the head. Hit me on the head. Again. Breach of faith.

I was not doing all that well in terms of the where-to-place-my-bets department (the one big exception being my wife). I was not consciously aware of keeping score. However, my neural memory bank has done a pretty good job of keeping track of my misjudgments. That's why, whenever I find myself thinking that something or someone is true and trustworthy, an amber button lights up with the warning, "YEAH, BUT."

I more than understand why so many of my friends in the world of advanced degreed professionals, including mainstream clergy, have walked away from classic tenets of Christianity. Authoritarian abuses by dishonorable "Christians" have defamed ideas like the authority of Scripture, obedience and repentance, the existence and nature of Heaven and Hell. The biggest trust casualties have been the notions that all people are in need of salvation and that faith in Jesus Christ is necessary for that salvation. Almost all books, movies, and intellectual thought have taken dead aim at religion in general and

Christianity in particular. The Weed is always alive and well in the back of my own mind whispering, "So, what is all THAT telling you?"

The first thing that tells me is a warning against once again putting my faith in the wrong things. On the other hand, since "everybody knows" all the negative things about Christianity, my yeahbutology meter also goes over into the red zone regarding anti-Christian skepticism.

Whether it's Christianity or its challengers, I never stop turning the coin over. And over. And over. All of this is to say that there has always been a big part of me that identifies with Doubting Thomas. But like Thomas, for some reason, I do come to rest on Jesus. This memoir is about why I do this.

The Growing Of A Yeahbutologist Into A Pastor

One of the compelling things to me about the Bible is how it continually runs against the clichés of life. Back in the day, as we say, each high school graduating class published a yearbook of photos and memories. These yearbooks often had a section called "Voted Most Likely," classmates whom the rest of us voted as most likely to succeed in one thing or another. Most of the heroes in the Bible would have been voted as "LEAST Likely to Succeed." Me too.

Years of faith struggles had taken many forms. My wife was a pastor's kid and for years I simply tagged along to church with her. Actually, there was nothing simple about it. Every Sunday after church I would make sarcastic comments about the stupid things the pastor said and the mindless sheep who simply took it all in. She never took the bait. Ann simply nodded to let me know that she was still awake. She still does that. One Sunday in church, we were sitting on the end of the pew when I felt a tap on my shoulder. For quite a while thereafter, I assumed that the tap had come from one of the ushers. He asked if I could help out because they were short-handed. From that moment on, I had a permanent job and suddenly "I" was part of "them."

Months later, the pastor learned that I was in the field of education. He asked if I would consider teaching the faith to teenage confirmands. I thought he must have been out of his mind. I said something along the lines of first needing to get my own faith act together before I messed it up for others. His reply was that the best way to learn something was to teach it. Plus, his offer came with the requirement that we teachers meet with him weekly. The following year, I was asked to serve on the church Council. Apparently that tap on the shoulder had literally called me off the bench for more than the offering plates.

Before long, my wife and I bought our first house which was in another town and so we moved to a closer church. Soon I was teaching teenagers again. And serving on the church Council again. And singing in the choir and reading the scripture lessons again. My volunteer resume changed late one Saturday night. The phone rang and it was the pastor. I could barely understand him because he had an advanced case of laryngitis.

"Dave, you're a speech therapist, right?"

"Yes."

"You treat voice problems?"

"Yes."

"I need help with my voice."

"Can't."

I explained that there was nothing that could be done at the moment. It would simply have to run its course. "You'll lose everything by morning."

He cleared his throat, "So, um, could you take the service for me in the morning?"

I thought he was joking, so I teased back. "Yeah, sure."

His response was something like, "I really owe you one. Thanks." And he hung up.

Eight hours later I finished leading the first church service of my life. Afterwards, I was greeting worshippers at the back of the sanctuary like I had seen the pastor do each week. An older woman who was one of the senior leaders in the church was four handshakes back. Her eyes were locked on mine like a heat-seeking missile. She was an Army full colonel and I immediately became a junior officer again, instinctively wondering where I must have screwed up. She stepped forward, looked me in the eye, officially pumped my hand and said, "You have a calling."

I thanked her for her compliment but said I was sure that there must be a lot more to being a pastor than just leading a worship service. She sort of came to attention and bored a look straight through me, like other colonels had done. "I did not mean it as a compliment. How you deal with God's call is your problem."

She did a right face and left me with a red one. She marched off and left me to greet the next person who had an expression like, "Ooo, um, yeah, sorry about that."

My greater fear was having to tell my wife that I thought I might have offended this particular person. That's because this colonel had always been one of Ann's most revered instructors in her nurse's training.

My only hope of a reprieve was what Ann had once said back when we were seriously dating. I distinctly remember kind of making a "note to self." This PK (pastor's kid) said she never again would want to live in the glass house of a pastor. That wasn't because there was any danger of me becoming a pastor. Rather, this was more in the context of saying that she was glad I was going into any field other than the ministry. But, on our way home, she said that she actually agreed with the Colonel. I almost drove up over the curb. Still, we both agreed that with a new mortgage, a baby and a tenured teaching position, how in the world could we afford my return to school?

Three days later, after he recovered his voice, the pastor stopped by the house to thank me.

"I hear you also got a little talk by The Colonel," he said. "Don't let it bother you. She can be a little direct at times."

I chuckled and he added, "And, whatever you do, do not listen to her advice. You don't want to be pastor, believe me."

That last remark really threw me for a loop. I thought a pastor would have encouraged a church member to enter

the ministry. I wondered if I had flunked my altar
audition the other day.

"You're telling me to NOT go into the ministry?" I said.

He said, "Not if there is any way you can avoid it."

"Well," I said, "that shouldn't be too hard. I never took
any classes in college that would get me into seminary.
I've just gotten tenure with the school system, we've
racked up close to a million dollars in medical costs, we
have a mortgage, and because of our sick child, Ann and
I can't both work at the same time."

He kind of pursed his mouth in deep thought. "Yeah.
About that. I've also come over to tell you that our parish
has an old scholarship fund for members who want to
enter full-time ministry. (Dot number one). It would
cover all expenses. But, again, I would advise you not to
do it."

I had no idea what to say. I had no idea what to think
or what to feel. I think I must have looked a little
confused. He filled in the space. "The ministry is all about
personal sacrifice. For you, your spouse, your kids. It
quite often can be really tough. You need to give this
some serious prayer, thought and time. If you still decide
to look further, get back to me about that scholarship."

Two weeks later, presumably out of the blue, the school
district offered me a temporary, new, experimentally
funded position. It would not have predictable hours or
clear responsibilities. I would have to be comfortable
with uncertainty. But the hours would be variable and
flexible. And, my salary would remain unchanged. (Dot
number two).

One week later in church, the guest preacher was an elderly, blind pastor. He was focusing on a Bible story about another blind old priest who was helping someone hear God's Call. The story goes that when the young boy heard God call out to him, he assumed that it was someone else speaking his name. It wasn't until this had happened three times that it was revealed to the boy that it might be God calling him. In the story, the blind old priest was named Eli. The boy was Samuel who would become the first prophet. In my case, the blind old preacher was the elderly father of The Colonel who two weeks earlier told me that I had a Call. This was the third time in as many weeks that something unusual had lined up about a Call to ministry.

I was beginning to connect the dots. I decided that if God might possibly be involved in all this, maybe I should give seminary a chance and see how things went, one academic term at a time. I fully expected the Seminary to say that I didn't have the necessary qualifications. Older, second-career seminarians were not something I had ever heard about. If I were turned away out of hand, then this might tell me that I was connecting dots that really weren't there, after all. I was surprised when the admissions officer told me that they had had some good experiences with what was jokingly being referred to as "retreads." In any case, the first year for every new seminarian was a trial period for both the seminary and student to see if this was a good fit.

Fast-forward four years. My father-in-law had recently retired as a pastor and he was granted special permission to conduct my ordination. I sat in the front pew as he preached from the elevated pulpit. He waited until all the paper shuffling, coughing and throat clearing faded away.

"I have known Dave, now, for most of his life. He walked into ours when he was all of fifteen years old." He rolled his eyes, "And he hasn't left since." Chuckles from the congregation. He was just getting started.

"So, I knew him when he was a teenager. I knew him when he started college, when he interrupted his studies to enlist as a soldier, when he returned to college, when he became a speech and language pathologist. I remember when he came, hat in hand, to ask permission to marry our eldest daughter, Ann. Of course, I've known him as the father of our granddaughters, Karen and Kirsten." I was like a balloon that was inflating with pride.

"I remember when Dave came to the same office where he once told me of his wishes to marry our daughter. This time, he came to discuss maybe entering seminary." This veteran speaker really had a way of building to a peak.

"For close to twenty years, I have watched Dave move through all these steps in life. And now, today, I stand before you as I look at him, and I can't help but think to myself ...." Here he paused, as if in deep reflection. There was not a sound throughout the congregation as even the littlest children stopped fidgeting.

He had our attention as he finished his thought. "I stand before you as I look at him ......" I was swelling with humble pride as he approached the pinnacle of his accolade.

"I look upon Dave, and I can't help but think to myself ..... " I held my breath.

"I think to myself .... how odd of God."

He had just stuck a needle into the balloon of my inflated pride. The whole sanctuary erupted in laughter.

So now the guy with all the questions would become the same guy with all the big answers. I would spend the next thirty years proclaiming as truth the most amazing claims in the history of human thought. I would preach that God actually existed and that all humans are infected with sin; that God came to Earth as a human baby; that this Jesus grew up to offer his life to pay the price of our sins; that everyone lives eternally and that trusting Jesus is the only way to avoid Hell and enter Heaven; that repeated, deliberate refusal to obey God's commands and refusal to repent can cost a person his salvation; that all of this is true because the Bible says so. How odd of God, for sure.

I almost feel like I was being put in my place, but not necessarily by my father-in-law. In maybe the oldest book of the Old Testament, a man named Job had been hurling at God accusatory questions about his unfair sufferings. God finally answers in anger and tells Job that he's about fed up with all the questions. "Why do you talk without knowing what you're talking about? I have some questions for you, and I want some straight answers. Tell me, since you know so much (Job 38:2-4 The Message)!"

The odds that I would ever wind up in a pulpit would have been virtually non-existent if you had asked me. It would never have crossed my mind to even consider something like this. For one thing, I had worked hard at a career with which I was quite happy. For another thing, religion and I had not been on good terms lately. But over the years, I've noticed in my reading of the Bible that few, if any, of God's servants have applied for the job. Usually, these appointments were a surprise to anyone who knew these people. The recruits were often the ones who were the most surprised.

Go figure. How odd of God, indeed. And now, with all my instinctive yeahbutology, I was newly ordained just in time for everything in society to begin coming apart. Why not? I entered adulthood by graduating from a big-city high school in America's most explosive year since the Civil War, 1968. I got to be part of all that, even as a soldier on my own university campus. Now I would serve my entire ministry during what Church historians are calling the most globally tumultuous era of religion in the last five hundred years. In America and Europe, these times are called "The POST Christian Era", as if Christianity itself has become, in some sense, a past thing.

To oversimplify a highly complex matter, I think it means that most people, including most Christians, no longer see Christianity as essential. I call it TIOLI Christianity: Take It Or Leave It. My sense is that most people who do see Christianity as important, nevertheless presume the competence to define it any way they want. Consumers increasingly do the same thing with medical matters and other highly specialized issues. But water still seeks the lowest level. Do-it-yourself theologians usually define things on their own terms, usually in their own image and only as it suits their personal wants and needs. Maybe that is why religion these days is so often thought of as a man-made, cultural matter. Supernatural things like Heaven and Hell are sounding increasingly bizarre, especially in these days of such amazing scientific and technological advancement.

My own timing in all cultural things has always been a problem. Whether it's fashions, music, clothing, food, or even philosophies, I always seem to get interested long after that thing has passed. When I applied to seminary, nobody told me that we were already in the POST Christian era. Pretty much everybody I had known was Christian and had gone to a church. In college, I had never taken religion courses and so I had never even heard of The Post Christian Era. By the time I found out about it, it was old news. It wasn't until I had been a pastor long enough to ask where everybody was going that I found out that my whole career had been on a sinking institution. The truth is that the number crunchers and cultural commentators hadn't start making a big deal out of this until twenty years after I was ordained.

If our culture is post-Christian, my guess is that it is post anything that is unseen. Most Americans these days, especially formally educated people, and most especially scientists, like to think that they only believe what they can see or understand or prove. I think I am largely that way about day to day matters, controversial issues, politics and policy. Like so many my age, I was raised and educated in the world of science. The year after the first American blasted into orbit, I was in sixth grade. Among all the sixth graders in my school district, one of the guys I never knew would one day become an astronaut to fly on three Space Shuttles, George "Pinky" Nelson.

Later, in college, my first two academic degrees were in the scientific fields of Speech Science, Pathology and Audiology. I studied research design and methodology, acoustic physics, fancy hi-tech instrumentation, the anatomy and physiology of neuroscience, principles of oral maxillo-facial surgery and brain injury, child development as well as counseling, operant conditioning and biofeedback strategies. I spent the next fifteen years diagnosing and conducting therapy and research with people who had disorders of communication.

After fifteen years in the natural sciences, I became a pastor with major weekly functions of teaching and preaching the fundamentals of faith. Sometimes, though, as I was preparing my sermon, I would step outside myself and imagine someone off the street looking at me and what I was saying. Sometimes, against the backdrop of our culture, the ideas would seem ludicrously out of place, things you rarely heard out-loud like sin and Heaven and salvation, and Hell. Or, I would be up in the pulpit and a thought would cross my mind, "Who in the world do you think YOU are to be talking so confidently about things you have never seen? How can you be so sure that all of this is really true?" In trying to ferret out the truth, assurance of eternal life was always what was at stake, not just for me but more importantly for everyone listening to me.

Throughout thirty years of wearing the robes and trappings of a Christian pastor, I sometimes was a little haunted by the fool who strutted around in *The Emperor's New Clothes.* Periodically, I actually had nightmares of finding myself naked in the pulpit! With all these big ideas that I was parading around, could people see through my wise-sounding pretensions? Who did I think I was? I could hear echoes of what Jesus' boyhood neighbors even said about him:

"He went away from there and came to his hometown, and his disciples followed him. And on the Sabbath he began to teach in the synagogue, and many who heard him were astonished, saying, 'Where did this man get these things? What is the wisdom given to him? How are such mighty works done by his hands? Is not this the carpenter, the son of Mary (Mark 6)?'"

I have wrestled with all kinds of serious matters which have always come down to the same question of that eleven-year-old: is it all really true?

PART III

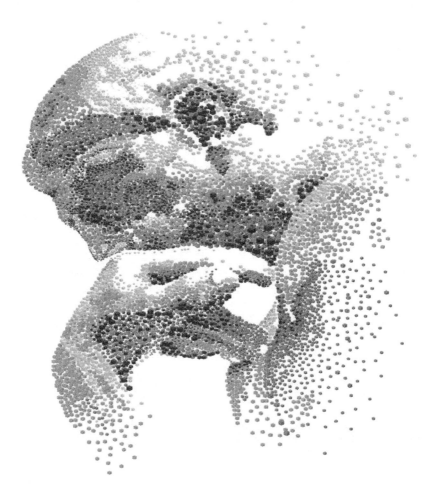

THE WAY I THINK

Chapter Eight
How Things Look to Me

I LOVE A GOOD MUSICAL. One of my all-time favorites is *Fiddler on the Roof.* Long after I fell in love with it, I discovered that it is the story of how I myself came to be an American. My mother's mother's side of the family was German Jewish in the White Russia area called Odessa. Their little village was eventually routed by the Czar in another Jewish liquidation. They migrated through Chicago to the prairies around Bismarck, North Dakota in the 1800's. The musical is the story of one family making that forced move from the same region as my family, to the same region as my family, at the same time as my family. The parents, Tevya and Golda, like so many others, brought with them a small sack of seeds with which to plant a new life.

Two generations later, my mother and her identical twin sister (and I do mean identical) were born to Matilda and Dave Rieker. And the seeds continued. This grandfather, after whom I was named, became a seed buyer in a number of lonely little whistle-stops along the rail lines. By the time he died, he had become an assistant grain advisor for the North Dakota Public Service Commission. After the Second World War, his eldest daughter (by fifteen minutes), my mother, was a student at the University of Minnesota. She would meet and fall in love with my father who just happened to be a horticulture student. I came along, and from my earliest memories until I was in third grade, I would ride along with him as he travelled the Bay Area of California selling, what? You guessed it: seeds. Decades later, I would become a pastor who recited, preached and taught all the things Jesus would say about seeds. The most frequent verse was one I would read hundreds of times at graveside services: "Unless a grain of wheat falls into the earth and dies, it remains alone; but if it dies, it bears much fruit," (John 12:24). Always with the seeds.

That's the way people like Tevya and Golda say it, "always with the seeds." Mom grew up speaking Yiddish until she was thirteen. Because of this, my sister and I would later unwittingly commit a major cultural sin. In high school German classes we would unwittingly pronounce things the way mom taught us. That was "low" German when we were supposed to be learning "hoch Deutsch," high German.

I know every word of *Fiddler on the Roof*. One of my favorite parts is at the beginning of the musical where we are introduced to several characters in the village of Anatefka, which could have been our ancestral home. One of these people is Yenta the Matchmaker. She proudly tells one father that she has finally found a match for his son. The father, however, is less than impressed with her choice because everyone knows that the girl is half blind. Yenta suggests that the man's son himself might not be all that much to look at. She says, "The way she sees and the way he looks, it's a perfect match!"

Without my glasses, I'm about half blind. With my glasses, everything I do see is through strong corrective lenses. This chapter is an attempt to help the reader understand why some things look to me the way they do.

In the Western world there has been an ever-increasing optimism in almost limitless human capabilities. The idea seems to be that there is nothing that humanity can't do, and that science and technology can solve just about anything. The upshot of this pride was articulated by the late (and I do mean late) Stephen Hawking, maybe the most brilliant theoretical physicist who ever lived. He was fond of saying that there is no longer any need for God, since we have figured out the most important mechanisms of existence. He had a marvelous way of coping with a horribly debilitating degenerative disease. But his indefatigable spirit could not eclipse the fact that no human brilliance could cure his disease and no human effort could save him from death. As far as not needing God, I think he was a brave man to have said that when he knew that he was perched at the very end of his earthly life. No mortal, however wise in his own eyes, has ever managed to overcome the limits of his own existence.

I am an awe-inspired beneficiary of human achievement and I can't begin to imagine what will be accomplished even in the next generation. I am a technogadgetologist of the first order. One of my greatest regrets about dying someday is that I will not be around to see all the amazing technical developments to come. Even so, I am not holding my breath to see anyone ever be able to end crime. Or end all disease. Or eliminate war. Or create the perfect human being. Or cure death. Or create life. Or capture whatever it is that leaves the body at death. Or control the nature of his or her existence beyond this life. It seems to me that since the Age of Enlightenment in the 1700's, humanity has been in its adolescence of stunning accomplishment and even more stunning misperceptions of invincibility, self-importance, self-centeredness, and self-sufficiency. In the venerable *Scientific American*, science journalist John Horgan articulated such a mentality when said, "Barring catastrophe, we can keep exploring *ourselves*, discovering *ourselves*, forever (italics mine). Even if we transform *ourselves* into a cosmic computer dedicated to figuring itself out, *our identity crisis* will not end," (December 1, 2018). Methinks, perchance, the shoe doth fit.

My thinking is driven by a few perspectives of a different sort which:

1. distinguish between important matters and ultimate matters,
2. focus on the long term (it's not about the here and now),
3. do not place humanity at the center (it's not about us),
4. accept that there are limits to human ability,
5. accept that not all questions can be answered here and now,
6. maintain vigilant scrutiny of my thinking (keeping my brain on a leash),
7. accept some time-tested measure outside myself as the standard of scrutiny,
8. value the importance of humility,
9. recognize the inadequacy of proof as the standard of ultimate things,
10. accept reasonableness as an alternative to proof,
11. try to understand difficult things by comparing them to accepted everyday parallels.

Chapter Nine
The Difference Between IMPORTANT and ULTIMATE

THE MAN-EATING REPTILE GROWS each time I tell the story. At last count, the serpent was over fifty feet long and weighed upwards of six hundred pounds. At least. The truth is, between the terror of that moment and the fog of years, I really cannot recall the actual numbers.

The time I was most afraid of being killed by a wild animal was not the time wolves were sizing me up on a remote island in the Lake of the Woods. It was not the night my bride and I were encircled by luminescent green eyes around our honeymoon campfire on the north woods island of Isle Royale. There was that time, though, when a charging black bear turned my dark beard to silver. At two o'clock in the morning, I was outside our tent answering nature's call. Nature's call turned out to be a snarl. A black bear was crouched to the ground with its ears pinned flat back. It charged and I sprinted away from the tent of my sleeping family to a close-by brick shower building. For the rest of the night I pushed back against the door as the beast growled and tried to claw his way in. The only reason he didn't come through the steel door was that he may not have been all that large. Either that or he was just playing with his food. Later that morning I shaved and noticed streaks of silver in my beard.

In the wild, it was probably the predators I never knew about that were the greatest danger to me. Come to think of it, that was also true in congregations I served. It was even true once in a preschool nursery. As a speech and language pathologist in an inner city public school, I sometimes had to share sad diagnoses with very distraught parents. For example, I would be the one to have to tell them that their child needed special therapy. After one such conference, the team social worker seemed uncharacteristically rattled. She told me that the father she was sitting next to had had a revolver pointed at me under the table.

I exploded at her, "And you didn't SAY anything?"

"Like what? Duck?" she said. "That wouldn't have helped much considering where the gun was aimed!"

I truly do think that guy qualified as a wild predator. But that is not where I felt most in danger of being killed by a predator. In those days, I co-taught two classrooms of four-year-old children who had major communication problems. Many of these little ones also had physical, social and emotional issues which made it difficult to take them on field trips to places like the zoo. So we took advantage of one of the zoo's traveling exhibits that would come to us. This time they brought a parrot, four bunnies, one armadillo and a pair of hedgehogs.

And a python. Twenty little ones were all seated in awesome wonder when "Mister Snake" was brought out. The volunteer explained that Mister Snake was not dangerous because he had already been fed and was actually kind of sleepy. You could actually see the bulge of the huge rat that was even sleepier inside Mr. Snake. Many of the children had major fear issues, so the speaker wanted the children to know that they could trust the grown-ups there to only bring safe things.

Just to prove their point, she said, "Would you like to see Mister Dave hold Mister Snake?"

I don't remember having a vote. I also don't recall them saying anything about things being safe for the teachers. Since we were trying to teach the children how to deal with fear, I didn't think it was the best time or place to scream out something like, "You've got to be out of your mind!" I can't call to mind the actual dimensions of said beast, but I do recall that it took all of the five trained volunteers to drape it over my shoulders. My shoulders. The other thing I remember is that I almost buckled under the weight. When our little charges screamed with delight, two things happened. The leader sweetly reminded the children to be as quiet as they could so as to not startle our friend. That remark kind of startled me. Speaking about the head volunteer reminds me of a second head thing. That python had a head. I had no idea that snakes had heads that big. When the kids cheered, the python kind of extended straight up and leveled off face to face with me. Until then, I had also never thought of snakes having faces either. Then its tongue darted in and out and in and out and sort of tickled my nose. The kids liked that a lot.

"Boys and girls, how many of you have doggies at home? How do they give you a kiss? Well, Mister Snake wants to be friends with Mister Dave." The feeling was not mutual. The python straightened up above me and very smoothly settled back down in an embracing coil that pinned my arms to my side.

"Oh look!" said the volunteer. "Mister Snake is giving Mister Dave a hug."

I suddenly wondered how I would know if this thing was killing me. I checked out the faces of the volunteers and most of them were still smiling. But those were the ones who didn't seem to be making eye contact with me.

The python slowly and smoothly snugged me a little more. I clearly remember thinking something like, "They wouldn't let this thing kill me." It got a little tighter and I thought, "Would they?" It cinched it's noose a bit more and I thought, "I've never heard of any zoo animal killing a teacher. Certainly not in school."

To the only volunteer who was making eye contact with me, I motioned with my head to come closer. The squeeze was now on. I whispered, "You can get this thing off me, right?"

"Well, yeah. Usually," she said. My look must have signaled something because she added, "The snake is responding to your blood heat, because you're sort of turning red. What you need to do is relax."

That did not help me relax. I must have gotten redder because the python was getting tighter. Why wasn't anybody else looking concerned? Was I overreacting? How serious was this? Could I wind up dying here? Literally wind up? The snake kept tightening and I whispered a little more forcefully, "You need to get this thing off me. Right now, please. I'm not kidding."

All this while, with each slow constriction, I was trying to figure out if my world might really be coming to a very quiet end. I was whispering, after all. It wasn't because I was totally out of breath. Yet. I think I still could have screamed, but for some reason, I didn't. I clearly recall that what I was most concerned about was the kids. Even if nothing bad happened to me, my reaction could cause permanent damage to these emotionally vulnerable little kids. In retrospect, I think my voice reflected the difference between what was very important (my life) and what was ultimate (the kids).

The children never did pick up on the drama. It took the immediate, sustained and calm efforts of all five handlers to stroke the underside of that reptile and cause it to relax. No sooner did they return the snake to its box than they pulled out a saucer-sized, long-haired tarantula. "Maybe Mister Dave would like to hold Mister Spidey." I almost had an accident of another sort right there. I have always struggled with arachnophobia and so I passed on the offer.

Years later as parish pastor, I was almost daily sorting out important things from ultimate things. For a solo parish pastor, the pinnacle of the whole week is Sunday. Every day of the week is another step in preparing for the sabbath. Sermon preparation itself can easily occupy at least twenty hours. The writing of the prayers, the study of the assigned Scriptures, the careful selection of hymns to reinforce the given themes, arrangements and service design to include the help of others, the preparation for a children's sermon, and the design and production of a bulletin can take another twenty to thirty hours. All of that is in addition to classes prepared and taught, endless committee and administrative functions, hospital calls, multiple crisis and counseling sessions, funerals and weddings. Every one of these things is extremely important, especially for the people who are involved. All along the way, one glitch or another would threaten to make it all come apart. I come down with laryngitis. The bride drops her wedding dress in the mud as a car rolls over it, three hours before the ceremony. It takes constant effort to remember that no matter what happens to these super-important things, the world will indeed continue to spin.

December 15, 2013 was not totally unusual. I have lived through that kind of Sunday many times. Because we were approaching Christmas, the worship service also included a delightful play which was written by the choir director and performed by the children. In addition to planning and conducting a traditional worship service, I had also done a fair amount of rehearsing for the role of Mr. Schnoop. A great time was had by all and a holiday reception followed.

Then I led an hour-long adult Bible study. Just as I was concluding the session, I received an emergency call from one of the eleven police departments I served as a uniformed police chaplain. I suited up and rushed to a crime scene where the body of a University freshman had been discovered. My job was to find the parents and break the news. Officers have often told me that they would far rather deal with a hold-up than deliver death notifications. I would usually drive my own car behind a squad car. Just as we pulled up in front of the house, the officer would often turn on the flashing lights to get the attention of whomever was inside. Then, we would walk up to the door together while someone in the house peered out at two cops approaching, one wearing a clergy collar. All this would give that person a few seconds to brace for whatever emotional hit was about to be delivered.

When the door was answered, we would introduce ourselves and immediately ask if we could all be seated, in case the person should pass out from shock. Then, so that we didn't further confuse a person who might be looking for a way to deny the news, our training was to avoid saying vague things like the victim had "passed." We had to say that their son had "died" or had been "killed." And then my job would be to help pick up the pieces. I would spend the rest of the afternoon counseling the parents, family and friends. I was usually the last first responder on the scene with the family after everyone else had moved on. Eventually I did too. As a pastor, I often had to do some other heavy lifting before the day was over.

At seven o'clock, I was on stage with some of the world's most famous rock stars at a benefit concert for one of them who was dying from cancer. Four years earlier, he had attended a wedding that I had conducted. He asked me if I would be his friend and pastor to walk him home to Jesus over the next few months. The journey would take four years. Tonight, he asked if I would open the benefit concert in prayer.

When I went to bed that night, I reflected on all the important things that had happened that day. All of them very important. But not all of them were ultimate matters.

All through my years, there have been all kinds of different things which meant the world to me at one time or another. When I was a little boy, the denial or loss of some things could really wreck my day. How many times did I cry myself to sleep when a pet died? When I was trying to fit in as a young teenager, the appearance of my clothing or the failure of a homework assignment could make me want to stay home out of utter humiliation. In my late teens, I remember thinking about nothing else day in and day out than my girlfriend. The fear of losing her love could crowd out any other matter in the entire universe. Most adults who are reading this are chuckling right about now because we've all been there, done that, got the tee-shirt. But we've also come out the other side intact and we realize how none of that really was such big a deal. But those were indeed big issues to us when we were going through them and nobody was able to convince us otherwise. That's what a lot of teen suicide is all about, a permanent solution to a temporary problem.

But, even as adults, the loss of a job, a reputation, a family, or even our health can seem like ultimate things. That's what a lot of clinical depression, self-medication, divorce and adult suicide is about. As a pastor who has been through it all so many times with others, the thought of losing any of our children or grandchildren is more than I can stand. I can't imagine how I could go on, or that I would even want to. But almost everybody does go on. Many realize that not even these kinds of heartbreaks have to be the end of the world, especially for the one who is facing death.

Everyone knows that horrible things occur. Nevertheless, it only seems logical to me that whatever happens is what God has allowed to happen. Because of that, my trust in God sometimes nearly shatters at some of things that God could have stopped but didn't. My reading of the Bible and my experience as a pastor prevent me from uttering the sweet-sounding false assurance that "God would never allow (this or that) to happen." If God is all-powerful and all-loving, then I can only conclude that the things which God does allow to happen are not really ultimate matters: something else is. My guess is that what is ultimate to God is whatever impacts his eternity with us.

Throughout the Jewish, Christian and Moslem scriptures, the poor and oppressed are always to be cared for with generosity and grace. But all those scriptures and life itself has God himself allowing people to be poor and oppressed. While earthly suffering and injustice are clearly major concerns to God, he obviously chooses not to eliminate them. This tells me that, as important as such things may be, they are still not God's main focus. Again, this is not to say that these things are unimportant, especially in terms of what God clearly expects of us. The elimination of pain and injustice in this life is clearly not God's ultimate concern for the sufferer. It may, however, be an ultimate matter to God for those who inflict it and those who tolerate it.

Chapter Ten

It's Not About The Here And Now

ONE OF THE MOST IMPORTANT PREMISES in my thinking is that "the point of it all" has to be way, way beyond the fleeting things of the here and now.

That God would have everything be about the long perspective makes total sense to this dad and grandpa. Everything my wife and I have done with our kids and grandchildren has been to prepare them for the future. When our eldest daughter was all of five years old, Ann and I were visiting with another couple in our living room. We grown-ups were so deeply engrossed in our conversation that we didn't even notice Karen quietly and patiently standing off to the side for maybe a good five minutes or so.

Ann was the one who noticed and said, "Do you need something, Honey?"

"Well, I know you're busy and I don't want to interrupt," she said in a seriously teacher-like voice. "But I need to ask you something."

"That's OK, Sweetie," I said. "Thank you for being so patient. What would you like?"

"Well, I know you're busy and I don't need an answer right away, and it's OK if you say 'no' and I already checked and her mom is going to be home ..." She was bobbing her little head and counting things off on her fingers to make sure she hit all the bases. Our guests were in wide-eyed amazement.

"And I won't whine if you say 'no', but can I walk over to Amanda's and play at her house?" She wanted to seal the deal. "And I don't have to know right now ...."

Ann excused herself to negotiate the final details with our little diplomat. Our guests were almost in shock and I told them to expect a similar visit in the next few minutes from our three-year-old. Little sister Kirsten, as usual, was right on schedule with her version of Part Two.

Over the last few years, I had been working as a speech and language pathologist in a public school inner city special education preschool. One of the skills we had been trying to teach the children was how to use words instead of violence to get what they wanted. So Ann and

I imported some of those concepts into our own parenting. We taught our little girls how we go about deciding our answers, so they could know how to negotiate when they ask for something:

1. They can know that usually we want to say yes, if we can.
2. The first thing we ask ourselves is if the request is for something good.
3. The next thing we ask ourselves is if the request is safe.
4. The louder they ask, the more likely we'll say no.
5. The faster they need an answer, the more likely we'll say no.
6. We do not have to have what they think is a fair or good reason.
7. They can always use words to explain why we should reconsider.
8. We are the ones who will decide.
9. For the privilege of getting to negotiate with us, they have to accept our decision without complaining.
10. I can't recall, but there must have been a tenth thing.

Part of why we did this was simply to avoid the grief of constant badgering and whining. But the main reason we did this and almost everything else was to prepare our kids for handling the future. In this case, how to negotiate.

The default human perspective is usually about the here and now. And yet, almost everything on this Earth is neither here nor now. Almost everything is in the past and in the future. The popular astrophysicist Neil deGras Tyson has explained that if all the years of Earth were compressed into the one hundred yards of a football field, the entire span of Homo sapiens would occupy the thickness of the last blade of grass in the end zone.

Therefore, it makes eminent sense to me that, unlike most philosophies, the main focus of Christianity is not on the here and now: it's about an existence in an entirely different realm, perhaps in the least comprehensible dimensions of time. Sometimes, I wonder if this is precisely what the mind-stretching revelations of the Space Age are getting us ready to grasp.

On this Earth, every living thing dies. There is no exception to the rule. The temporary nature of all living things convinces me that earthly life is not the point of existence. In the grand order of things, it would seem to be an exceedingly inefficient use of energy and other resources that go into each human being, just for that being to be extinguished in a blink of time.

Virtually all cultures of every time and place have developed extensive awareness of existence after death. The forms and rituals are all different, but almost every person who has ever lived and the vast majority of those living right now sense that life somehow continues after death. To me, this seems something like an inborn homing instinct. To regard Christianity in term of one's lot in the here and now strikes me as shortsightedly missing the point.

Another reason I look to the "long game" is that this has been one of the most basic assumptions behind just about all our understandings in the natural sciences, from evolution, to geological processes, to nutrition and exercise, to global warming, to the stars themselves. The longevity of all creation is found even in Newton's First Law of Thermodynamics which says that the total amount of energy in a closed system cannot be created or destroyed, though it can be changed from one form to another. The popular astrophysicist, Carl Sagan, was famous for saying that every single person is made of "star stuff." What he meant was that some of the most precious things in our bodies like gold, silver and iron come from stars that exploded eons ago, billions and billions of miles away. What we see now is not what will be, what we do now will have major impacts in the future, and so many things that seem distasteful, senseless or destructive in the present are things that will actually help in the long run. In fact, without too many exceptions, whatever seems desirable in the short run will almost always be worse in the long run, and vice versa. It seems eminently reasonable to imagine that this would also be the case in matters of God. By extension, to deny the existence of God and the eternal consequences of our current stance toward God is the same mindset that denies the implications of our current environmental behavior on the state of our future planetary existence.

Over the years, I have buried several hundred people. So to speak. I never actually dug a single grave. It is more accurate to say that I have officiated over that many funerals. So I have spent a lot of time in and around cemeteries. As I was beginning to settle in behind the big desk at my new church, a crusty, gruff-spoken farmer walked in. He told me that he was the keeper of the church's cemetery. He pointed to his rusty red pick-up and said, "Saddle up, Padre. It's time to introduce you to most of the members of your congregation!" MOST of the members? Before long, I buried him as well.

One of the things I came to notice over the years was how most graves had long since become tombs of the unknown. The gravesites that I could see all had some form of identifying information. Sometimes it would just be some sort of index number. Sometimes just a first name. Sometimes just the relation to the one who purchased it like, "son." Some there hadn't lived long enough to even get a name. The oldest grave in our church's cemetery was an ancient weathered oak post on

which was nailed a metal nameplate that simply said,
"Our precious darling." The legend had it that this was
the grave of a child who had died on a passing wagon
train. Turns out that this was indeed the grave of a little
girl. In fact, this little mite was holding her baby sister. It
was fitting that she should be holding her now, since that
was how she had contracted her sister's deadly contagion
over a hundred years ago. There were gravestones that
were much more important-looking monuments to the
deceased. But few of them were remembered, much less
venerated by anyone on earth. After the immediate
survivors had long moved on, it was rare for any grave
to ever be visited again. Rarely did anyone know
anything about the person beneath the stone.

That is why, for our church's 125th anniversary, I wrote
up the history of our church cemetery. I created a play
about many of the characters after the fashion of
Thornton Wilder's *Our Town*. In our cemetery there was
"Octavia", who died of an appendicitis infection the day
before her wedding to the congregation's first pastor.
Beneath that grave marker she lays in her wedding dress.

But the discovery that stays with me most had to do
with a memorial that wasn't even in the cemetery. A
lonely flagpole flies the Stars and Stripes in the back far
corner of the church parking lot in town. That solitary
flagpole was erected in memory of the only congregation
member to be killed in action in the Vietnam War. Robert
Andrew Holan, Jr. was a First Lieutenant in Charlie
Company, 1st Battalion, 5th Infantry, 25th Infantry
Division. Just seven months before I enlisted in the
Army, he was killed by small arms fire on March 24,
1969. He died in Hau Nghia, South Vietnam, just twenty-
five miles west of the capitol known in those days as
Saigon. But now just two decades later, I could find only
one person in the congregation who even had a vague

recollection of him. No one in the entire town even knew of his sacrifice. That hurts me to this day. For the next fifteen years of my time in that church, I printed his story along with his confirmation photo on the back of the bulletin on the date of his death and again on Memorial Day weekend. Before long, few if any people will even know that the church history book or especially the play ever existed. My best efforts maybe saved a little bit of the stories in that cemetery for a relatively short period of time with a just few people. It may seem morose to people who expect otherwise, but the simple reality is that, despite what some romantic poets may say, nothing about our earthly journey has much if any lasting effect in this world. I have a haunting suspicion that my writings here may be a bit of a vain and selfish protest against my own evaporation. If anybody ever reads this, perhaps I haven't totally passed away for just a tiny bit longer. If so, I would be remiss in not thanking you for my temporary stay of total oblivion.

All of this is by way of saying that, like King Solomon, I see absolutely everything about this Earth as undeniably fleeting, like wisps of upward curling and dissipating tendrils of smoke. The way he put it was, "Vanity of vanities, all is vanity (Ecclesiastes 1:2)." This is not to say that our earthly deeds are unimportant. Everything has value in its own right, regardless of its longevity. Even vanishing smoke or what caused it can have long consequences in this world. In fact, I believe that the most important thing about our earthly actions is that they have eternal consequence, at least if Jesus was telling the truth. It was the Heaven-minded Martin Luther of the Middle Ages who said, "Even if I knew that tomorrow the world would go to pieces, I would still plant my apple tree." But in my thinking, there is a distinction between things that might be really important and things that are ultimately important. I am increasingly convinced that nothing on Earth is more than really important. Likewise, I am increasingly convinced that Christianity is about the eternal consequences of what we do or do not do, what we choose and what we do not choose, specifically in terms of what we choose to honor as the center of our lives.

It dawns on me that so many of the things that bother me in my faith struggles may be about matters that are only really important in our temporary existence, but which are not ultimate issues. In my experience, most people who have an awareness of God will grieve the death of a child by saying something like, "Why did God allow him to die?" But I have also known many horribly anguished parents who grieve hopefully. These are parents who believe that nothing has the power to end anything other than their child's earthly existence which they have always known is passing sooner or later.

One reason I struggle to hang on to my faith rather than just cut it loose is because of the possible eternal consequences. When I have counseled people who were contemplating suicide, I have advised them to not choose a long term solution for a short term problem. Likewise, I also don't want to make the mistake of walking away from God because of short-term problems, like things that I don't understand about God.

Chapter Eleven
It's Not About Us

IF THERE IS ANYTHING THAT HAS MOST STOOD
OUT for me in all the emerging immensities of space
sciences, it is that we are not the center of the universe.

When I assumed my first Call as a pastor, I had just
completed my employment as a speech and language
pathologist in the public schools. My last project there
had been to explore newly emerging computer
technologies to help non-verbal people communicate.
Now in my new career, I persuaded the church to
purchase a computer system which we could use in the
office to produce things like worship bulletins.

Soon we had a funeral for a lady I'll call Mary Sullivan.
I showed our church secretary how she could type up the
funeral bulletin on that nifty little television on her desk.

With the push of a button, out would come the bulletin
on another machine! Six months later, Alice Peterson

passed away. This time, I showed our secretary how all she had to do was find the last bulletin which we had done and simply change the name of the deceased. Just like that, a hundred bulletins for the funeral of Alice Peterson were in the hands of as many grieving family and friends.

As I was leading the service, my eyes, as usual, were scanning four or five lines ahead. Dead ahead, as it were, the Apostle's Creed was coming straight at us. It was written, as they say, thusly:

"I believe in God, the Father, Creator of Heaven and Earth
    And in Jesus Christ, His only Son, our Lord
    Who was conceived by the Holy Spirit
    And born of the Virgin ALICE."

In a fraction of the time it is taking you to read this, my imagination panicked its way through half a dozen things I might do. Most of them were along the lines of trying to distract people by doing something like passing out. I decided to just plough ahead and say it the way it was supposed to be said, that Jesus was conceived by the Virgin Mary. But everyone followed the bulletin and dutifully proclaimed in unison that it was their mother, their grandmother, their sister, their aunt who had given birth to Jesus Christ. This may have been the first time that I was grateful that only a handful of people were paying attention. Those few looked up at me with various expressions of concern, to say the least. Most people had no experience yet with computers in those days. No one had guessed that a "search and replace all" computer stroke had substituted the name of "Alice" not only for all instances of Mary Sullivan but also the Virgin Mary.

The error was particularly grievous since most people expect a funeral to be about the person who died. My primary job as a pastor is viewed by many as saying nice things, and only nice things, about the deceased. In any case, most people expect themselves and the deceased to be the center of worship that day. This is why almost all funeral bulletins are entitled, "A Celebration of the Life of (insert name)". I, on the other hand, have the bizarre notion that worship is to be of GOD. So my bulletins typically say, "A Celebration of Christ's Resurrection for (insert name)". Also, I do try to get the name right.

One of the best opening lines of any book outside the Bible was penned by Rick Warren in *The Purpose Driven Life*. He simply says, "It's not about you."

Perhaps the most well-known passage in the New Testament is where the Gospel of John says, "God so loved the world that He gave His Only begotten Son ....." (John 3:16). In an effort to tell people the profound truth that God loves us, much Christian preaching these days has unwittingly conveyed the idea that humans are the center of the universe and that we are therefore the most important reason for everything God does. But it has always seemed to me that even a theoretical possibility of the existence of God would place GOD at the center of things. It is the immaturity of the small child who naturally sees himself as the center of everything.

Though the Bible never said so, the earliest thinking of the Church was that everything, including the Sun, revolved around the Earth. It was a Catholic priest named Copernicus who gets most of the press for eventually correcting the record and insisting that we, especially Church thinkers, had it just backwards: the

Earth and everything else in the solar system revolves around the sun! Virtually all astrophysics these days is continuing the theme that not even our sun, or our solar system or our galaxy or even our neighborhood of galaxies are the center of the universe.

And yet, with all of this enlightened thinking, so many of the most advanced thinkers continue to judge reality as though the greatest things in the universe must answer to them in order to be declared as valid by them. This is nothing new. Thousands of years ago, the Old Testament had over a dozen passages that observed something along the lines of Proverbs 16:2 which said, "All the ways of a man are pure in his own eyes ..... "

I am no less prone to such self-centered thinking, especially when I try to come to terms with things about God which bother me, or which do not make sense to me. As I will explain later in this memoir, my greatest quandaries with God have to do with him allowing children to suffer at the hands of evil monsters. It occurs to me that, as precious as children are, maybe a big part of my problem is that I am placing children at the center of all things, as though their creator should be all about service to them. Especially where my grandchildren are concerned, I am abundantly and unquestionably guilty as charged. I unintentionally give them the message that, as far as grandpa is concerned, they are the center of the universe. As my energy and other resources wind down and their tastes go up, I will probably correct that misimpression.

Chapter Twelve

I Accept Limits To Human Capabilities

When I Was A Horse

IT MAY BE THAT SO MANY THINGS about God confuse me simply because they are above my pay grade. That's another one of those little things I learned in the Army. In some branches of the American military there is a relatively small group of officers sometimes referred to as mustangs. These are people who start out as privates, usually rise to sergeants and eventually become commissioned officers. I was a mustang. It's always been one of my proudest accomplishments to say that I worked my way up the ranks the hard way. Though I never fought in combat and would never be the decorated hero he was in my eyes, I took a perverse pride in outranking my dad. He became a Staff Sergeant and I became a First Lieutenant. So there.

Compared to other officers, mustangs often more quickly earned credibility among the troops, having come from their ranks. Mustangs were generally known for respecting the sergeants who had probably been their peers and mentors. A mustang could sometimes get the troops to do things because such an officer knew how to think and talk like everyone else. He could also be a bit of a respected threat to the enlisted folk, because this was the one officer who knew all their tricks and hiding places.

A mustang could also be in for some unexpected humbling. Becoming a commissioned officer is typically considered a promotion. Now, for the first time, most people have to salute the mustang and say 'Sir'. Now, for the first time, the mustang wears nicer uniforms and gets to eat in the posh Officers' Club. But before too long, the new mustang slams into at least two things that were heard a hundred times before:

"That is on a need-to-know basis and you do not need to know."

"That is above your pay grade."

In the case of the military, these kinds of answers were basically a nice way of saying, "You don't know enough to have an opinion." I only needed to hear one time that when they needed my opinion, they would give it to me. A corollary of that was what my captain told me when I griped about being advance-scheduled for an assignment on the day of my wedding. He replied with a line that apparently has long been used on others: "If the Army would'a wanted you to have a wife, they'da issued you one." We had to reschedule the wedding. I have been known to use that change in plans as the excuse for sometimes getting confused about our wedding anniversary.

I never liked being told that I did not have a need to know something. I did not agree with it. And nobody gave a whit what I thought. I was surprised to even hear full colonels say the same thing! I later discovered that this principle applied everywhere throughout life, especially in law enforcement, in all kinds of privacy matters, in litigation, in health care, in personnel management, in politics, etc.

When I am told this kind of thing, my prideful instinct is to take it personally, as though I am being told that I am not considered important enough, smart enough, trustworthy enough, mature enough, whatever enough to handle things. Most often, I am simply being told that, for some reason, I cannot have access to all the relevant information that would be necessary to have an informed opinion. A pastor may be an esteemed member of the professional community, but even a police chaplain on an active crime scene might not be privy to certain investigative information. Why might that not apply to matters of God? The scribe of the book of Deuteronomy put it this way: "The secret things belong to the Lord our God, but the things that are revealed belong to us and to our children forever ... (Deuteronomy 29:29)."

The Rocket Scientist

I remember seeing this poor guy sitting all by himself in the refectory. The refectory was the monastery-type term for a cafeteria in the seminary where I was in my second year of training to be a pastor. It was 10:45 in the morning and some of us had filed downstairs after morning chapel to meditate over hot-fudge covered homemade doughnuts. That was an important part of our training because one of the last things King Solomon ever wrote was, "Of making many books there is no end, and much study is a weariness of the flesh," (Ecclesiastes 12:12). I like to think that he must have intended to also mention chocolate.

The first sign that something was wrong with this guy was the simple fact that he was sitting there all by himself, with no doughnuts. Something was wrong or he was from out of town. In those days, only a few of us were older, second-career students, referred to as re-treads. He looked like one of us, except that I had never seen him there before. He looked like maybe he didn't want to be bothered. So I sat down across from him.

"Looks like you're new here," I said.

He just kept gazing out the window and kind of nodded.

I tried again. "Thinking about studying here?"
This time he shrugged his shoulders.

"My name's Dave," I said. "I'm in my second year." I extended my handshake and he accepted.

"So, you from around here?" I asked.

The man spoke. "Uh, no. Not really."

"Where 'bouts?" I said.

"California."

I said, "When I was a little kid, I grew up in the Bay area. You from there?"

"No, a little farther south," he said.

"L.A.?"

"Yeah, kinda near there," he said.

"By the way, I didn't catch your name," I said.

He shook his head. "Pasadena."

I thought I'd try to loosen things up a bit. "Um, isn't that where they have the Jet Propulsion Laboratory?"

He finally looked away from the window and made eye contact. "Yep, that's the place, all right. My name's Bob."

Now we were getting somewhere. "You didn't by chance work there, did you?"

Back to the window gazing again. "Yeah. Until maybe, what, seven o'clock this morning. Their time."

I just couldn't leave it alone. "So, what did you do at JPL?" I shouldn't have asked.

"Well, did you hear about a rocket yesterday that got lost after it 'slipped the surly bounds of Earth,'?" I recognized that from a poem called "High Flight" which the TV stations played at the end of each programming day around midnight.

I was excited to recognize what he was talking about. "Oh yeah! Something about a rocket engine nozzle that got stuck and wouldn't shut off."

"Yeah," he said, still gazing out the window. "That was our team. I was the lead engineer on the nozzle system." He had this vacant gaze as he just barely shook his head.

It felt like a good time to say something really insightful. All I could come up with was, "Oh."

His gaze out the window now tilted upward a bit. He got this quizzical look on his face as he gestured with his hand in a round-and-round motion. "I, I um, don't know. It, it just, just sort of kept, you know, going and going and going ....." He momentarily seemed to fade out.

After a few seconds he said, "You know, I've always kinda been interested in God, the stars and everything."

All I could think of saying was, "Ummm, have you tried the doughnuts?"

This time it WAS rocket science. An aerospace propulsion engineer with questions he couldn't answer, now turning God-ward. By this time, nozzle technology had long been tackled and had worked countless times. But this particular scene was emblematic of two things. The first was that there are limits to what humanity can control. Secondly, there is an instinct which some people have, to turn to God when they need something that cares and is outside of humanity.

Gloria

By this time of my life, I have amassed quite a collection of things which I do not even know about myself. Mark Twain confessed something about the limits of his own self-understanding which is a warning to all memoir writers. He said, "When I was younger, I could remember anything, whether it happened or not."

Not long after I became pastor of a congregation, one of the members mentioned that he periodically traveled a couple hours south to his tiny hometown to check in on his elderly mother.

"No kidding?" I said. "When I was in tenth grade, I dated a girl from your town!"

"What's her name?" he asked. "Our town's so small, we probably knew her."

"Gloria Hanford," I said. "Yeah, I was pretty smitten by her. Our church youth groups would get together at area retreats and that's how we met. She was really special, but she was a couple years older. So when she went off to college, we kind of lost touch. I've always wondered what became of her. Know her?"

"Oh," was all he said. "Yeah." I expected a bit of a more interesting recognition reaction. He wasn't offering any more information and I was immediately starting to wonder if I wanted to ask.

The silence felt a little awkward so I kept the line open. "She was a little on the shorter side and also had shorter hair. On the quieter side and really cute."

"Yeah, that was Gloria, all right," he said. "She was about ten years younger than me, but I remember her well."

Was. He said, "was." Of course he did. We were talking about quite a few years ago, after all. I said, "Yeah, we lost touch and sort of moved on in our lives. Guess that's kind of natural," I said.

His wife all of a sudden recalled something. "Honey, that wasn't the one with the car accident, was it? I think she had a name like that."

"Car accident?" I said.

Bill turned a little red. "You probably didn't know that she was lost in a car accident."

I felt a chill waft over me. "Do you know how long ago that happened?"

Bill searched his memory. At least, I think that's what he was doing. "I'm pretty sure it was when she had come home on break from the University." In her sophomore year she hadn't answered my last letter. By that time, I had become interested in someone else and I assumed that maybe she had as well.

Ellen tried to repair the bridge she had blown unintentionally. "You know, her widowed mom still lives in that same house. I'll bet she'd love for you to stop by. She could probably fill you in. We don't know a lot of the details."

Two weeks later, I had a pastor's conference in the large city I had lived in when I had dated Gloria. I skipped the second day of speakers and spent the whole afternoon in the archive department of the regional newspaper. I went through week after week after week of obituaries on microfiche rolls. Picture after picture of local guys and classmates killed in combat in Vietnam. My first classmate was killed there when we were in ninth grade. Actually, he had been held back so many years that he dropped out in the ninth grade when he became eighteen. Louie enlisted in the Army and apparently wasn't too good at that either. But not for long. Got himself shot dead, right off the bat.

Suddenly, there was her photo. The same one I had had from her high school graduation which I had attended. She had died two years later in a single car accident. The obituary listed the funeral home. I had to work up the nerve, but I phoned. I think this was the only time that I ever deliberately traded on my role as a pastor to get something for myself. I succeeded in prevailing on the funeral director to meet with me to see if he knew anything about Gloria. Turns out that he was the one who had handled her death. She had plowed herself at high speed into a massive oak tree at the end of the main residential street in town. She was found to be pregnant. And unmarried. She was buried at a tiny, untended graveyard a dozen miles out in the countryside. I visited her elderly mother who remembered me and was so glad that I took the time to stop by. I went looking for Gloria's grave. Just before the sun set, I found her. The flat grave marker was long since grown over in this tiny, forgotten cemetery. I pulled weeds all around it and wiped the faceplate clean. That's where I laid the white rose I had brought along, after I removed the thorns.

I shared all this with my parents. They remembered Gloria quite well. "This just makes it all the more amazing," said my mother. That was not exactly the reaction I had expected.

Dad said, "We were always taken with how much Gloria reminded us of your Gloria back in California when you were a little boy."

MY Gloria? I was drawing a total blank.

Mom said, "She was your special favorite sitter. Her name was Gloria. We were instantly struck by how your new Gloria was a total spitting image of her: exact same height, they were both kind of petite, and the absolutely identical brunette hairstyle. They even sounded alike."

"I think she was probably your first crush when you were all of four years old," said Dad. "She went on vacation once. She always called you Davey and so she brought you back a Davey Crockett T-shirt and raccoon tail cap. You would not take them off. They became your second skin."

Now I had to correct their memory. "No, the shirt and cap came from Brownie."

They looked quizzically at each other. "Brownie?" said my mom. "Who was Brownie?"

I said, "Brownie was from England and she's the one who brought me the presents."

There was a pause as each searched distant memories. A light bulb went off and Dad said to Mom, "Oh, I know what he's thinking about!" As if I wasn't sitting right there in front of them. "That sales rep from London!"

Mom remembered too. "Oh, sweetie," she said to me, as though she was speaking again to her little boy. "I don't know why you're confusing her with Gloria. No, Brownie was a sales associate with Dad's work. Because she was visiting from overseas, we had her over for supper one night before she flew back. How strange you would remember her after just that one evening."

Dad was connecting something and he said to my mother, "Wasn't that about the same time as Gloria?"

Mom didn't have to give it much thought. "I'll bet you're right." That's not something my mom usually said to my dad. She gave me this endearing mommy look and said, "We still keep discovering things about his little head."

I weighed in. "I don't suppose you could let my little head in on whatever this is?"

Dad picked up the thread of the story. "Like we said a minute ago, Mom and I were taken with how much your friend Gloria resembled your babysitter Gloria. All we could figure was that you must have subconsciously been attracted for that reason. Especially after what had happened to your first Gloria."

"I don't even remember that Gloria," I said.

"There is no way that you forgot her," Dad said. "You absolutely adored her. And she felt the same way about you, Dave."

Mom said, "Afterwards, you were so traumatized that you didn't speak again for weeks and weeks. We took you to specialists and we didn't know if we were going to get you back. Eventually, you slowly began to talk again. And even grew up to be a speech therapist yourself, of all things. Go figure."

I was even more confused. "What do you mean that I was traumatized 'afterwards'? After what?"

The endearing mommy tone again. "You really still don't remember, do you, honey?"

Before I could ask again, Dad said, "I think Mom and I are kind of reeling right now ourselves, at how Gloria and Gloria continue to match. Your babysitter also died in a single car accident. You cried and cried and cried. You were inconsolable."

Mom said, "Of course, you would have had no way of knowing this, because we were careful to talk only after you had gone to bed. But Gloria died by driving into a concrete bridge. We suspected that she committed suicide. Turns out she was pregnant. Strange, but it was only after we figured this out one night, after you went to bed, that you stopped talking."

Time and again in my own life, I have banged my head against some door which locks away things that I can never know. Maybe there are profound reasons why some knowledge is above my pay grade.

The ancient Greeks talked about humans defying the gods and opening Pandora's Box. From out of that box flew all kinds of things into the world. The lid was slammed shut, trapping only the one virtue of hope from entering the world. At about that same time, their Hebrew neighbors across the pond were telling a similar tale about how the first humans defied God. They ate the fruit of the forbidden Tree of Knowledge of Good and Evil. Ever since, one of the things we have most wanted our children to learn is the difference between good and evil. A criminal court refuses to hold a defendant accountable if he does not know the difference between right and wrong. As far back as we have records, almost all peoples and cultures have highly prized the acquisition of knowledge, especially of good and evil.

I have always had a haunting suspicion that we are doomed to struggle with dangerous knowledge because of some cookie jar that we have opened. The birth of the atom bomb comes to mind. To paraphrase Jonathan Swift, knowledge always seems to circle the globe several times before wisdom even gets its boots on. And so we have lamented about losing our innocence.

Father

Until I was a young adult, cars were always stalling out or refusing to start. A lot of the time, it was a matter of the carburetor developing something called vapor lock. Dad would have mom sit behind the wheel while he popped the hood and unscrewed this thing that looked like a big metal cake pan cover on top of the engine. Then he would tell mom to pump the accelerator three times and wait while he sprayed something into the carburetor. "Don't turn the key until I tell you," he would instruct mom. Then he would stick a screwdriver into said carburetor to hold open something called the butterfly.

"When I get the butterfly opened, I'll tell you to turn the ignition." Mom was paying very, very close attention, but she didn't say anything because dad didn't want to be interrupted.

His impatience at not being answered by Mom must have gotten the better of him. He gave the carburetor one last spray and yelled at her, "I said, 'OK'?" Figuring she must have missed the cue, she fired the ignition, floored the gas and darn near blew my dad to kingdom come. I doubt he said anything about heaven when something

like a fireball filled the engine compartment. The living remains of Dad slowly walked around to Mom's driver side window. Most of his curly blonde hair and both his eyebrows were completely singed. His face was totally blackened by soot. Quietly and very deliberately he put his face right up to Mom's: "I didn't say 'Now'". It did not help that she almost died laughing while he stood there smoldering.

My dad knew everything. For a number of years, we lived on nursery farms. Things were always breaking down. A gate would fall off its hinges. A tractor wouldn't start. The coal-fired furnace would go out. Dad fixed everything and could build anything. I knew that I would never learn all I needed to know in order to be a grown-up. I remember asking him how he knew how to do everything. He said that you learn simply by trying and that by the time I am an adult, I will have learned what I will need to know. But as an adult, I learn a lesson from my little self about what it means to be a child who knows he is a child.

When his apostles asked him how to pray, Jesus didn't say anything about mental focusing, or how they should kneel or fold their hands or close their eyes. He started off by telling them to pray to "Our Father who art in Heaven." I assume that would have made them God's children. Experimental science would begin by asking if this notion has what is termed face validity: on the face of it, does it seem reasonable at all that human beings could actually be children of God? But right off, there is a problem in suggesting that children would even have the ability to make such an assessment in the first place. On the off-chance that Jesus may have meant this to be more than figurative imagery, I do what theoretical physicists do: I develop what they refer to as a thought experiment. This experiment asks what we would be able to understand if we actually were the children of a creator.

When it comes to human intellectual capacity, I try to imagine, in human terms, how developed we might be as children, relative to God. Obviously, if there were a god who created everything and all the eons of time, then our chronological age, relative to God's, would not even be on the charts at all. Yet, we do have at least some ability to think and speak. Relative to the Creator whom the Bible says called all things into existence through words, I would imagine that our language abilities compared to God's would be somewhat modest, to say the least. As a speech and language pathologist, I take note of our ability to string together ideas and words. So, compared to our Parent, my thought experiment would place us no more than around twelve to eighteen months of age. This would also mean that we would be just beginning to learn how to move ourselves around. The history of transportation technology would agree with this. We would also be in the very earliest stages of learning how to be around others, knowing where our stuff ends and other people's stuff begins. History, crime, war, current events and family relations confirm that we've got a long way to go in this regard as well. We would also just be learning what we should do and what we can do, and the difference between the two. One thing we would be quite adept at is trying to assert our will over that of our parents. But our self-awareness, our ability to stand back and see ourselves as others see us would be just emerging.

What can a young toddler understand of the parents' ways? Though the emotional and cognitive abilities of the child grow phenomenally over the years, who has not noticed the inability of teens and even young adults to "get it?" From a young age and all the way through to full maturity, many if not most of these emerging people project an unquestioned assumption of superiority over their parents and all other authorities. Until maturity of the brain somewhere in the mid-twenties, there are a multitude of things that the emerging person is not even capable of knowing, almost regardless of intellectual powers.

Every single day, staggering scientific gaps and discoveries are announced about all kinds of fundamental phenomena. This very morning, as I write these words, National Geographic on-line announced a provocative new theory to explain something called The Great Nonconformity ("Earth is missing a huge part of its crust. Now we may know why." Robin George Andrews. January 1, 2019). Since at least the late 1800's, earth scientists apparently have known that somewhere around one-fifth of the Earth has been missing, but there has been no scientific consensus about why. One example, near Las Vegas, is Frenchman's Mountain where one and a half billion years of rock is simply missing. On the one hand, such announcements justifiably speak to humanity's phenomenal capabilities to even be aware of such things. On the other hand, compared to what is yet to be discovered of just the known universe, humanity's mental powers may still far short of even an embryonic stage of development. If there were a being who created it all, it makes total sense to me that what we can know might be infinitesimally insignificant.

Chapter Thirteen

Not All Questions Can Be Answered Here And Now

IT'S PROBABLY NOT TOO FAR OFF the mark to say that I might be a bit of a party-pooper. At this moment, I am sitting in a hotel lobby in the middle of one of the fanciest convention hotels in one of the world's most exciting and powerful cities. All day long, people have been feeling sorry for me because I don't have a ticket to the big affair tonight in the main ballroom downstairs. The truth is that I'm happily here by choice. I would rather be sitting right here all by my lonesome, with a nice glass of wine, writing this book and reading someone else's.

So maybe it's just because I'm a natural kill-joy that I sometimes have concerns about all the Christmas gift hysteria. When I see people, especially children, so focused on what they're going to get, I worry that this undermines the virtue of self-sacrifice which embodies Christ's birth. I know whereof I speak. I resemble that remark. When I was a kid, my family opened our gifts on Christmas Eve. Our family's evolved rituals for that day drove me absolutely nuts. My folks seemed to go out of their way to find every possible excuse to delay the opening of the presents. I remember thinking that it was as if they didn't care!

First of all, we had to go to church. That seemed totally unnecessary because we had gone to church earlier that week. So what was the point? Since we usually went to the early service on this evening, we would come home and have to have supper. And, no, not a quick, light supper but one that Mom wouldn't start making until we got back. And what was Dad doing? That was another thing. So that we kids wouldn't shake, rattle and roll apart the packages under the tree, and to increase the suspense, Dad would keep all gifts out of sight and wouldn't even wrap them until that night. While Mom was preparing supper, he was somewhere wrapping up the gifts. Then, after supper, we had to do the dishes. And then we had to get in our pajamas, which took Mom and Dad forever. Finally, we would all gather around the tree. But, oh no: first Dad had to read the Christmas story! Didn't we just hear that in church?

So, along with the virtues of delayed gratification, our parents really did teach the true point of Christmas. Because of our relatively modest standard of living, our gifts were not particularly extravagant. But in this boy's mind, it was nevertheless the presents that took center stage. I have to admit that in terms of what I was actually experiencing and feeling, what registered was that, when it came to Jesus, it was about waiting.

A big part of Christianity really is about waiting, living in the between times. To paraphrase an ancient response, Christ came once, still things are not perfect, he will come again and everything will be complete. The New Testament says that now we see like in a cloudy mirror but that one day we will know perfectly. Therefore, what is assumed is precisely the human inability to answer some and maybe most questions at the present time. The lack of answers about God does not necessarily have to mean that something is false or wrong about God, but that the answer may well be premature.

Christianity shares the frustration of delayed answers with every field of inquiry, including all branches of science. Some scientists believe that eventually we will have enough information to understand everything. Recently, a major scientific endeavor has been to find "the" T.O.E., the "Theory of Everything." Every now and then, one group or another will claim that it has finally discovered the holy grail in its pet theory or discovery. To me, such a claim seems like a fool's gamble because that bet so far has had no winners. There are many who believe that science will eventually be able to create life and cure death. These same people will undoubtedly acknowledge that, to date, we have not actually created life. But they would add, "yet." We have not cured death. Yet. We have not eliminated crime and war. Yet. We have not eliminated the problems among human beings. Yet. We have not discovered other sentient life in the universe. Yet. But many human progress optimists trust that sooner or later we will. These too are people of faith, who live in the between times and who trust in the eventual emergence of things they hope for and expect.

Chapter Fourteen
I Accept A Need To Keep My Brain On A Leash

It's Not Always Ice Cream

IN MY UNDERGRADUATE MAJOR of Speech Science, Pathology, and Audiology, my special interest was in matters of brain injury. My focus was learning how to diagnose, treat and do research on communication disorders caused by central nervous system disorders like strokes, injuries and long term neurological diseases like Parkinson's. On my twenty-first birthday, one of our best friends gave me a fairly heavy plastic bucket that was all wrapped in aluminum foil and sealed with a tight lid. It was about the size of ice cream bins which ice cream stores use.

"Be careful," said my friend as he slowly lifted it over to me. "It kind of sloshes a bit in there."

"I'm almost afraid to ask," I said.

He looked like he was trying to keep a straight face. "Don't worry," he said.

When someone tells you not to worry, this is sometimes precisely when you do need to worry. I pried off the lid and found a human brain floating in a tea-colored brine of formaldehyde. This was not meant as a prank because my friend was beaming at what he had managed to accomplish. "Your very own brain!" he proudly said. I wasn't sure how to take that - either the gift or the remark.

My friend was an art student who had just finished a class on sculpting human anatomy. Apparently, the program would procure specimens like this from the medical school. I can't recall how he came to be the custodian of this blessed thing, but now I had the honor. I was a little nervous because I was fairly certain that it might be illegal to possess a human body part that was not my own. I didn't know whom to safely ask, so I spent some time trying to figure out how to get rid of this thing. I could not think of a single way that wasn't disgusting, disrespectful, or discoverable. Now I knew why our ninth grade English teacher made us read Edgar Allen Poe's "The Tell-Tale Heart." For the first time in my life, I could identity with a guy who went insane because of body parts he had hidden in his house.

And so, with us, the remains remained until I could figure out a safe way to somehow relocate them. As newly marrieds, Ann and I never had a lot of living space, but now we had to find room for three brains between us. We didn't want to keep it in our bedroom, or the kitchen or the bathroom. Over the next three years, wherever we lived, we hid our brain in the front closet, right underneath our coats and everyone else's who would stop over. I don't want to think that this is how the social custom may have developed where the host always greets guests by taking their coats.

This same friend helped me move our belongings in a U-Haul trailer out to Denver for grad school. My brain rode on the floor of the back seat, right behind me at the wheel. Half-way along Interstate 70 in the middle of the night, my worst fears came true. A Nebraska state trooper races up behind us with flashing lights and pulls us over. I do not recall exactly why he pulled us over. Maybe some routine road check. I am trying not to soak myself with sweat or anything else as we wait. And wait. And wait. Finally, he gets out of his cruiser, saunters up to my driver's side window and wants my license and registration. While I am looking, he starts looking as he scans everything in the darkened car with his flashlight. He checks out my friend sitting next to me. He checks out the backseat that is piled with blankets and pillows. And he shines the flashlight on the floor of the backseat. I am trying to look normal while frantically searching my imagination to find some way to answer a question he might ask about a foil-wrapped ice cream bucket. I cannot think of one single thing to say. The truth itself will seem crazier than anything I can make up. Fortunately, he does not ask. Apparently, whatever he's looking for does not fit in a large ice cream bucket. He returns my license and registration and wishes us a safe drive.

The brain spent the next year in the front closet of our tiny apartment in Married Student Housing. At the end of graduate school, I was called to active duty for several months. My brain could not go with me, which one helicopter instructor may have surmised anyway when I nearly blew us out of the sky with an artillery barrage. In all the excitement, I apparently had mistakenly designated our own position as the target location. Meanwhile, back home, my new wife made it equally clear that my brain would not go with her back home to Minnesota. Fortunately, I had developed a good relationship with one of my professors whom I could risk asking if he might want an extra brain. He was more than happy to add this to his pathophysiology collection.

As memorable as this adventure was, I have found that keeping track of my own brain has been much harder than keeping track of someone else's floating in a bucket. When things about God perplex me, my temptation has always been to try and figure things out. The problem is that I don't trust my brain any farther than I can throw it. As a pastor, a student of history, and a life-long owner of my own brain, I have come to believe that most of us perceive what we already believe. Especially when it comes to religion. With not much effort at all, I can rationalize or justify almost anything. I have learned that I always have to be on guard about confusing my imagination with what's really out there.

In high school I was a debater where I was trained to argue both sides of any issue on the spot. As a result, things flip on me all the time. As soon as I have an opinion about something, I instinctively begin considering the opposite side of the issue. Of all the things I have seen on classroom blackboards, the one thing that most stays with me is the exercise of the three dimensional cube. Stare at it for a few seconds and keep trying to figure out which side of the cube is closest. Right before your eyes, that cube on the blackboard will seem to rotate another side to be closest. Then it will rotate again. And again. And again. That's exactly how my brain works when I try to focus on confusing things, especially things that confuse me about God. Sometimes, I feel like the proverbial jackass that died of starvation between two mounds of hay because it couldn't decide which one to eat.

And then there's the problem of my intelligence. I am constantly reminded of my limits in all kinds of things that other mortals do without breaking a sweat. I have always wanted to be a white haired, pipe-smoking chess aficionado in a tweed sport coat with leather elbow patches. I'm part-way there. I've got the white hair and I am going to buy that jacket. But I can't get my mind past the other two things: the cancer causing pipe and the game of chess itself. I have a number of chess books. But I have never gotten past the first chapter on opening moves. And, I have never won a chess game. I especially avoid kids who want to play. They are the most dangerous ones because they may not yet have developed a sense of generosity and nobility toward lesser mortals. Since I cannot scratch the surface on so many earthly things, how can I possibly make much sense of things that are beyond the cosmos?

Also, I have never stopped marveling at all the places my brain can lead me on auto-pilot. After forty years of duct-tapping emotional leaks, my neural plumbing finally sprang a major leak. A.K.A. a mental breakdown. Six years of subsequent therapy revealed to me the most amazing ways that my brain and my mind could go AWOL without my awareness, much less my permission. My still incomplete list includes things like totally blocked memories, explosive flashbacks, natural sedation by way of turning off awareness of pain and most other emotional sensations, self-destruction, nightmares upon nightmares, and perceptions and conclusions that can be totally off-base. My breakdown was the reward for having stuffed everything while projecting the facade of a well-adjusted, highly functioning pastor. I had developed a reputation for being particularly good at helping others deal with their own issues. "Doubtless you will quote to me this proverb, 'Physician, heal yourself (Jesus Christ to skeptics, Gospel of Luke 4:23).'"

Anybody who has ever dreamed should be well-acquainted with the brain's ways of running amok. Even when we are sound asleep, our brains can produce full-length motion pictures. Our Academy Award-caliber dreams can include scenery, plot lines, dialogue, action, and maybe even music and sound effects. These films can rival the work of a Hollywood production team of hundreds of the world's most trained, experienced and creative geniuses. And all within a fraction of a second.

The Sleep Study

Speaking of sleep, I recently discovered that my brain can also trick me into thinking that I'm awake when I'm actually asleep! Somewhere between my membership into clinical depression and the marvels of hearing loss, I also got introduced to the wonderful world of sleep apnea. I was sent to a sleep study clinic where I was wired up from head to foot with all kinds of sensors, electrodes and wires which were glued onto every inch of my body. The technician told me that she would be video-tapping me and recording all my sounds from the lab next door. In case I wouldn't mind being stared at all night in bed, she added that she would also be watching me through that tiny little window there. Then she told me to go to sleep. Like I usually do. Right.

I could not fall asleep for the life of me. Every time I moved I would set off some little alarm. I carefully experimented with all kinds of contortions to adjust my legs, my arms, my shoulders. I lay there, wide awake, and tried to think relaxing thoughts. When those didn't work, I went to monotonous thoughts. I decided that I was keeping myself awake by thinking too much. So I tried to not think. Worst idea of them all. After a while of trying to think of nothing, I thought to myself that I was doing a pretty good job of not thinking. Until it dawned on me that to realize I was not thinking must mean that I actually was thinking, after all.

Suddenly, there was a quiet rap on the door and the technician quickly entered the room, flipped on the dim night lights, and walked over to adjust some settings on my equipment. She didn't say a word to me and I thought she was acting a little brusk. So I apologized for messing up the test.

"I'm sorry. I just can't fall asleep. Must be all the wires and things and being observed and all."

"Not at all," she said. "You've been in deep sleep for quite a while now."

I couldn't believe her. "No, really, I can tell you every thought I've been wrestling with."

She said, "I could show you the video and some of the brain tracings. I've been monitoring you for a specific problem we call hypnagogia. You get stuck in the transition from wakefulness to sleep. Kinda cool, huh?"

She could tell I wasn't entirely convinced with this explanation. She held out her wrist right in front of my incredulous face. "Here, look at my watch." Four hours had passed. But just that fast, my next thought was, "YEAH, BUT, how do I know that THIS isn't a dream?" I was off and running again.

My brain is also pretty good at taking detours in lots of ways when I'm fully awake. Sometimes, I look back on something really wrong which flitted across my radar and I am totally flummoxed that I hadn't reacted to it. "What in the world was I thinking?!" Sometimes the answer is simply that I wasn't thinking at all, most often because I wasn't paying attention. Sometimes, the answer is more troubling: it may have been that what I noticed actually seemed normal or OK because my moral or ethical or faith lenses needed adjusting. When that dawns on me, my reaction will become something more like, "How could I have ever thought that way?"

These kinds of experiences remind me of two things: to not think too highly of my own mental powers, and the need to always keep my brain on a bit of a leash.

The Earth Is Not Flat, After All

But, I have also learned that keeping my brain on a leash means that I also need to be skeptical of my skepticism. On the morning of Alan Shepherd's first orbit, I learned that sometimes the emperor really does have clothes. He really did see a round (ish) Earth, after all. Or, so they say. (Just kidding: I'm a believer).

Newton's Third Law of Motion has it that for every action there is an equal and opposite reaction. The human body has many muscles arranged in pairs where one serves as a counter-force to the other: one set of muscles grasps and another set releases. Otherwise, your arms would lock-up. Likewise, if my first impulse is to question the truth of something, then my next impulse is to question the question. Things might not be such a struggle for me if I were just a yeahbutologist. I could look at something, say "Yeah, BUT what if ..... ?", walk away and simply leave it at that. I think that is why so many people walk away from faith once they find a good killer question. But as wired as I am to be a yeahbutologist, I am also mindful of the collective wisdom of the ages.

For all these reasons, and perhaps many more, I know that I need to verify my thoughts with some more reliable standard of measure outside myself. There's something fundamentally illogical about expecting the brain to keep a leash on itself. It makes about as much sense to me as trying to lift up oneself in a basket. That is why I try to hold myself accountable to something outside myself, an anchor that is outside and apart from me. That is why I, all three branches of our government, and our entire legal system regard the United States Constitution as the inviolable be-all-and-end-all. But for cosmic challenges which transcend our nation, it makes sense to me to seek something much, much older, far more tested, which has been revered by peoples from all classes in all cultures in all forms of society in all times. That is why I have chosen the Bible as my anchor, my tether. This is why I try to be especially careful whenever I am tempted to dismiss, altar, or creatively nullify anything in that Bible anchor which might otherwise make me uncomfortable.

Chapter Fifteen

Why I Have Chosen The Bible, Warts And All

STRANGELY ENOUGH, EVEN THOUGH it is things in the Bible that so often perplex me, it is the Bible itself that I have come to trust as the standard of measure outside myself. Even more surprising is that the troubling things are often what finally sell me on the Bible's trustworthiness!

Impressed By "Contradictions"

A lifetime of rugged farming had given big, old George a pair of baseball gloves for hands. When I handed him the thin, flat wafer during Communion, he sometimes couldn't find it. This living oak had seen pastors come and go for nigh unto a hundred years. He told me that at his age he wasn't planning on breaking in any more preachers. He worried that with my work load, I might burn out before him. So, he decided that his mission was to get me out of the office. Without any advance notice, he would have his wife call me and tell me to be at the farm in an hour. He would have me pile into his candy-apple-red, 1964 Pontiac Bonneville convertible and he would floor it across three or four counties. If I said anything about needing to get back to work, this would only confirm his idea that we needed to add on another hour.

Early one spring on a Wednesday, he broke with tradition and called me ahead of time. On Saturday we were going on an all-day trail ride with the Valley Horse Club. So, he wanted me at the farm by eleven to break in my horse. She hadn't been ridden since the last time I was on her four months ago. "So this time, Willie, be sure to get your sermon done before the weekend." I was Willie because my grey hair and goatee reminded him of an ancient rock star by the same name.

One hour later found me right where I had been ordered to be. He had gotten the horses ready, and all that remained was, "Saddle up, Willie!" Old farmers in my congregation liked to say "saddle up" a lot. But I have short legs. It's all I can do to reach up high to grab the saddle horn, balance back on one leg in order to hoist my other one high enough to get my foot into the stirrup, and do a one legged hop-up into the saddle.

The horse spooked, bounced me up off the saddle a bit, and then she slipped in the deep mud. I somehow managed to stay with the saddle, though just a few inches above it. This meant that the horse hit the ground first with me following a split second later. While I was still on the way down, the horse was on the way back up, slamming me hard into the saddle and shattering my tail bone. The horse apparently thought that she was the one that got the worst of it, so she bucked me off, right over her head and into the six strands of barbed wire fence. Finally, she slipped in the mud one last time. And fell on top of me.

At the moment, I didn't quite think of this as a Bible study. But as I look back on it, this horse gave me an answer to a question that had pestered me for years. Not infrequently, one Gospel will describe something one way and another Gospel will describe it in a different way. Critics will sometimes seize upon these different descriptions as proof that one or both of them are fake. If the Bible disagrees with itself, the reasoning goes, then how can it be trusted as reliable? One of most often cited examples is how Jesus rode into Jerusalem just days before his crucifixion. Three of the four Gospels say that Jesus rode in on a young colt. One Gospel says that he rode in on a donkey AND a young colt. Skeptics claim that Jesus obviously could not have ridden on two animals and one animal: it would have to be one or the other.

To the contrary, in law enforcement, detectives will become suspicious when two or more people use identical language to describe something. Identical answers are not natural and suggest artificially planned lies. When accounts seem to differ, the first effort is to see if there is any way that they could be compatible. For example, the accounts of Jesus riding the colt neither say nor imply that he rode only a colt. He could have ridden one and then the other. Why in the world would he have done something like that? Well, the colt was described as one on which no one had ever yet sat. That is where my shattered tail bone detects a truth.

Jesus was about to parade through a crowd of at least tens of thousands of cheering people. Anyone who is familiar with young, unbroken equines knows how predictably skittish they can be. I learned that truth the hard way. And believe me, it was truly hard. Apparently, young colts in unfamiliar situations are sometimes calmed by being accompanied by the mother. Jesus could have gently ridden the young colt up to the crowd, whereupon he may well have transferred to the older animal.

But why would he have even bothered to start out on the colt at all? Because doing so would have fulfilled one of the critical Old Testament prophesies which said that the expected Messiah would arrive sitting on a donkey's colt. This is just one instance of where the Bible proved itself reliable, precisely where my own mind had judged it and considered dismissing it as UNreliable.

The same thing happens time and again when I dive deeper into so-called contradictions in the Bible: most of the time, the so-called contradiction reflects my false assumptions and lack of contextual knowledge. Typically, I find that the problem lies not with the text but with me as the reader. One of the most revealing techniques for me these days is something that was not available when I first planted my seeds of question: to simply query the question among the multitude of Internet users. A myriad of perspectives will materialize in a nano second. I will always disagree with a lot of the entries. But almost always, I will also come across some helpful perspectives, including some that I had not been aware of, even in my own areas of expertise.

The Bible Doesn't Whitewash Its Heroes

The validity of the Bible also comes through in the troubling way that it describes its own heroes. Again and again throughout the Old Testament, the Chosen People are slain by plagues. They themselves record these disasters as being the punishment of God for their own faithlessness. Abraham twice misrepresents his wife as his sister and exposes her to sexual abuse in order to protect himself from foreign kings. God punishes Moses' disobedience by refusing to let him enter the promised land. King David commits adultery and first degree murder of Bathsheba's husband. At various points, Jesus derides all of his apostles in ways that no pastor would ever dare speak of the members of the congregation. At one point Jesus rebukes his chief apostle, Peter, and calls him "satan." Peter denies Jesus three times at the point of arrest. The apostle Thomas becomes Doubting Thomas. The treasurer of the apostles is the Judas who sells out Jesus for thirty pieces of silver and then commits suicide. The apostle Paul describes himself as the worst of sinners. The hero of the New Testament, Jesus Christ, is not only put to death, but is put to death by the will of his Father, God in Heaven. This is not the way people would make up fictional legends about their heroes.

The Bible Doesn't Sugarcoat the Sale

Another way that the Bible establishes its validity to me is that it does not sell itself well. Some of the wealthiest and most powerful preachers try to dress up the message of Jesus as some kind product that prospective customers would want to buy. Slick marketing is necessary to make the Bible turn a profit because the prophets ruin all the fun. Jesus even more so. It is all, in fact, a tough package to sell "as is." To readers who usually measure things according to personal benefit in the here and now, the Bible mainly offers present sacrifice and future benefits. To be one of God's Chosen People is a dangerous thing.

Scripture clearly and repeatedly says that following Jesus and his teachings will lead not to success in the present life but most likely suffering and sacrifice. Such was the fate of every single person who penned those words and most of Jesus' named followers. Again, who would make up these things if they wanted to sell the program? As a preacher, I often wondered if anybody was really listening to the words when I saw that the people were still remaining in the pews. I often said this exact thing from the pulpit and all they did was chuckle and sit there!

The Bible lays it all out, "warts and all." If the Bible presents the warts, then I assume that it accurately presents everything else as well.

Chapter Sixteen

I Most Easily Warm Up To Humble Things

MY CLINICAL TRAINING in major hospitals involved learning to administer certain tests to teenagers who had different kinds of developmental challenges. In this case, the one who was having challenges was me. I was nervous and awkward and the testing involved technical instrumentation and somewhat complex procedures. The patient was a sixteen year old boy who had some level of intellectual difficulties. So they said.

He earned the title of patient because he really was. He sat quietly for me as I fumbled everything into place. I had just started explaining the procedure to him when my clinical professor came around the corner with a dozen medical students in tow. Showtime.

In his professorial vocal splendor, he gravels out a masterful salutation. "Well, well, well. What do we have here?" he says as he takes the field before his dutiful audience.

The portly professor in his white lab coat pulls up a chair right between William and me. Dr. Hansen mops his balding head, thoughtfully removes his black, horned-rimmed glasses, and clears his throat twice in a harrumphing manner. He bends forward close to the face of the teenager, stretches a wide smile across his very superior countenance and he bobs his head in an all-knowing ingratiation.

He clears his throat a couple more times and graciously deigns to welcome the boy. "So tell me, Johnny, what are YOU going to be when you grow up?"

William looks at me with question written all over his face. I explain, "He meant to say William."

"That's right, Johnny. So what ARE you going to be when you grow up?"

William kind of squinted his eyes and tilted his head to offer the only answer he could think of. "A man?" The boy timidly looks back at me with an expression that asked if he got it right.

Twelve medical students muffle coughs and chuckles and one of them drops a clipboard. Dr. Hansen, for once, is at a loss for words. Which does not stop him. A couple more harrumphs and he dismisses himself. "Yes, yes. Of course. Very good. Well then. By all means. Carry on, Mr. Garwick."

Whether it's politics, sales, social settings, or most especially religion, few things impress me less than "look at me" people. I am immediately suspicious of anyone who puts on a show, who acts totally unreal and who tries to make himself the big, impressive center of attention. Especially when that person is supposed to be about some other serious matter. Allergic reactions especially kick in when it's a religious leader who struts the role of the privileged BMOC (Big Man On Campus). I have a hard time seeing Jesus when the person who is supposed to be reflecting him looks more like Caesar and acts like Elvis Presley with a message of "Aren't I something important?" A big red flag goes up when a person has to advertise all the great things he has accomplished and how much others appreciate him.

My friend, Cowboy George, would usually want to take the convertible out for a ride when the "relative's humility" was low. It was his way of saying the weather was good. The lower the relative humidity, the more likely I want to be outside. To the contrary, the lower someone's relative humility, the less likely I want to play with that person or his ideas.

I tend to discount the value of an idea in proportion to the self-impressed arrogance I perceive in the "enlightened" thinker. All the way from Greeks like Plato, to Oriental thinkers like Confucius, to European Enlightenment philosophers like Kant and Rousseau, to political philosophers like Marx, to early American philosophers like Thoreau, to modern eastern mystics and New Age channelers, the stereotype of the wise one is always of a high-minded brainiac who is above it all in some elevated plane of self-impressed "smartdom." Think of Thoreau who could contemplate on Walden Pond because his mommy was cooking his meals and hanging out his dirty laundry back home. Or Karl Marx who could wax so eloquently about the unfair labors of the masses while he was being financially cared for by some sugar daddy who was bankrolling him.

Christianity certainly has produced and continues to produce more than its own share of self-impressed celebrities. However, I see arrogance as a clear contradiction to the message and model of Jesus. Most other philosophies cannot be held accountable to an ethic of humility when that virtue is not fundamental to their namesakes or teachings. But Christian scripture is consistently clear that followers of Christ are not to lord things over others (Matthew 20:25). At times, I'm not at all sure that I would have personally liked the apostle Paul when he wrote things like, "I wish that all of you were as I am (1 Corinthians 7:7), " and, "I urge you to imitate me (1 Corinthians 4:16)."

But most of the time when Paul points to himself, it is by way of self-deprecating things he says about himself:

"I am the least of the apostles and do not even deserve to be called an apostle, because I persecuted the church of God(1 Corinthians 15:5)."

"Christ Jesus came into the world to save sinners — of whom I am the worst. But for that very reason I was shown mercy so that in me, the worst of sinners, Christ Jesus might display his immense patience (1 Timothy 1:15-16)."

I see Paul recognizing his own inconsistency. He says, "By the humility and gentleness of Christ, I appeal to you - I, Paul, who am 'timid' when face to face with you, but 'bold' toward you when away (1 Corinthians 10:1)." He admits his own bafflement about himself: "I do not understand what I do. For what I want to do I do not do, but it's what I hate that I do (Romans 7:15). " He even goes so far as to attribute some disability in himself as caused by this exact character issue: "In order to keep me from becoming conceited, I was given a thorn in my flesh, a messenger of Satan, to torment me (2 Corinthians 2:7)."

Though legions of Christians have puffed up themselves in the name of Christ, both the Old and New Testaments are clear about the need for intellectual humility.

"Trust in the Lord. Lean not on your own understanding (Proverbs 3:5)."

"Whoever trusts in his own mind is a fool, (Proverbs 28:26)."

"At that time Jesus declared, 'I thank you, Father, Lord of Heaven and Earth, that you have hidden these things from the wise and understanding and revealed them to little children; yes, Father, for such was your gracious will (Matthew 11:25).'"

"Where is the one who is wise? Where is the scribe? Where is the debater of this age? Has not God made foolish the wisdom of the world? For since, in the wisdom of God, the world did not know God through wisdom, it pleased God through the folly of what we preach to save those who believe. ... For the foolishness of God is wiser than men, and the weakness of God is stronger than men. For consider your calling, brothers: not many of you were wise according to worldly standards, not many were powerful, not many were of noble birth. But God chose what is foolish in the world to shame the wise; God chose what is weak in the world to shame the strong; God chose what is low and despised in the world, even things that are not, to bring to nothing things that are, so that no human being might boast in the presence of God (1 Corinthians 1:19-31)."

I notice at least two things about these admonitions to intellectual humility. The first is that the issue is not just about humility before other people: it is about humility before something greater than oneself, specifically greater than all humanity itself. The second thing I see is that as far back as we can read, there have always been people who have been self-impressed with their intellectual prowess as the final arbiter of all things. Jesus, his messages and messengers in the Bible are consistently of the self-less humility that speaks to me.

Chapter Seventeen

Seeking Proof Barks Up The Wrong Tree When It Comes To Ultimate Things

My First Lesson About Proof

FOR A WHOLE HOUR, my little sister and I would sit on the floor in front of the tiny TV set. Life must have been good since we had a TV set. Who knows if it really was an hour? We couldn't read clocks yet, but we knew when television shows started and ended. We knew precisely when to put on our Mickey Mouse ears. Our parents surely must have loved us if we even had our own Mickey Mouse ears.

At the end of each show, the timer for the end of the day would begin its countdown for what lay ahead. Annette Funicello and Cubby O'Brien and all the other Mousketeers formed up and slowed the pace way down with the sadly sincere benediction:

"Now it's time .... to say goodbye .... to all our company."

The tempo slowed even more: "M - I – C." My sister and I would shout out with the Mouseketeers as we waved back at them, "See you real soon!"

Even slower. "K - E – Y."   Then the adult Mouseketeer leader would say, "Why?"

We would shout back with the other kids, "Because we love you!"

"M.   O.   U.   S.   E."

The detective show, "Boston Blackie," was next up and I would begin a close watch on the time, as told by the sun. This was when the late afternoon California sun would just begin to dim. I could have told you the exact second every single day "when the deep purple falls over backyard garden walls," as the hit pop song put it about that time. I had to know this because it was in the coming hours of darkness that all the emotional shrapnel of World War Two would ricochet through my family. I've always identified with the children of London who, not too many years before this, had huddled in the bomb shelters during Hitler's nightly bombing raids.

At the time of this writing, a lot of academic research is discovering that major experiences in a person's life, especially in the earliest years, can actually cause structural changes in the brain. I would not be surprised if my yeahbutology is something that was hard-wired from those experiences. To this day, I still experience my own version of sundowner syndrome. I cannot be home alone as the sun goes down. I need to be around people. The neurons for these hours were soldered in place every day of every year until I was in my teens. That's part of why most of these words have to be written in coffee houses.

Starting in those hours and sometimes for two or three solid days and nights thereafter, our parents would hurl thunderbolts of heinous accusations against each other. Frequently they would make my little sister and me tremble in front of them and demand that each of us choose whom we would go to live with. All my life I believed that if I could just prove who was telling the truth, then I could figure out what to do. If I could know the truth of my parents' mutual recriminations, then maybe I would know which one to love the most, whom to live with, what to say, what to feel, and most importantly, whom to trust. This was the myth of my hope well into my adult years, until both my parents died. That search grew into a frantic futility that drove me to the absolute brink of almost beating them to that punch.

I eventually came to the conclusion that, even as a pastor, I never would be able to prove what was true and what was false in the rival claims of two such wounded warriors. The truth I discovered was that proof is highly overrated and sometimes impossible to determine.

The Most Critically Important Things In Life Often Cannot Be Proven

Ironically, I would one day find myself in a county jail facing the sheriff himself, his chief deputy, and the head jailer who told me that they "just wanted the truth." I had received an urgent call from County Emergency Dispatch to report to the jail immediately. There had just been an armed escape. I was in the first months of my first position as a volunteer law enforcement chaplain. It was beyond me why they would want the Sheriff's Chaplain to be involved in something like a jail break. On arrival I was asked to report to Interview Room A which is when and where I found myself facing a tribunal of senior officers. They all looked somber as they each flipped through a file folder. I greeted them and took a seat.

The Sheriff spoke. "Pastor Garwick, according to our logs, it looks like you've been meeting with Inmate John Smith. Is that correct?"

When I said that this was true, the Chief Deputy asked the next question. "Are you aware that Smith just escaped with a deputy's firearm?"

I said something like, "I had heard that there has been an escape, but I didn't know the details."

"You want to stick with that story?" said the Chief Deputy.

"Well, yeah?" I said. "What's going on?"

The Chief Jailer said, "You saw him only yesterday, according to my recollection."

Especially since I was a volunteer, I was beginning to think that I wasn't being paid enough for this. "Is there a problem with that?"

The jailer looked over his files and ran his finger down some kind of a list. "Here's the thing, Chaplain. According to this, you were the last person to meet with him before his escape this morning."

The three supervisors looked at one another and cleared their throats. The Sheriff took control. "Here's the problem, Dave. Apparently when you met with him yesterday, you were overheard saying, 'The truth shall set you free?'"

My mouth dropped open, my eyes went bullseye and the three cops exploded in laughter. They got me good. I had just passed the initiation hazing and I was now one of them.

The truth will set you free. It was Jesus who said that. But when Pontius Pilate first interrogated Jesus, what Pilate said was, "What is truth?" Biblical scholars do not have a consensus on whether Pilate meant that cynically or sincerely. I am of the mind that he meant it sincerely.

My YEAH, BUT mentality is what probably led me to choose a course in Logic as my first, and only, course in Philosophy in my freshman year at the university. Of all the things which must have been covered in that course, the one thing which stuck with me was the notion called "tautology." I came away with the idea that the pinnacle of proof was when everybody agreed that something was always true under all circumstances and with no exceptions. Like two plus two equals four. Of course, I had not yet come across a nifty little ditty called "Gödel's Incompleteness Theorem." That principle states that

certain claims, even in mathematics, are true but
CANNOT be proven. That idea had already been
accepted since 1931 and, to this day, it is inspiring some
of the most cutting-edge work in physics.

It is not always true that you will die if you drink and
drive. But it is a tautology that if you jump off a cliff, you
will always, everywhere, fall to the Earth, no matter who
you are or what you think, and there is virtually no one
who would disagree with that. Who is still alive, that is.

Anything less than that may be called reasonable,
defensible, it may be called interpretation and may be
called opinion, but it cannot claim the status of a
tautology. I figured that I had finally found a standard
that I could apply to everything that claimed to be the
truth, especially in matters of faith. I thought I had
stumbled on to the key to unlock the truth of all
competing claims in all things. All I had to do was to
figure out if there was any conceivable exception to the
truth of the claim or if there were any credible people
who disagreed with the idea. If so, I could simply discard
that idea.

It made sense to me that the most important ideas
would, by definition, rise to this highest level of truth.
But to the contrary, I have never discovered any idea
about God with which most people agree. Some scholars
don't agree that Abraham and Moses even existed. Those
who do believe that Abraham and Moses were more than
legends do not all agree that they really were messengers
of God. Most people believe that Jesus and Mohammed
existed, but, beyond that, even their followers don't
unanimously agree about almost anything else
concerning them. In the realm of religious ideas, I have
found that every claim is soon answered with, "Well,

that's just your interpretation. Your 'truth' is not my 'truth.'"

But how can it be that nothing said about God can rise to the same the level of certainty as gravity? All people agree that gravity applies to everybody, everywhere, at all times. Why wouldn't that apply to something infinitely more important like the one who presumably would have created gravity? This gap between what I think should be and what appears to be the case provides the energy which drives my Yeah-But-what-if thinking.

That incident in the county clink was something that had started a decade earlier when I was starting to train for the ministry. In our second year, each of us was being assigned one term of experience as a student chaplain in a nursing home and another term in a hospital. I was one of a few older students who had come from a previous career. In my previous life as a speech and language pathologist, I had already spent a fair amount of time working in nursing homes and hospitals. It was decided that I should try out some less familiar setting. I was given a list of seven alternatives and I was asked to rank order where I was most and least interested. I marked "prisons" as the last place I ever wanted to see. So that is precisely where they assigned me. For both terms.

I reported to a state prison and was immediately assigned to "deadlock", to work with the most violent prisoners. I was terrified. I was advised to avoid stepping over a yellow line in front of the prison cells. That was so these guys couldn't grab my scrawny neck and drag it through the bars. Five days later, I was told that I would be preaching the Sunday sermon to another group of prisoners who were cleared to attend chapel. My assigned text was Jesus' words, "The truth will set you free." Twenty gargantuan men with arm muscles bigger than my thighs proceeded to file in on that first (and I was afraid last) prison Sunday. They focused on me with rapt attention, and I felt like a side of beef inside a cage of pent-up carnivores. But to my relief, several of them kept encouraging me by answering back, "Amen, brother," "lay it on me, preacher man," "You say it like it is, Reverend!" I never felt so connected to a congregation in my entire life. I loved it, except maybe the part where I took prayer requests. Some of them requested prayers for the painful death of this prosecutor or that judge. This was where I learned the art of spontaneously crafted public prayer. I would come to refer to this as I.O.D., Inspiration On Demand.

My training in that first facility continued by doing individual pastoral counseling. I learned in a hurry that most of the prisoners were guys who were wanting me to get things for them, to do things for them, to put in a word for them with this warden or that guard. All such things were strictly prohibited. So, they would try to win my sympathy by convincing me how they were innocent and had been framed. I quickly realized two things: the futility of trying to figure out what was true and the fact that nobody would care what I thought. Eventually, I developed a little orientation speech for when I first met a prisoner. It went something like this:

"I'm really happy to meet with you, but I need you to know that I am strictly prohibited from doing any favors for you. I am not allowed to get stuff for you or bring stuff to other people, I cannot take messages to other people for you and I can't bring messages to you. Judges and wardens and guards don't care anything about what I think because they look at pastors as just do-gooders with soft heads anyway. I do not have access to any information about your case, so you can tell me anything you want and it won't make any difference to me. You can even lie if you want to. I wouldn't know the difference and, like I said, nobody would care about my opinion anyway. But I'm here to chat with you whenever you want."

That little speech cut down my caseload a bit. And it would leave me to deal with guys who weren't trying to game me so much. They became some of my favorite people because they could be so authentic when they had nothing material to gain.

I really took to this kind of ministry, and went on to serve thirty years as a volunteer law enforcement chaplain. It probably makes sense that someone like me, who is always trying to determine what is true, would be attracted to law enforcement which is all about determining truth from falsehood. I discovered right away, though, that except in the most extreme cases, I was absolutely lousy at figuring out who was telling me the truth and who was leading me on. Fortunately, my particular role in law enforcement would only rarely be about having to decide what was and what wasn't true. In my typical role, it usually did not matter much whether or not someone was telling me the truth, as long as I was telling them the truth.

But there were other times in my ministry when it did matter to try to determine the truth in the total absence of proof. Over the years, I served two churches and both were located just off highways in small towns that were each ports of entry to a large city. People on the run and other bad actors looking for trouble in big cities sometimes hang out in such port towns. Easy-to-spot churches are often "targets of opportunity" because churches are supposed to be welcoming to the stranger, particularly those in apparent need.

Two teenage boys were passing through on their way home on a summer hiking adventure. They had plum run out of pocket change and were looking to earn enough for a motel room. I had no proof about their story or who they really were. They were kids. Obviously, they were just trying to get home. It occurred to me that an unemployed social worker in the congregation might have the perfect home to put up the boys over the weekend. We had talked about these kinds of needs before. The parable of the Good Samaritan always guided our thinking (Luke 10). Based on my description and recommendation, she and her husband were more than willing to offer these boys a little shelter. Their two pre-teen daughters really liked these Huck Finns and were sad to see the boys move on after the weekend. Two days later, police visited my office on a lead. These two boys were escapees from a juvenile facility in Kansas where they were being held on suspicion of first degree murder.

Most judgment calls were never that dramatic. There were plenty of needy people who came to our doors requesting money for food, shelter or gasoline. Through the generosity of a few anonymous people in the congregation, I was able to maintain a small "Pastor's Discretionary Account" of a couple thousand dollars. It was up to me to use these limited funds in the most responsible way for those who really needed help. The flip side of that privilege was the responsibility to protect these limited resources from theft by scam artists.

Through lots of experience, I learned that many of those who came to our doors actually were pretenders. But not all of them. That was the challenge. Unless I had major suspicions of immediate consequences, I almost never had much confidence that I really could know who was telling the truth and who was not. Occasionally, we could clearly spot a thief, such as the person who hit us three times over four years and had served two jail terms as a result. I could check peoples' driver's licenses, write down license plates, check with other congregations and check with police. But unless it was clearly obvious that someone was trying to scam us, we usually decided that we would rather give money to a scammer than risk turning away a genuinely needy person. Jesus himself once warned about mistakenly pulling up good wheat when trying to pull up weeds (Matthew 13:24-30).

These kinds of judgment dilemmas were all because of our inability to decide what was true and what was not. Whenever I suspected that a request was a scam, I almost always wondered if I was being the innkeeper who denied shelter to Mary and Joseph on Christmas Eve (strange how many would show up at our doors in that same cold season). On the other hand, when I took people over to the village motel and covered their room for three nights, somebody would invariably say that I was a naive sucker. And when I would tell myself that, for Pete's sake, it was only money, another voice would counter, "Right, money that you don't have anymore when that next young couple's baby needs diapers."

There were other times when I did have to decide what was true, when I had no way of proving anything for sure. The most frequent situation was in pastoral counseling. An accused teenager would make a strongly believable case in which she denied that she had done anything wrong. A man would make a compelling argument that he had done nothing of which he was accused. Next up, the accusing woman would make an equally convincing case to the contrary. On the spiritual level, it could be almost impossible to talk about repentance and forgiveness when I had little confidence that somebody had actually done something. At the practical level, it was almost impossible to explore alternatives when there was no agreement about what problem needed solving. For example, how could I help the person seek a counselor when I was far from certain that she needed counseling to begin with?

Sometimes I could wish that I had some court of law that could prove which things were true or not. But that also is wishful thinking. In a court of law, a whole cast of characters line up competing arguments and evidence. Sometimes, each side will hire equally impressive experts who are each paid big bucks to compellingly say opposite things. Often, it is a group of people called a jury who have no experience in the subject matter who have to decide which highly technical expert is correct. At the end of the day, the accused may be judged guilty or innocent. Even so, the verdict is only the best guess possible under a set of rules. It may not be the truth of what actually transpired. The ones who know the most often do not agree on what really happened. Proof is elusive even here.

The Most Essential Things About Christianity Cannot And Will Not Be Proven

When I was dating the golden haired lass who would become my wife, my dream could have slipped through my hands by hanging on too tight. I constantly felt threatened by the fact that my girlfriend had all kinds of other options that I thought could easily be more appealing than me: highly charged career options with required extended school opportunities away from me, other guys who were wealthier and better looking. I would get so jealous every time I thought any guy even noticed her, especially if she did so much as even recognize that he existed. At her wit's end it was my mother who told me, "If you had any brains at all, you would take pride in the fact that with all those choices, you are the one she has chosen to go with!" And she really did end the sentence with a preposition.

In the later years of counseling parishioners, I came to view jealousy as one of the most deadly cancers of relationships. Sometimes the lack of trust was justifiably earned by the suspect's untrustworthy behavior of betrayal, secrecy, lies and repeatedly broken promises. Most often, though, the jealousy reflected the unhealthy needs of the one who was suspicious. To the insecure mind, there was virtually nothing the suspected person could do to prove their love. Yeahbutology ruled the jealous mind. Every answer would BE answered by something like, "Yeah, but how can I know for sure that you didn't _____?" No answer was enough. To the one who had already decided to not trust, any resolution of one jealousy crisis would only be the prelude to the next.

So it is with religious claims. Even the Gospels say that there were no eyewitnesses to the most important thing about Jesus, the act of resurrection itself. When I was an eleven-year-old stargazer, I only had to wait a few minutes for my flat-earth question to be answered by someone's direct observation. Not so with the big God questions. The Bible claims that at the end of all things Jesus actually will appear in a way such that every single knee will bow and agree that he is God Almighty (Philippians 2:10). Unless and until that happens, total agreement on the big God questions will probably always stay just out of reach.

Since we live in a "prove it" world these days, there have been a lot of Christian thinkers who have tried to prove that Christianity is true. This usually has not worked for me. I can pretty easily find some fatal flaw in any argument which forces the issue back to faith again. For example, to prove that Jesus really is God, a believer might point to a lot of things which Jesus himself said to show that he himself believed he was God. The reasoning here is that, in saying such things, Jesus could only have been wrong if he was simply misinformed, or if he was deliberately lying, or if he was completely deluded. But not even his enemies typically believe such uncharitable things about him. The only alternative would be that he must have been telling the truth.

But that logic fails when it is pointed out that no one knows if Jesus himself really was the one who said all these things. How do we know that someone didn't put those words in his mouth? All we know for sure is that these claims were made by whomever it was who penned the New Testament. And there is endless debate about who many of those people actually were. The Book of Hebrews is one of the most important scriptures about who Jesus was and there isn't even a claim as to who penned those ideas.

If we even knew a lot about the writers, the human authority behind such fantastic claims still might not go too far with a yeahbutologist like me. People and organizations I've known up-close have betrayed my trust on all kinds of important matters. All kinds of people and movements which are connected with Jesus have a vested material interest in him being who he said he was. This is especially true of religious organizations. But even so, there is one little fact which jams the gears of suspicion to a full stop for me. The original penmen of the Jesus claims only got one thing for their efforts: horrible execution, time and time and time again. Not one or two of them, but virtually all of them.

To me, the most essential and unique ideas of Christianity have to do with the claim that Jesus was God in the flesh, and that his death and resurrection will achieve never-ending joyous life in Heaven for all who trust and worship him. Not one of the people who first recorded these ideas saw any proof of that when they chose to stand by these promises through torture and death. Similarly, until we die, there simply is no way to prove any of this. The essence of Christianity cannot be a matter of proof.

Jesus himself was reported to have said the same thing to the apostle who would not believe without seeing: "Because you have seen me, you have believed; blessed are those who have not seen and yet have believed (John 20:29)."

I think that the inability to prove the most essential things about the Gospel is exactly as it should be and how it has always been intended.

My family roots are from the Old West where a deal, and the deal-maker, could be dead on arrival if either party didn't believe that "a man's word was as good as his handshake." President Reagan liked to borrow an old Russian adage which says, "trust but verify." It is important to know that he used this Russian wisdom for the purpose of working with the Russians. He was referring to negotiations with adversaries, not with those who loved him. He probably did not take this approach when dealing with his wife. Legal contracts are commonplace in business. But people often feel uncomfortable drawing up formal contracts with close personal friends and family.

My childhood years taught me the horribly corrosive lesson that I could not always trust the important people in my life to not harm me. Trust has always been a big struggle for me and may well drive my yeahbutology. Serving as a pastor in a highly political church is not a healthy venue for someone with those kinds of trust issues. Assuming anyone's friendship in such roles is a risky thing. I have learned the hard way that it is usually risky to trust almost anybody without being somewhat vigilant.

It dawns on me that maybe my yeahbutology is some version of "trust but verify" with God. But then I wonder, if this is what I'm doing, am I essentially treating God like some kind of enemy? Apparently, I may not be the first person who has ever thought of that. The apostle Paul wrote that it was when we were ENEMIES of God that he settled the score with us through the death of his son (Romans 5:10).

The most well-known verse in the New Testament is John 3:16 which says, "God so loved the entire cosmos that he gave his one and only Son ..." So, I'm treating like an enemy someone who loves me? What amazes me is that anyone could cook up a story about God choosing to love this kind of world, considering how his own so-called followers treated him. My thinking is that such a thing is so preposterous on the face of it, that no one would try to sell it as true unless it really was true.

It makes sense to me that a love-based God would want our affiliation not because we can verify what he said but simply because he was the one who said it. I committed my love and my entire earthly existence to my wife long, long before I knew most things about her. I seriously doubt that she would have given me the chance to do that if I had insisted on verifying everything she said and claimed to be. It makes sense to me that if a personal God existed who was about love, then such a God would give us not one other thing that we could depend on, other than himself and for his sake alone. He will not allow us to trust his hand in creation on the basis of someone claiming to find an ark on a mountain in Turkey. He will not allow us to believe that Jesus rose from the dead on the basis of being able to prove it or verify it like one would have to do with an enemy. In fact, Jesus said that "If [non-believers] won't listen to Moses and the Prophets, they're not going to be convinced by someone who rises from the dead (Luke 6:31).'"

Chapter Eighteen

Reasonableness As An Alternative To Proof

What I Do Not Mean By "Reasonable"

FIRST OF ALL, JESUS AND HIS TEACHINGS often seem anything but reasonable to me at first glance. Hence, my yeahbutology.

There are two rather different ways that the word "reasonable" is used. In one way, to say that something is reasonable is to say that it is fair. For example, "I think that was a very reasonable thing you asked me to do." In that sense, so much of what Jesus said is totally unreasonable, totally unfair. To wit, we are to love our enemies, we are not to resist someone taking our belongings, we are to endlessly forgive without regard to apology, we are to be satisfied with last minute workers receiving the same pay as those who toiled all day, and we are to give to whomever asks.

There is another sense of what it means to be reasonable. For something to be reasonable, it must be rational, answerable to reason. There again, I think that the vast majority of formally educated people in western civilization today would say that the most important claims of Christianity do not make sense: that someone could be both God and human at the same time, that a virgin could conceive without human intervention, that someone could rise from the dead.

However, in the following discussion, I will claim that, upon deeper reflection, even the Gospel's most difficult aspects can make as much sense as any other system of thought. This position says that biblical claims about Jesus cannot be legitimately dismissed as irrational. But that is not the reason I follow Jesus as my Lord and Savior. Reasonableness is simply my effort to explain the thinking part of my belief. I suspect that the substantial reason I follow Jesus may be more akin to sheep which only follow the voice that they recognize as their own shepherd.

Secondly, I do not presume that what seems reasonable to me would necessarily seem reasonable to everyone else. Even Jesus said that sheep that are not of his flock are not able to recognize his voice. My understanding of the Old and New testaments is that God allows people to decide what does and does not make sense. In fact, God even requires each person to choose whether or not to follow him. This is most clearly articulated by Joshua, the successor to Moses, who said, "... if serving the Lord seems undesirable to you, then choose for yourselves this day whom you will serve, whether the gods your ancestors served beyond the Euphrates, or the gods of the Amorites, in whose land you are living. But as for me and my household, we will serve the Lord (Joshua 24:15)."

What I Do Mean By "Reasonable:" The Principal Principle

As a pastor and police chaplain, I've had to pick up too many pieces of broken lives and broken hearts because someone has unnecessarily died doing something really stupid. This is where I am not going to share a story. I don't want those pictures in anybody else's mind. Suffice it to say, I've developed a bit of a short fuse in that department. A generally healthy, non-addict who plays with drugs is somewhere near the top of my judgmental list. And when children pay the price, that gets to me in a big way.

But a retired elementary school principal once mentioned something she taught her little ones: "Always remember that whenever you point a finger at someone, you've got three other fingers of yours pointing back at yourself." I call this the Principal Principle. I have since discovered so many times that when someone does something that doesn't seem to make any sense, it doesn't take me any time at all to recall having done something like that myself.

For example, I love to kayak and I'm kind of a safety nut. I'm especially big on people needing to wear flotation devices. I struggle to have a graceful reaction when someone drowns because they weren't wearing a life jacket .... until I remember the time when my kayak pulled me into Lake Superior in a seventy mile an hour gale. And I was not wearing a life jacket.

But let me not hesitate to add in my own defense that I was not actually kayaking. The evening before, I had pulled my boat way up onto the rocks. Way up. Apparently not way up enough. The next morning, I awoke in the cabin to the angriest storm I had ever seen on Superior in thirty years of vacationing there. Suddenly, a loud rapping on the door. In heavy oilskin storm gear, the caretaker was trying to hang on to the screen door and was yelling over the howling wind, "Is that your kayak out in the lake?" Sure enough, about a hundred yards out, my swamped boat was ducking in and out of towering waves. But it looked like each crest was somehow drifting my boat shoreward. So, when it got closer, I carefully picked my way down the cliff rocks, timing my dodges to avoid massive breakers which were crashing into the shoreline.

Just as the kayak washed ashore, I ran down to grab the bow rope loop, only to discover that the boat was filled with a few hundred pounds of freezing water. I discovered this just as a rolling breaker slammed into me. Because of the thirty-seven degree water, my hand had frozen, immovable inside the rope loop. When the breaker receded, it effortlessly dragged the kayak back into the deep as it dragged me down. And out. And under. The next breaker slammed boat and bumbler into a high, jagged cliff, turning both of us over and over like a washing machine agitator. I distinctly remember realizing that I was done and thinking, "Darwin wins again." I was consumed not with fear but by embarrassment. It was not my life that passed before my eyes but what I could imagine in the headlines: "Idiot Sleeps With The Fishes." Another wave washed us both up onto the shore once more, just as the caretaker scampered down to find me. He unlooped the rope from my frozen hand and ran for cover as the next breaker washed in. I had just enough energy to crab-crawl farther up the rocks. The whole incident took less time than it took you to read this script of stupidity.

To this day, I have no idea what compelled me to do something so unbelievably and certifiably foolish. Obviously, though, it must have seemed like a good idea at the time. Death is generally not a learning experience for the main actor. At times, I have wondered if I was allowed to survive so that I could come to realize that every unreasonable action does indeed have a story behind it. As a police chaplain, we described fatalities in two ways. DOA meant they got to the hospital and "died on arrival." In the very worst cases, there was no point in sending them off. These ones were DRT, dead right there. That should have been me. No one who knew anything about me would have been able to figure out what on earth I was doing in my kayak, without a life jacket, in a major gale on the coldest, deepest, largest and most deadly of the Great Lakes. As Kurt Vonnegut never tired of saying in *Slaughterhouse-Five*, "So it goes."

Since I'm still a little short of complete perfection in all things, my three thawed fingers periodically do get a bit of a workout pointing back at me. My most rehearsed refrain has become, "there but for the grace of God go I." I have found few things where this doesn't apply. Those three fingers have shown me how so many apparently unreasonable things really can make sense. When I talk about my three fingers leading to "there but for the grace of God," something else dawns on me: is my yeahbutology somehow all about me pointing my finger in accusation at God? Because, if that is the case, maybe I should see where the other three fingers are pointing. When I do this, sometimes those troubling things about God begin to make a little more sense.

I'm finding that it's not proof that carries the day with me, but the reasonableness of what I had thought was unreasonable. Troublesome things about God can begin to make a little more sense to me when I see:

One finger pointing back to similar things in myself, and/or

One finger pointing back to other things in this world which are generally accepted as true and reasonable by most people, and/or

One more finger pointing way, way back beyond myself, to the long-term perspective.

The Principal Principle I: The First Finger That Points to Myself

I remember my dad telling me that he and his buddies did not know that they had been in something called the Battle of the Bulge. Weeks later, newspaper deliveries caught up with them and they really felt bad for the poor suckers they read about. Which, unbeknownst to them, WAS them. I had a little of that experience after I had made the first of my three trips to lands of the Bible. Our little band of travelers arrived in Israel the Spring of 2001. As a former Army officer, I was acutely aware of all the military activity around us. But I had nothing to compare it to, and I figured that this was just the way things usually were in this part of the world. We didn't know it, but it turns out that we had just walked right smack dab into the beginning of what history books would come to refer to as The Second Intifada (uprising) of the Palestinians against the State of Israel.

Patrols of heavily armed teenaged Israeli soldiers roamed everywhere. Around every hill was an Israeli tank which tracked us with its slowly traversing barrel. Military checkpoints were everywhere with heavy machine guns trained on us from high vantage points. Some cities would suddenly be off-limits. Maybe it was the PLO, the Palestinian Liberation Authority blocking our way into Bethlehem. Other times it was the IDF, the Israeli Defense Forces blockading entry into Jericho. Teams of roof-top Israeli snipers followed our every move inside the plaza of the Western Wall (few made the error more than once of mistakenly referring to it as the Wailing Wall). Other than that, we neither saw nor heard any threats at all, since our tour leaders were quietly and constantly changing our itinerary away from dangerous activity. For all we knew, we were simply experiencing everyday Jerusalem.

Our first night there was where my first finger got bent back on me. It was nighttime at the end of a fifteen hour day when we were shuffling down the steep wooded hillside of the Mount of Olives. This was the exact place where Jesus' exhausted apostles took a break while he walked a couple hundred feet away to pray at the Garden of Gethsemane. The story goes that he had asked his followers to keep watch, but that when he returned, he found them all fast asleep. In his disappointment, he asked them why they couldn't stay awake and keep watch for just one hour. He left them with the same instructions and went off once more to pray. When he returned, he found them sleeping again (Luke 22:39-46).

I had always told this story in my sermons to contrast the faithfulness of Jesus with the unfaithfulness of those he died to save. Jesus himself expressed his own judgment on them. Now I was right where that had actually happened and my disdain for the clueless followers grew even more. On the hillside we were shown how the crowds of Passover pilgrims would often have to camp out here on the ground because there was not enough lodging in the city. This is where Jesus said that foxes have holes but that the Son of Man had nowhere to lay his head (Matthew 8:20). But there were a few caves on that hillside where some lucky travelers could find a little shelter. It was maybe 10 PM when our guide took us in to one of those caves. It had long since been designed as a retreat spot with lighted candles and folding chairs. We all took a chair and quieted down as our guide, Hannah, read the passage about Jesus and those sleepy apostles. At least, that's how she started. I don't know how far she read, because I myself dozed off in exhausted slumber right after she began. I awoke when she said something like, "That concludes the reading." And that also concluded any future opinions in my sermons about the irresponsibility of the apostles on that hillside. So much for pointing fingers. This was one of those times when what had once seemed unreasonable to me groggily became reasonable. I saw the same thing in myself.

The second day was our short hop to a suburb called Bethlehem. But first we had to drop off our guide, Hanna, because Israelis were not allowed into Bethlehem at that time. Soon, our tourist bus was winding its way up the switch-back road to Bethlehem. Half way up, we were stopped by a patrol of Palestinian gunmen. They were somewhat insistent in their "invitation" that we get off the bus. They asked us to line up beside it. The gunmen faced us. Was this it? Were we about to be shot? It all seemed so routine. There was no drama at all. Our bus driver showed no concern. But then again, Ahmed himself was Palestinian Muslim. The leader of the group asked for our attention. He simply wanted to tell us what was going to happen. That got our attention. He then guided us through a barricade of debris and boulders. On the other side, he helped us onto a different, beat up, light blue, repurposed school bus. The rest of his squad stayed behind as he alone boarded the bus with us. Soon we were winding our way up the narrow roads, and he proclaimed, "Now you are all feeling safe and having wonderful time, ARE YOU NOT?!" On cue, we dutifully responded in unison, "Yes!"

Since those gunmen pointed my finger back on myself, I now I have some appreciation why hostages usually don't fight back.

The Principal Principle II: The Second Finger That Points Beyond Myself to Other Things That Seem Reasonable in Everyday Life

"And you tell that pig right there next to you to move in front of the counter. If he tries any hero stuff, I'll blow YOUR head off right where you're standing." Pig is what angry people called cops and soldiers in those happy days. This was a hold up. But it was different from anything I had been trained for as a hotel front desk clerk. This was a telephone stick-up of all things! This guy had called the switchboard and had asked to be connected to the front desk. Somehow, he knew that I was just about to make "the drop." At irregular times on this late night shift, I was to bundle up most of the accumulated cash from the cash drawer, put it in a white canvas cloth bag, and drop it in a rotating slot on top of our safe. The guy's timing was perfect. Just as I bundled up the cash, but seconds before I dropped it, he made the call.

I couldn't see the bad guy, but he clearly could see me. I had never been robbed before, but the element of an unseen predator added to the terror. My knees were literally knocking together. I hadn't told my security guard anything because my chattering teeth made it impossible to talk. I froze on the spot with the phone stuck to my ear. The voice on the other end said, "This is the last time I tell you, man. Do it! Now!"

I obeyed and looked over to my security man, an off-duty cop who was standing to the side of the office area. He was monitoring the whole thing. "Clint, the guy on the phone says he'll shoot me if you do anything." To the switchboard operator who was tucked into the switchboard cubicle off to my other side, Clint pantomimed the dialing of a phone. What did I just tell him? Was he trying to get my head blown off?!

The voice cut back in with urgency, "You tell that pig one more stunt like that and I'll take you out without another warning, sucker. I mean it. Don't push me."

"Clint, he saw you. He's going to kill me."

"That's right, sucker. Now you tell the pig and your operator I want both of them standing right out in the open next to you. Do it now! I ain't telling you one more time!"

All of a sudden, screaming squad cars assaulted the parking lot from all directions. A dozen heavily armed officers breached the lobby entrance with massive precision. The episode ended as quickly as it had begun. Just like that. A pair of high-powered binoculars were soon found in a phone booth a block away. Apparently, the caller had his partner manipulate side mirrors on parked cars so that, from a safe distance, he could make the call, watch me and control me.

This happened while I was working my way through college as the youngest night auditor in the history of a regional hotel chain. Since the job title included the word "night", I typically worked the middle of the night shift. They called that the graveyard shift, and the irony was not lost on me this particular evening. Like most night auditors, I also served as the front desk clerk and the night manager. My post was on the front desk of this high-end hotel in the downtown of a major metropolitan city. In addition to run-of-the-mill crime, nightly urban adventures also included periodic bombings. That entertainment was provided by anti-government terrorists who were, oddly, protesting against war. In just fifteen months, there were forty-thousand bombings, attempted bombings and bomb threats throughout the country. One night, I was receiving a printed message from one of our hotels. The teletype machine was key-clattering away, word-by-word-by-line-by-line when it suddenly stopped in the middle of a word. Hours later, we found out that the other property that had been sending the message had just been blasted off-line by a bomb. One afternoon, I sprang into action as the helpful person who called the police bomb squad. They were more than happy to blow up a guy's suspiciously unattended brief case. It turned out that it included, not a bomb, but rather a few thousand dollars' worth of his personal music collection. The man also got arrested, jailed, arraigned, and fined. That was partly because he threatened to kill me.

The drama never ended on this job. That is why we were regularly briefed by the police on what to do and what not to do if things went bump in the night. And things often did. We were told to give the bad guys whatever they wanted and not to resist them. We were not to hold anything back because that could make things worse. We were not to do anything to make them nervous. We were to do everything we could to help them feel OK and not threatened. We were not to try to signal for help until after the bad guys had left.

Our manager stressed these rules over and over and over. Until the morning that he was grabbed by one of three gunmen in our crowded lobby. On their way out the door, my boss started to resist. One of the gunmen shot him, point blank. A guest behind him fell to the floor. Somehow, our boss hadn't been hit. But he was dragged out the front door to the waiting getaway car which squealed away. A couple blocks away, the burglars pistol-whipped him and tossed him out of the speeding car onto the curb where he sustained a minor concussion.

Meanwhile, back at the lobby, the guest who had been shot was conscious and terrified and balled up in the fetal position, curled around his clutched stomach. When his clothes were torn away, an unrecognizable piece of smoking lead was resting on top of his abdomen. The bullet had gone through the man's briefcase, a folded up newspaper and several layers of clothing, including the heavy overcoat that he had draped over his arm. His only injury was a minor first degree burn on his stomach from the spent round.

When I am tempted to point my finger at God's apparently unreasonable ways, it does not take me long to see similar things in everyday life which many people easily accept as reasonable. The hold-up situation is a good example.

When Jesus told his apostles that he was going to be executed, Peter was shocked and told his master that he would never let this happen. Jesus responded in an equally shocking way. He turned on Peter, called him Satan, and told him to get out of the way (Matthew 16:23). I have always felt a little sorry for Peter. The poor guy gets a tongue-lashing from Jesus simply because he's trying to defend his boss. If I had been there, I would have thought that Jesus was making no sense at all. Jesus followed up by telling Peter that the problem was that Peter had his priorities turned around. "You are not setting your mind on the things of God, but on the things of man (Mark 8:33)." It is not recorded if Peter said anything in reply. If I had been in Peter's sandals, if I had had the courage to say what Peter said, I myself would have been speechless. That's because my mouth would have been hanging open in utter astonishment. I would have been thinking, "What?!?!?!! You're telling me that God WANTS you to get executed?!?!?" This is another example of something that is so ludicrous by earthly standards that no one would write it unless it were true in the most unimaginable way.

If the chief of the apostles didn't think that Jesus' words made any sense, it's totally understandable that others would have trouble as well. Almost all people who have ever lived on Earth would say that the most reasonable thing is the prerogative to defend what is yours, and if necessary to do it with force. According to the Bible, however, Jesus says all kinds of things about violence which most people reject as totally flying in the face of common sense. We are not supposed to exchange an eye for an eye? To the contrary, we are not even supposed to return fire, but rather turn the other cheek. Not only that, but if someone steals from us, we are not supposed to resist him. We're supposed to let him have what he wants. And if that's not enough, we're supposed to give that guy something else in addition. If all of that isn't enough to blow your circuits, how about this: we are to actually pray for our enemies and do them good (Luke 6:27-30)!

Who would think that this makes any sense at all? I have no question that if more people really paid attention to what Jesus actually said, most American Christians would choose guns over the ways and means of Christ. After all, our founding fathers wrote into the holy scripture of America that there was only one mechanical device that was important enough to enshrine in our nation's operators' manual. It wasn't the plow and it wasn't books or pens or ships or eating utensils. It was guns. The reason why guns were the only mechanical device included is because it is self-defense that makes sense to most people.

But then there was that hold-up. It certainly did not occur to me at the time, and I doubt that this was their reason for doing so, but the police department was telling us to do exactly what Jesus told us to do. They trained us to not resist and to give whatever our enemy demanded. In at least this case, Jesus' non-violent approach was the one that law enforcement had taught us was the most reasonable one. I would doubt that such an approach is the most effective way to materially advance and impose oneself or one's nation against the will of others. But the fact is that most law enforcement agencies say that at least in hold-ups and hostage situations, Jesus' approach is not only reasonable but preferred. This is not to suggest that Jesus did such things for the same reasons as the police. I would hazard a wild guess that there's at least an outside chance that a god might have reasons well beyond my grasp. All I am saying is that what I had once rejected as unimaginably unacceptable about God, might well be something that I have otherwise found to be reasonably acceptable in other aspects of my life. Specifically, I have discovered everyday parallels in my own experiences of parenting, science and the military, which will be discussed in the next chapter.

The Principal Principle III: The Third Finger That Points Way, Way, Way Beyond Myself to the Long-Term

When I watch action movies, I kind of feel sorry for the bad guys, even though they almost always outnumber the hero by magnitudes of order. In the storyline, these characters had been specially picked, highly trained and phenomenally weaponized. They seem to be a really well-oiled machine. But as soon as they come on screen to face our hero, every single last one of these fighters gets horribly wiped out. In a matter of seconds. Not one of them seems to be able to hit the broad side of a barn. Or duck. Everything our hero throws their direction seems to connect. Aaaaaand, as they say, that's a wrap. Just like that. Eight hundred and thirty-six dead guys in the record-setting body count of *The Lord of the Rings: Return of the King.* It's like their whole life was just so they could be a target for one inglorious obliteration. That's all there is. Nothing more than that. A lot of their acting careers don't have much better longevity and benefits. Seems like a lot of effort for not much to show. Even the costuming seems like a waste. It all seems so short-lived, so short-sighted.

The previously described armed robbery at the hotel also makes a point about time. I find it helpful to consider the extremely long-term perspective when something about God seems absurd. I subscribe to a Christian notion that the most important thing about earthly life is how it affects eternal life. If there is even an outside chance that there is eternal life and that Jesus will be the one to decide my eternal fate, then it would be in my long-term interest to heed his consistent prohibitions against violent self-defense.

In that hotel hostage robbery, after-action reports decided that the manager's self-defense almost cost the life of a bystander. The fact that no one was killed was attributed to the fact that nobody else resisted. But the reason that Jesus prohibited violent self-defense was not because it was the safest practice. Said attitude got him nailed to a cross. And not just him but thousands and thousands of his followers then and since. I can only guess at the reason for his non-violence commands, even in the middle of brutal military occupation. But I don't think it's because of improvements to earthly things.

Though no one was killed in that hold-up, not a single person was saved from death. Everyone in that story has since died or soon will. Including yours truly, though the category I belong to may have changed between the time I wrote this and the time you read it. My reason for trying to heed Jesus' non-violence commands is not about temporary earthly gain. It's about who Jesus is to me and how all this affects my eternity.

It was probably fifth grade where I first learned about near-sightedness. This was when our family moved from the North Dakota Badlands. Dad's friend had a gigantic eighteen-wheeler moving van. They disassembled the plywood sales office from my Dad's tree nursery and placed the whole structure, one piece at a time, on the truck. And then, the biggest surprise of all to a ten-year-old boy: I got to ride up front with Ernie all the way across the prairies to our new home. Well, actually, our new home had been with us the whole way. The best part of the trip was that Ernie made himself pull over for coffee every couple hours or so. Make that chocolate milk and pie! I thought I'd died and gone to Heaven.

Eventually, we arrived. I have no memory how that eighteen-wheeler did it, but somehow we found ourselves up and over a steep and stoney trail, across railroad tracks and into a stand of woods. This is where our little house in the woods was reassembled, right next to the train tracks, just inside the woods, two miles outside the nearest little town. And there we lived for two winters, all four of us, in a one-room plywood box, painted fire-engine red, with no plumbing, no phone, and no electricity. It had a flat roof where Dad made me practice my clarinet when the weather was warmer. Thirty years later would find me prowling those same roads as a pastor in the next town over. Maybe I should have said "haunting" because I later was told that my family and I had long ago become the Ghosts of Greenville (name changed to protect the curious). We earned our place in infamy because of how we made our move after a couple years. Apparently, no one knew that we had moved until some time later, when the cabin was found abandoned. I'm guessing that this may have occurred somewhere near Halloween. All kinds of bizarre rumors of murders, abductions, disappearances and ghostings started making the rounds. Local teenagers sort of consecrated the cabin as a haunted house and soon the whole thing became a local legend. I was totally unaware of any of this until I rose from the dead to reappear as the new pastor in the area some forty years later. Mercifully, the fire department eventually burned down the shrine as a training exercise.

Our family didn't have a whole lot of stuff, but our first Halloween led to something that we had in abundance. That afternoon, when my sister and I were playing outside, we heard the fragile mewing of an abandoned little kitten. It was trying to hop from one railroad tie to the next. We named her Spooks. Somehow, she eventually found herself with three little ones of her own, two females and a male. Until the male had kittens. I remember Dad trying to explain that. Four cats now became thirteen in this one-room kingdom. And every one of them was female. Long story, sudden end, don't ask. We were told that Dad adopted them out as mousers to some farmer.

Our new place had an unpaved, dirt driveway which rainstorms always turned into a small version of the Grand Canyon. Those ruts would solve my first problem with eyeglasses. When I was diagnosed with nearsightedness, I was told that I would probably have to wear these things for the rest of my life. We had just moved from near the Theodore Roosevelt National Park where our spectacled President was immortalized as "Old Four Eyes." I didn't like the image. I remember feeling claustrophobic, like I was now going to have to spend the rest of my life looking out through smeared windows. That's when it dawned on me: Dad usually didn't come up the driveway until well after dark. I carefully placed my glasses in one of those ruts. Worked. Like. A. Charm.

This may have been my first lesson in shortsightedness. We were temporarily living in that plywood sales office because my folks were in tough financial straits. My dad had been self-employed, and I seriously doubt they would have had health insurance, especially the kind that covered glasses. So, there were no more eyeglasses for awhile, which is exactly what I wanted to achieve. Until I found myself as the new kid in class, placed right up front beside Mrs. Angel (who was anything but) so that I could see the blackboard. To mangle a Jewish folk proverb, "Too soon shneaky, too late shmart." I probably got a few lectures from my parents about being 'penny wise and pound foolish.'

The glasses did indeed stay with me the rest of my life, but not without some effort. Since I moved to a new school every year, there was always somebody trying to separate the new kid from his glasses. Becoming a pastor didn't change that. In fact, it was the very fact of being a pastor that almost cost me my glasses a second time. In the Introduction, I told the story about almost losing my glasses along with my nose on which they rested. That had something to do with the Green Bay Packers. A second near-miss was a little better positioned, this time in a hospital. I had driven a parishioner downtown for a lovely afternoon of diagnostics. For several hours I waited in the hectic lobby with my nose in a book. Make it the Bible. I do know that I was wearing my black clergy shirt with that little white collar tab. I clearly remember this, because that's what got me in trouble.

A shadow suddenly dimmed the pages because one of tallest guys I had ever seen was towering over me. The old guy's face was beat red and he was shaking from head to foot. I noticed one other thing because it was at the level of my nose: both his hands were clenched into fists. I was quick to figure out that he was either monstrously angry or he was about to have a medical episode of some sort. Or both.

I said, "Can I help you, sir?"

"I just want to know," he said with a quivering voice, "where in the hell you get off calling yourself Father!" I punctuate that last line with an exclamation mark because I don't think he really was asking a question. I also didn't think he was exactly in the mood to discuss the finer points of Jesus' words in Matthew 23:9. He did, in fact say, "call no man your father on Earth, for you have one Father, who is in Heaven." So the tall man did have a point. But I chose not to split hairs. Especially mine.

My instinct was to try to defuse the situation with a little humor. So I said, "Well, to tell you the truth, I get off calling myself father because I have two daughters."

That particular choice of words had an effect more along the lines of gasoline on a barbecue. "And you have the damn gall to admit it!" he said.

In seminary they try to teach you how to be an insightful listener. I may have missed that class because I apparently tossed a little more fuel on the fire. I explained that if I didn't admit to having fathered two children, their mother would not be too happy.

I noticed people starting to move away from us when his next escalation included describing me as the male offspring of a female canine. Quick to discern a need to try a different approach, I told the man that I was a Lutheran pastor, not a Catholic priest. He almost swallowed his tongue and nearly tripped over it in effusive apologies. He had no way of knowing that some time ago, I had actually been converted to his position in a way that was infinitely more powerful than anything he had been threatening to do. That also occurred in a hospital.

Our second daughter had been born with absolutely no complications. When we went to get her up for the second Sunday of her life, we were dumbstruck to discover her unresponsive in her sweat-soaked crib. She was a dusky blue. We decided that we could drive her to nearby Children's Hospital faster than waiting for an ambulance. Minutes later, a cardiologist was on the scene. A couple hours after this, one of them told us that we were looking at heart failure. He said that if baptism were important to us, we might want to arrange it rather quickly.

My wife and I answered in unison: she said "yes" and I said "no." Two hours later, both our families gathered around our parish pastor who did baptize her in the hospital chapel. My wife had rendered my objections moot, sort of like tank treads might do. I initially had refused baptism because I could not admit the possibility of losing our precious baby. If I admitted that possibility, then I was giving up. As a nurse, my wife had been through this before with others. In her own crushing grief, she nursed me with gentle reasoning: the fact is that we might well be saying goodbye to our precious, precious baby girl any time now. It was time to get ready.

With her big sister always bravely standing guard, this child would survive many, many operations and pacemakers in the months and years to come. One of the most crushing days of my life was the first time we surrendered her into the arms of the anesthesiologist to take her away for a major procedure. This horrible moment was one we would go through again and again in the years to come. We had been told that there was maybe a one in ten chance of her surviving the operation. Same thing with the next two operations. Each time the anesthesiologist took her away, we watched her go through the doors for maybe the last time. Each was a long procedure. We always waited in the same chapel where she had recently been baptized. Hours into one of those surgeries, her surgeon came into the chapel. He was never known for nuance and he was still in his scrubs covered with her blood. "We've done all we can. She's in God's hands." It was like the ancient hymn which says, "God himself is with us, all within keep silence, prostrate lie with deepest reverence." And so we did. Many, many times.

Even though he was a large man, this surgeon's hands were unusually small. For tiny places. This was the man who held our daughter's life in his own small hands. When he said that she was now in God's hands, it slowly dawned on me that God was her real father, not me. I was her daddy. He knew her before I did and he loved her more than I ever could. At this moment, she was right where she always had been and always would be. In retrospect, that is where and that is when my first sermon came together, years before I became a pastor. It would become my Fathers' Day sermon which I would always end by wishing everybody a Happy DADDYS' Day.

From that moment on, everything in my world has been about the long perspective. I see everything here as temporary and in service of the long haul. Ever since, my Christian faith has been articulated by the apostle Paul's conviction that, "If in Christ we have hope in this life only, we are of all people most to be pitied (1 Corinthians 15:19)." This is the touchstone for how the most difficult things in the Gospel begin to make sense to me. This is how we parents would be able to dare trust our child to a God who might well allow her to pass from this phase. She is God's child who is and will be safe where that child has always been. Our "heart child" would grow up to become a nurse in that same hospital. Her big sister would grow up to be a researcher in another children's hospital.

This is why, when I point my finger at God, I am slowly and still inconsistently learning to look for the long perspective from one of my other back-pointing fingers. I have mortal near-sightedness. So I never presume that I really know what the long perspective is in any particular case, even in retrospect. But almost always, I am able to imagine a number of possible scenarios. The upshot is that if even I can imagine possibilities, it is certainly reasonable to think that God is doing things now for purposes downstream. This, in fact, is one of the most basic notions throughout the Bible.

Chapter Nineteen

Finding Parallels

Finding Everyday Parallels In Parenting

IN THE EARLY YEARS after World War Two, my father was one of millions of returning veterans. Every one of them was struggling to find his niche for a living. Dad's unfinished university training was in horticulture, and the only job he could find in California was as a seed salesman. I liked his job because he got a company car. We always were the only ones on our block to get a brand new car every single year. Dad would sometimes let me ride along as he introduced new lines of seeds to various merchants. Sometimes this would take us to orchards, like an apricot grove I will never forget. Ever. The farmer set a ladder up against a tree and told me that while he and my daddy did business, I could pick all the apricots I could eat. I did. I would like to meet that guy and have a little talk with him. To this day, I cannot stomach the fruit of my misadventure. I was all of eight years old, when, for the first time in my life, I begged my mom to take me to a doctor. I was that sick.

Dad's clients also included pet stores. From time to time, he would bring home interesting pets. Few of these little visitors seemed to survive too many days. There was a beautiful bird that was pure white, except for a bright red trickle down its breast. It died of a heart attack. Dad said that the red trickle was just the way its feathers were colored and had nothing to do with its death. Next, there was the green parakeet. Petie flew out the window. I don't think the guppy was with us long enough to get a name. But she was, as they say, "full with child," or more correctly, full with lots of children. You could actually see these tiny little things in her belly! Until one morning when they were suddenly all gone. Mommy told me that she had had her babies. So where were they? When my mom said that the mommy had "had" her babies, apparently she could have meant that a couple different ways. Kind of like the cannibal who told the missionary that he'd like to have him for dinner. Sometimes mommy guppies eat their babies. I'm glad I got over that by the time I was old enough to have kids.

Turns out that guppies are not the only ones which do things like this: so do mother hamsters, burying beetles and sometimes cats and dogs as well as father bears, father cats, father lions, and father sharks. Other ways are also strangely effective in promoting their species. Immediate abandonment of newborns apparently works for snakes, lizards, turtles, moths, butterflies, rabbits and harp seals. Panda mothers typically give birth to twins, only to abandon one in favor of the other.

Humans offspring, however, typically survive because most parents remain to nurture and, if necessary, sacrifice themselves for their young, America's abortion industry notwithstanding. Placing their young ahead of themselves is the typical human instinct regardless of culture, era, gender, number of adults or genetic relationship. The Judeo-Christian understanding is that God made humans in his own image. There are endless notions about what that could mean. Sometimes, I think our species came to nurture its young because this may be the best way to understand how things are between God and us. The nurturing parent model speaks not to some impersonal universe of random happenstance that has nothing to do with us. The typical human process, rather, reflects a deliberate, personal, nurturing, sustaining, loving and self-sacrificing parent. I find it curious that the only time Jesus gave instruction on how to pray was when he said that we are to say, "Our FATHER ..." Some call this the Lord's Prayer. Roman Catholics may be on to something when they refer to it as the Our Father. In his last prayer, Jesus called the Father "abba." It means something akin to "daddy."

So many of the most confusing things about God begin to make sense to me when I consider how a healthy, loving parent nurtures his or her child. Admittedly, my personal experience is limited in that I have only grown up once and with only one particular set of parents. I have raised only my own children. I have helped raise only my own grandchildren. But decades as a therapist and as a pastor have also given me a front-row seat to observe many other parents up close. So many of my own tussles with God, and so many of the struggles between God and his children in the Bible, resemble dynamics in parent-child relationships. No matter how old they are, children are often incapable of understanding why their parents treat them the way they do. The typical response from the elder is, "Someday you will understand." This kind of remark is part of the same toolbox which includes other devices like, "I'm doing this for your own good," and "This is going to hurt me a lot more than it hurts you." The tool which most cut me to the quick was my dad's watery-eyed silence whenever I seriously disappointed him.

The long road to one of Dad's greatest disappointments with me began when Mom and I became a driving team. When I was in second grade in the Bay area, Mom was an Avon cosmetics door-to-door saleslady. Sometimes, she let me walk along on her sales calls. Eventually, she saved up enough money to purchase a black, 1950 Ford Club Coupe. In this car she was dauntless. When it stalled at a busy intersection, an impatient man behind us just laid on his horn. When nothing she did could wake up Black Beauty, Mom turned her attention to the guy behind us. She ordered me to stay put while she stormed her way back to him. Suddenly the honking stopped and I heard her voice above the San Francisco traffic. "I'll tell you what, Mister: you start my car for me and I'll honk your horn for you!"

At just over four and a half feet tall, she couldn't see over the steering wheel without sitting on several pillows. She typically steered by closely following the car ahead of her. One afternoon, she got pulled over for suspected drunken driving. Well, yes, she told the officer, she did know that she had been weaving back and forth. But that was because she had been avoiding potholes like that car in front of her had been doing. The cop had her step out of the car to see that there were no potholes. Apparently the guy in front had been drunk. Mom got a warning ticket. That's what she told Dad.

She was the parent who taught me how to drive. Dad refused to get in the same car with either Mom or me behind the wheel. That's why I was surprised when, on my first day with a driver's license, he let me drive myself to school in our massive, eighteen-foot long, 1959 Pontiac Catalina. After school that day, I had fencing practice. Our coach was the coquettish, first year German teacher, Fräulein Mueller. She's the reason why some people have noticed a faint, southern accent in my own German. On our way to the parking lot afterwards, I noticed that her little Volkswagen "Bug" was parked directly across the row from my tank. Our cars were faced away from each other. She playfully mocked my new wheels by clutching her manual transmission into neutral and revving her little engine like a dragster. I responded in kind, goosing my accelerator three times. But my four thousand pound behemoth was in reverse. Before I realized what was happening, I had slammed my car that many times into the little Ford Falcon next door, as it were. Speaking of doors, both of them fell off the other car, as well as its front fender and rear quarter-panel. Kind of reminded me of those cut-away pictures to show the interior of a new car. I think Fräulein Mueller said "auf wiedersehen" as she waved and puttered off.

I slinked my way back to the main office where I discovered that the newly dead Falcon belonged to none other than my English teacher. Mr. Larson was a real nice guy. He even insisted he could find his own way home. Eventually, a nice letter appeared in my school file, commending my honesty, if not my driving ability.

Our all-steel car hardly had a scratch on it, though that would change in time. I was terrified about having to face Dad who had been working at home that day. I decided to simply walk right in, sit myself down, and just come right out with it. No excuses. As it turned out, I didn't quite get to the sitting down part. With stoic objectivity and not one other word, Dad said, "Let's go out and see what you did."

He was striding ahead of me, and the next thing he said was something like, "So where did you put it?" The car was gone. I was sure I had left it in the driveway. Apparently, in my preoccupied rush to just get things over with, I must have left the car running. This time I put it in neutral, like I should have back at school. We had a driveway that sloped down to a steeply descending street in a neighborhood called Northern Heights. The key word there is "heights." The police report eventually said that the car had rolled backwards until it got down to the street. At that point, the steering wheel must have rotated back and forth a couple times to put the car into something like an "S" pattern. Which is how it backed up onto the Schneider's front steps with the long Pontiac tail fins punched through their front door.

I don't recall any charges being pressed in my wake of destruction that afternoon. Dad told me that there was no point in him saying much because everything was pretty obvious. Hopefully, the lessons were learned. Besides, it was all due to a series of weird things that would probably never happen again, anyway. The only question was how much of my life it would take for me to pay him back for all the damages. The honest truth is that I really do not remember much of what followed. My guess is that I don't recall much because my parents forgave me. If this is the way it is with God, what I learned is that I do not get what I have coming. I do not get what I deserve. I had screwed up, I had confessed, and by the grace of my parents, they were the ones who decided to forgive me and give me the dignity of trying to clean up some of the pieces. That has become my best understanding of how things work between God and us.

Finding Everyday Parallels In Science

The human-made things which are furthest from the Earth are two spacecraft that were launched about the same time in 1977. The first one was named Voyager 2 and the last one launched was Voyager 1. As with some things in the Bible, that last statement might well look like some kind of error, most likely a typo. But it is not a typo: Number 2 did launch first. Believe it or not, despite its illogical appearance, there is a good reason why that actually does make sense. As I write this, I can't help but recall that two thousand years earlier someone said that the last will be first (Matthew 19:30). In the case of the Brothers Voyager, it was actually planned that the second launched vehicle would soon catch up with and surpass the first one because of the geometry of its launch. As a result, the last-launched Voyager 1 did, in fact, become the first one in line.

What's more interesting is that these spaceships each carry a golden disc that describes all kinds of things about Earth and its inhabitants. But these discs deliberately omitted some critical information. The designers of those discs intentionally excluded some things that have been fundamental parts of virtually all human civilizations. There is no reference to death or war. Or a higher power of any sort.

Question: what's the point of the discs? Answer: In case there's somebody out there who might come across these spacecraft. So many serious scientific experts who exclude any reference to a greater extraterrestrial (God) are the same people who sent these golden discs in the hope and the expectation that there really might be. Such life-forms are usually imagined as significantly greater powers, which they would have to be in order to divine what these discs are all about in the first place! This effort parallels SETI, the search for signals from extraterrestrial intelligence. The growing consensus among scientists is that other life must exist, based only on the probabilities afforded by the sheer enormity of the known universe. This, without the tiniest shred of any kind of evidence. One significant difference from Christianity is that thinkers like the late Stephen Hawking often warn that higher powers from beyond this world will probably be hostile. As opposed to God who so loved the world that he gave his only son to save it.

My point is that, especially regarding faith in things not seen, the science community and the faith community may have more in common than many think. The idea of the atom had been around at least four hundred and fifty years before Christ, but it was not actually seen until 1981. Christians, including thousands of highly acclaimed scientists have always said that the invisible God himself became visible a lot sooner than that, as far back as 4 BCE (Jesus Christ). At the time of this writing, the overwhelming consensus among astrophysicists is that most of the universe, as much as eighty-five percent, is made up of invisible matter. Even if this invisible matter is eventually seen, the fact is that highly advanced scientific minds have long been comfortable hitching their star to a universe that was largely unseen. This is less surprising when I discover that a number of these people are also well publicized believers in the fundamental tenets of Christianity. It was at Nobel Science conferences that I heard experts like John Polkinghorn, the famous British theoretical physicist and mathematics professor from the University of Cambridge. He later became an Anglican priest who wrote *Quantum Physics and Theology: An Unexpected Kinship.*

An example of such science-faith kinship is a statement in *Scientific American* which said,

"... the central question in quantum mechanics [of which] no one knows the answer [is]: What really happens in a superposition - the peculiar circumstance in which particles seem to be in two or more places or states at once? .... For decades, researchers have stalled at this apparent impasse. They cannot say exactly what a superposition is without looking at it; but if they try to look at it, it disappears." ("Quantum Physics May Be Even Spookier Than You Think." Philip Ball, *Scientific American* May 21, 2018.)

Try reading things like that alongside biblical prophesies which seem to talk about things simultaneously having happened in the past, in the present and in the future. Or about dead men like Moses, Elijah, and Jesus appearing and then disappearing as soon as they are recognized.

I listened to Leslie Wickman who had been corporate astronaut for Lockheed Martin Missiles & Space where she had worked as a rocket scientist and engineer on NASA's Hubble Space Telescope and International Space Station. With a Ph.D. from Stanford in human biomechanics, she had been professor and dean at several universities. She went on to write *God of the Big Bang: How Modern Science Affirms the Creator*.

I later became aware of Francis Collins who became the head of the historic Human Genome Project and thereafter Director of the National Institutes of Health. Throughout his stellar career in genome research, he traveled the road from atheism to evangelical belief. After decades of studying the DNA code, Collins was intrigued by the thought that these codes could literally be the language of God. He authored a book called, *The Language of God: A Scientist Presents Evidence for Belief.* In that book he referred to his professional membership in the American Scientific Affiliation which includes several thousand scientists whose papers typically show strong support for scientific consensus like evolution, ancient geological processes and global climate change. At the same time, since its inception in 1941, these same scientists all subscribe to the fundamental historic creeds of Christian belief.

Going back a lot further than this, the Vatican's Pontifical Academy of Sciences has its roots all the way back to the 1600's. Certainly, and even intentionally, not all of its members are Christian, though obviously many are, such as its first president, Galileo. It's membership includes forty-six Nobel laureates and has included scientific giants like Ernest Rutherford, Max Planck, Otto Hahn, Niels Bohr, Erwin Schrödinger, and Charles Hard Townes.

As I was writing this book, R.J. Berry passed away. He had served as Professor of Genetics at University College London and was Fellow of the Royal Society of Edinburgh and the Institute of Biology. He served as President of the Linnean Society, the oldest scientific biological society in the world, the British Ecological Society, the European Ecological Federation, the Mammal Society, and Christians in Science. He wrote *Adam and the Ape, God and the Biologist, Science, Life and Christian Belief,* and *God's Book of Works.* He also edited *Real Science, Real Faith* in which he included chapters from eighteen high level scientists from a wide variety of fields who were strong Christian believers.

I do not doubt that the vast majority of scientists and advanced degreed people these days are not traditional

Christians. But this may simply reflect the current general culture. In earlier times when western culture was more homogeneously Christian, so were the dons of all fields. Regardless, it is significant to me that in these days when profession of faith can be a career killer, there are more than a few traditional Christians in the higher halls of science.

As I said in the opening of this book, even as an eleven-year-old, I instinctively picked up on the central role of faith in the field of science. By the time that Alan Shepard was rocketed into orbit, not one scientist who unquestionably believed in the roundness of the Earth had ever actually seen the roundness of the Earth. But the scientific community was nevertheless sure enough of it that they banked everything on it, including the life of Alan Shepard himself. Of course, an amazing number of previous scientific findings had all reinforced one another in establishing the veritable certainty of the roundness that they eventually did see. That same process is essentially what develops the notions of the religious community and its believers. Proposals are compared to observations, observations reinforce and challenge each other, believers proceed on their best understanding, and periodically adjust their notions. That's what this entire book is about.

Finding Everyday Parallels In My Military Experience

Many years into our marriage and well into middle age, my wife and I saw the movie *Legends of the Fall*. It was the story of how World War I tore apart a Canadian family. The father had been a highly decorated hero from wars gone by. Before Canada joined the Allies, the young men of this family felt duty-bound to answer the call and join the fight against the German Kaiser. Their father knew the realities of war and sternly forbid their adventurism in a fight that was not their own. They went anyway and suffered horribly. As we walked away from the movie, I fumed and sputtered about the testosterone-flooded stupidity of young men like that who would rush into the carnage of war for things like glory and fame! My wife just stopped in her tracks and stared at me with incredulity. The upshot was that, at least in my case, memory also seems to have diminished along with testosterone. She was absolutely dumbstruck at how I could have forgotten how I myself had done precisely the same thing when I was the same age. And did it to her.

To this day, I honestly do not know what in the world my nineteen-year-old self had been thinking. At least that's what I told my mom and dad. That's also what I tried on my girlfriend who had this notion that she should have gotten a vote on our plans for the future. Somehow, she would eventually calm down enough to still accept my marriage proposal two months later – the night before I shipped off, with one hour notice, for basic training in the middle of a war. So ended my Christmas break in my sophomore year at the University of Minnesota.

Maybe that student thing was part of it. College students were exempted from the draft until graduation. But it was rumored that college deferments were in jeopardy. I must have figured that if I enlisted in the National Guard, then maybe I could at least finish college. Sure enough: one month to the day after enlisting in the Guard, deferments were suddenly cancelled. One week later, guys my age who were not already in service were thrown into the very first birthdate lottery for immediate draft. Those with my birthdate were among the first drafted. I had escaped the lottery, purely by thirty lucky days.

All of that is in hind-sight. Nobody knew that any of this was going to happen. Therefore, at the time of my enlistment, I couldn't use any of this good fortune to defend myself from my incredulous family. I truly don't recall why I enlisted without telling anyone ahead of time. I probably knew what they'd say. Or, this may have been my first documented case of temporary insanity.

All I remember is walking into the Armory and following the signs to the recruiting office of something called the 1st Battalion, 151st Brigade, Light Field Artillery, 47th Infantry Viking Division. A really nice sergeant welcomed me along with two other guys. This was the friendliest he would ever seem. The next thing I recall was the three of us raising our right hands and repeating after him:

"I do solemnly swear that I will support and defend the Constitution of the United States against all enemies, foreign and domestic; that I will bear true faith and allegiance to the same; and that I will obey the orders of the President of the United States and the orders of the officers appointed over me, according to regulations and the Uniform Code of Military Justice. So help me God."

It was some time afterwards that I learned that I had just enlisted in America's next "jump status" National Guard artillery outfit. I'm not sure I recall Sgt. Larson mentioning that. This meant that we had twice as many drills because we would be the next Guard combat unit to go to Vietnam if necessary. A few months later, when I was in basic training, my unit was indeed activated. I only heard rumors of why they were eventually turned around mid-flight and returned home.

I had always been raised to respect my elders, teachers, cops, my pastors. But such authorities were generally nice to me, and I was taught to trust that they were looking out for me. This Army business was a whole new thing. As a rule, most of these masters weren't particularly nice, they didn't care all that much what I thought, what I felt, what I wanted or when I figured things might be most convenient.

I now received the most intense schooling on what it meant to live under someone else's authority, to live for something greater than myself, to serve not my own interests but the larger mission, to not let my brother fall, to not leave the other one behind. I share my military experiences specifically because there was absolutely nothing remarkable about my service. My lessons are the very same ones learned by anyone who has served under arms.

So much of what confuses me about God can sometimes make a little more sense when I understand him in the context of my military experiences and knowledge. This makes sense to me because, for some reason, life-and-death warfare of one kind or another seems inescapably interwoven at all levels of existence. Though I am no fan of war, the Old Testament claims that when God broke into history, the recruiting of a people and a land actually was a matter of constant warfare. Likewise, in the New Testament, when Jesus was spreading his Gospel and when he was crucified for doing so, it was all tangled up with the brutal oppression of the Roman occupation. It was Jesus himself who is reported to have said that all of creation and the destiny of the entire human race is actually a matter of cosmic battle. These cosmic struggles are reflected in humanity's endless combat, at all social levels, despite the most intense efforts of the best minds to avoid it. Contest and combat have always had the biggest draw for entertainment as depicted in all forms of competition and media through all eras and all cultures.

I have chosen to be among those Christians who call Jesus "Lord." This means that, just as in the days of kings and queens, we are subjects under his authority. We also call him "King."

PART IV

MY FAITH CHALLENGES

Chapter Twenty

Coming To Terms With The Hiddenness Of God

SOME OF THE MOST TREASURED manuscripts in writing and music are copies that retain the author's scratch-outs and multiple revisions. I'm thinking of Beethoven's Fifth Symphony, the original score of which is littered with scratch-outs, write-overs and notes-to-self. On the other hand, when you read a book, especially one by yours truly, you often see little of what the author has actually written. For most authors, many words, maybe even most words, are often deleted in editing along the way. The wonders of modern electronic typing save the reader from some of my misfires. I am no Beethoven, even in the realms of mistakeology. On my first draft, I had titled this section, "How I've come to ACCEPT the hardest things about God." I changed that to "How I've COME TO TERMS WITH the hardest things about God." Coming to terms simply means that these are things that can make sense to me, whether I like them or not. The apparent hiddenness of God is one of these things.

Something May Have Saved My Life

Early in my pastor years, when I was on the road by myself, I would sometimes stay overnight in monasteries. I enjoyed the serenity of participating with the monks in their evening prayers. One time in Washington, D.C. I wangled an invitation to stay at a Franciscan monastery. The hard part was finding a cabbie to drive me there one late afternoon. The monastery was located in a dangerous part of the city. When we arrived, I barely got out of the cab before he wished me good luck, warned me to get inside before dark and sped off.

I walked through a vine-covered archway and found myself standing in a huge courtyard of statues and huge, variously shaped shrubs. A massive stone cathedral wrapped itself around the courtyard. A long, sheltered corridor of arches was lighted by open flame torches leading toward the buildings. Nobody was in sight as the late afternoon was quickly retiring to an early twilight. All was so quiet that I could hear leaves falling on this October day. I had no idea where to begin looking for an entrance. Since my duffel bag was heavy with books, I stuffed it under a bush while I snooped around.

One of the statues moved. Obviously, one of the statues wasn't a statue. An absolutely ancient looking woman, hunch-backed to less than four feet tall, limped over to me. She was dressed in tattered black rags like something off the stage of a Charles Dickens play. Long, tangled gray hair fell on either side of a deeply creviced, pale white face with an usually long nose. In mid-October this had to be a Halloween audition of some sort.

She went right to where I had hidden my duffel. "I help you. With that," said a breathy, gravelly voice.

Why not? Nothing was making sense. "Oh no, ma'm. Please. That's gotta weigh over a hundred pounds. I'll do that," I said.

She ignored me and galumphed over to the duffel and picked it up like it was nothing. She walked back and faced me straight on, eye to eye. Raising her free hand, she pointed to steps leading up to a massive, dark, fortress-like alcove. "When they come. They go there."

I followed her through the portico of arches past one torch after another. When we got to the steps, she said the same thing. "When they come. They go there."

And up the stairs we went. There must have been fifty steps. But she led the way, and never let the heavy duffel touch the ground. She was not the one who was winded when we got to the top. Not even putting the duffel down, she looked straight ahead at massive, heavy wooden, double doors. She pointed to an almost hidden doorbell. "When they come. They press. That."

So I did. Almost immediately one of the massive oaken doors creaked as it slowly opened. There stood a middle-aged monk. "Ahh! You must be the prodigal son I spoke to on the phone! Welcome, welcome!"

I turned to thank my ancient valet who had been standing so close beside. The monk said, "You seem to be looking for something."

"I was just wanting to thank the lady who helped me find the door," I said.

My host leaned out a bit to look around. "A lady, you say?" He peeked out once again. "Funny, I didn't see anybody with you."

"She was quite elderly and kind of had a hunch-back. Almost looked like a homeless person." I was sure that he would recognize a familiar character from my description. I was expecting him to say something like, "Oh, so you met old Hestor!"

I was a little surprised when he said, "Hmmm, doesn't ring a bell. Maybe one of the other brothers knows her. I spend too much time cooped up in the office. We'll ask tomorrow at breakfast when I introduce you around." As though he suddenly remembered what the moment was all about, he extended his hand to me, "By the way, I'm Brother Thomas. I'm the Assistant Abbott around here. I'm the one you talked to on the phone." Brother Thomas fully looked the part in his rope-belted, course brown robe with its huge, cowled collar. His girth was only a little less prominent than the stereotypic Friar Tuck, but his bare, sandaled feet did complete the effect.

I introduced myself and told him how gracious he was to let me camp out there for a couple days. My host said, "To tell you the truth, my friend, I was beginning to get a little worried about you showing up. We don't usually have too many people show up around here after the sun starts to go down. Not the safest neighborhood these days."

"Yeah," I said. "That's sort of what the cabbie told me."

Brother Thomas raised his eyebrows. "I'm surprised you were even able to GET a cab."

I handed him my business card which displayed an embossed, deep red Jerusalem Cross. When I got ordained, I had adopted this symbol as sort of my professional brand. There are dozens of variations of this cross design around. So I was surprised to see all the monks here wearing that absolutely identical cross. As he escorted me to my little cell room, we passed a number of medieval suits of armor, swords, halyards, and shields, all bearing that identical cross.

The next morning I met up with him at breakfast. Before he introduced me to the others, he explained that the major role of this monastery was to train monks to be the caretakers for all the shrines assigned to the care of the Franciscans in the Holy Land. I would come to discover each of those shrines replicated in full scale on the grounds of this facility. Each younger monk I was about to meet was here to train for the care, maintenance, and use of just one of those shrines. This would be his responsibility for the rest of his life. The elderly monks were those who had returned from a lifetime of such duty in Israel. Later in the day, Brother Thomas would have someone lead me way, way, way down into the increasingly dank catacombs to see where their deceased predecessors were entombed.

"Brothers, I would like to introduce a guest among us," said the Assistant Abbott to the thirty or so brothers. "Pastor Garwick, would you be so kind as to tell us a little about yourself?"

After I introduced myself, Brother Thomas spiced up the breakfast. "Our new friend here experienced something of a mystery last night when he came to us.

I'm hoping some of you might be able to shed some light on this."

He had their attention. "Do any of us know anything about some Good Samaritan, elderly, homeless woman who hangs out around here?"

No one showed any observable reaction. Everyone just kept looking at him. "Anybody? Anything at all?" A few brothers looked at one another and a couple shrugged their shoulders. He focused his attention to get somebody to say something. "Brother Andrew, you probably know the surrounding neighborhood best. Does this ring any bells with you?"

A slender, black haired brother with a freshly trimmed dark beard was in his mid-fifties and spoke with a deeply rich voice. "Not off-hand, Abbott. Was there a problem with this woman?"

"No, no. Not at all. In fact, quite the contrary. Seems she walked up to the pastor here as he was trying to find our entrance, around 5:30 or so last night. Carried his luggage all the way up the west entrance steps. He turned to thank her and she was totally vanished. I'd just opened the door and was standing right there while he's looking all around for her. I didn't see a blessed thing at all. Strangest thing. Hope our friend here doesn't mind me saying so," and he turns to look at me. "But you did look a little …" he groped for the word, "…. uncomfortable?"

Now a short, rotund brother with thinning hair and black, horn-rimmed glasses chimed in. "Excuse me, Brother Thomas. But when did you say all this happened?"

"Oh, I don't know. Somewhere around 5:30, six o'clock maybe?" Then something seemed to dawn on the Abbott. "Yes, I think that's about right, because it had just gotten dark."

The deep and dark Brother Andrew said to me, "My friend, others might say that you are rather fortunate to be here at all this morning."

"Lucky?" I said.

Brother Andrew seemed to consider his next words for a moment. "I don't know how much you dear separated brethren are into things like guardian angels and such." Here he paused and shifted his gaze away from me. He locked eyes with the Abbott and did not take his eyes off him. "But, around here we don't talk all that much about luck."

At that monastery I was among people who were accustomed to a world of visions and visitors. Such things have not been my experience. Even during that brief walk with the mysterious old woman, I don't remember it even crossing my mind that I might have been experiencing some kind of supernatural visitation. When I have prayed to hear or see something, it more often feels like I'm talking to myself. Some prayers seem answered, most don't appear to change anything, and sometimes things just seem to get worse. Good things sometimes happen to bad people and sometimes bad things happen to good people.

Hardly anyone has claimed to have ever directly seen God. I sure haven't. Well, at least, not that I'm aware of. This was the biggest problem for the apostle nicknamed Doubting Thomas. The hiddenness of God remains one of the biggest stumbling blocks to people who need to "see it to believe it." Sometimes, as a pastor, I have felt like I've been representing an absentee landlord. More than once I have wondered why a god would play hide-and-seek if he wants the world to know him.

On the other hand, I've read about all kinds of things which everyone knows exists, yet no one perceives. There are some colors that only shrimp can see. There are types of snow which only Eskimos can even perceive, with words that can be found in no other language. Most people could be surrounded by such things and not even know it. If told that these things were present, a person would either not believe it or say that it was invisible.

The fact that something is invisible to most people does not mean that it does not exist. As discussed earlier, even the highest reaches of science have long since come to terms with being certain of what cannot be seen. That, according to the New Testament, is the very definition of faith: "Faith is the assurance of things hoped for, the conviction of things not seen," (Hebrews 11:1).

It was recently discovered that there is more gravity in the universe than can be accounted for by all the objects that can be seen. A new consensus has emerged that upwards of ninety per cent of all matter in the universe is unseen matter. At the time of this writing, there is absolutely no consensus as to how this could be possible. The lack of explanation does not cause most scientists to doubt the existence of all that matter. Two thousand years ago, whoever penned the New Testament book of Hebrews had written that, "what is seen was NOT made out of things that are visible" (Hebrews 11:2).

So much for the eyes. God's silence also bugs me.

The Bible says that God and his heavenly hosts have audibly spoken many, many times in the past. How I wish that he would even just once speak to me with intelligible words. I want to be sure that I am not mistaking echoes of my own thoughts for his. I know people who always like to say that "God told me to do this." Usually these people tell me that they did not actually hear a voice as such. To my query, these people invariably say that they "just know" it was God speaking. So often, what they report God saying not only doesn't sound like something God would say, but sounds like something that this person would say.

If I sound skeptical of what other people think they're hearing, I am far more scrutinizing of myself. When my grandson Ollie turned nine, he received some more art tools because he always loved to draw. One morning, he had been closely following a drawing lesson on TV while I cleaned up the kitchen from breakfast. Suddenly I heard his plaintiff wail from the living room, "Grandpa, you don't respect my art at all!"

I called back, "What are you talking about? I'm one of your biggest fans!"

"Then why did you do THIS!?" he bellowed in a tearful rage. He held up the remains of the drawing he had been working on for so long. The evidence was clear: my footprint embossed right in the middle of his work.

I was aghast. "How could I have stepped on that and not even heard it?"

"'Cause you've got big feet and you're deaf!" A verbal stomp to the feet and an upper left hook to the hearing aids. Merciless. He was enraged, disrespected, and crushed. And I was once again reminded of all the things in this realm that are right before my face, but which I neither see nor hear. I assume my cluelessness is even more so with the things that God does and says.

Post script: I convinced the artist to let me try taking his mangled masterpiece to the nearby copy center. We made another nice, smooth copy on which he could put his final touches.

Are The Answers To My Prayers Simply Me Seeing What I Want to See?

Because of my creative misperceptions, I have wondered if there is a god who really has answered my prayers or if I'm just seeing what I want to see.

But how could that be the case when my prayers so often seem to go unanswered or are followed by the exact opposite of my wishes? There is also the phenomenon of "the last least likely thing." Sometimes, I think and think and think and try to figure a way out of some problem. I talk to others and then think some more. Finally, it dawns on me to try practicing what I preach, about first turning to God in prayer. In situations like this, people will often say, "Well, I suppose the least we can do is pray." To the contrary, I often tell people that prayer is the most we can do, not the least. For those who at least hope that there is a living God, prayer should not be the last resort, but the first resort. Yet, I'm embarrassed to admit, I myself too often resort to prayer as the last refuge.

When I do remember to pray, a couple things sometimes get my attention. It is not uncommon that, within seconds, circumstances will happen or a thought will occur that will immediately answer the question or solve the problem. I sometimes notice something else: occasionally the answer is something that has never occurred to me or to anyone else I have asked. Furthermore, the solution may be the last thing that would ever have crossed my mind. Sometimes, it is the last thing I would ever have chosen, even if it had been laid out as one of several options. When this happens, it definitely is not a case of me simply hearing what I want to hear, of me talking to myself. In these cases, it seems to me that the solution had not presented itself up to this point, until I had prayed. Up to this point, all my thinking had been a matter of me talking to myself. But when I speak these words to God, things often do seem to change. This sort of thing has happened again and again. Lots of other people have relayed to me that same experience.

But still, why do I never hear an audible voice from God? As soon as I write these words, it dawns on me how ludicrous it is that I, of all people, should be asking that question. In the very years that I was studying audiology, I was getting my own hearing blasted in the Army. I earned my "cannoneer's ears" through six years in the field artillery, three of which were up close on the left side of a 105 mm howitzer. When I finally got hearing aids in my sixties, I was astounded at birdsongs that I hadn't heard in decades. Periodically, I have to ask my wife what is making this or that sound, as if I'm new to these things. We always joke about how I'm always hearing people say the most unusual things. I often only hear part of a word and have to make a guess based on context. Especially when I can't read the speaker's lips, my best guess can be pretty funny. Sitting beside me in the car, my wife will sometimes say, "You thought I'd say something like THAT?!" I can imagine God himself saying that as well.

So, I am always failing to hear things that even mortals speak. But even humans with extremely sensitive hearing cannot hear things that other ears can. Dog whistles come to mind. No human has ever heard one, but any dog can. In the same way, only trained musicians can hear certain musical features. There must be all kinds of audible things which most people cannot hear. Why might this also not be true of God's voice?

Kitten Logic

I love the way kittens play hide-and-seek. At some point, when they can't get away, they will run under a piece of furniture. Part-way. Their little back half will be sticking out, but as long as they can't see you, they really believe that you don't exist.

Some celebrity scientists have decided that because they now can peek under the couch, God does not exist. Because science has figured out how things work, these people see no need of God to explain natural phenomena. Obviously, no one needs the idea of God in order to explain how a telephone works. But to explain its physical mechanisms is not to deny the existence of those who put it together. The fact that we hear a voice through a telephone speaker does not negate the existence of a living speaker on the other end. Of course, that assumption changed with the development of artificially synthesized speech. Kindly note that this intentional confusion is the wonderful product of human ingenuity.

Ironically, it is the phenomenal work of scientists which gives me so much confidence in the actual existence of God. Science displays the immensity, the fine-tuned complexity and the incomprehensibility of the universe and the human creature. For me, it is science which provides some of the most compelling evidence of a creative being. I think it would eclipse the demands of Christian faith, itself, to believe that the integrated complexity of the human being spontaneously organized itself into existence, and in such a short period of time. For me, it makes as much sense to suggest that a tornado could sweep through a parts warehouse and a passenger jumbo jet would emerge, even gradually over millions of tornados.

Chapter Twenty-One

Coming To Terms With Unfulfilled Promises

A LITTLE TEASE WAS DOING THE ROUNDS this Christmas. What would have happened if, instead of three wise men, there had been three wise women?

They would have asked directions,
arrived on time,
helped deliver the baby,
cleaned the stable,
made a casserole,
brought practical gifts, and
there WOULD be Peace On Earth.

There would be peace on earth. Yeah, there is that. One of the biggest reasons why Jews reject Jesus as the Messiah is precisely because he did not bring peace. Yet, as a pastor, I would begin every Christmas season by leading my congregation in reciting the words of the prophet Isaiah who described what the Messiah would do:

"For every boot of the tramping warrior in battle tumult and every garment rolled in blood will be burned as fuel for the fire. For to us a child is born, to us a son is given; and the government shall be upon his shoulder, and his name shall be called Wonderful Counselor, Mighty God, Everlasting Father, Prince of Peace. Of the increase of his government and of peace there will be no end … (Isaiah 9)."

But, there has been no peace. To the contrary, the Church of Jesus Christ and countless people representing him have been a source of a tremendous amount of self-serving violence all throughout history. Even the righteous, peaceful presence of Christianity has stimulated monumental violence and suffering. Being faithful followers of Jesus has brought on martyrdom for self and family. It was Jesus himself who promised as much when he said,

"Do not think that I have come to bring peace to the earth. I have not come to bring peace, but a sword. For I have come to set a man against his father, and a daughter against her mother, and a daughter-in-law against her mother-in-law. And a person's enemies will be those of his own household (Matthew 10:34-36)."

So, how could Jesus really be the one? This was the question asked by his cousin. John the Baptist was languishing in prison. Of all people, he especially might well have been recalling the prophecy that the Messiah would be recognizable because he would free the captives from prison. I could imagine John praying, "Any time would be good now." What he did have his friends ask Jesus was, "ARE you the one who is to come, or shall we look for another" (Matthew 11:3)?

Act two: he got his head chopped off.

The yeahbutologist in me asks how Jesus can really be the one, if he fails one of the most important ways to be recognized as the Messiah. Sometimes it's hard not to wonder if that train just ain'ta comin'. The Christian answer is that the promised peace is something that will happen in the future, at Jesus' Second Coming. The yeahbutologist rolls the eyes and says, "Right." Even the ones who walked with Jesus and knew him best expected delivery of the promises right around the corner.

But like Karen Carpenter sang, "Still, I look to find a reason to believe." One thing that does catch my attention is that the Bible itself does not try to hide the unfulfilled status of so many of God's promises. The book of Hebrews says that all the heroes of the faith died without having seen their promises fulfilled. Then that passage explains why this was important:

"… but having seen them and greeted [these promises] from afar, [they] acknowledged that they were strangers and exiles on the earth. For people who speak thus make it clear that they are seeking a homeland. If they had been thinking of that land from which they had gone out, they would have had opportunity to return. But as it is, they desire a better country, that is, a heavenly one. Therefore God is not ashamed to be called their God, for he has prepared for them a city (Hebrews 11:12-16)."

The fact that promises have not been fulfilled apparently is not an embarrassing problem from the Bible's point of view. That inconvenient fact seems to be intentionally highlighted. Furthermore, a number of commendable things are described which occurred specifically because the promises were not immediately fulfilled. In fact, the Jews know better than anyone else that, throughout the Hebrew scriptures, every one of God's promises were fulfilled gradually over the course of centuries. Deferred gratification has always been the way. From the liberation out of Egyptian slavery and later Babylonian exile, to the granting of and then return to the Promised Land, to the return of Elijah and the arrival of the Messiah, the story has always been one of great expectations.

My yeahbutology notwithstanding, maybe it's not unreasonable to hope that the fulfillment of peace has already begun. Throughout all my growing up, it was almost a forgone conclusion that we would all die soon from nuclear war. My science teacher uncle, who knew more about more things than any mortal I have ever known, built a fallout shelter three basements deep. I will never forget one October day when gym class was halted and all of us were made to sit on the floor. Over the previous week, some kind of impending showdown had been building just off our Caribbean shores. Everybody with a newspaper or a radio knew that we all were less than twenty minutes' flight time for an enemy nuclear missile from Cuba. Over the speaker system, we listened to a live radio broadcast. At that very moment, American and Soviet nuclear warships were confronting each other, awaiting orders to open fire. History books eventually called this the Cuban Missile Crisis.

I remember sitting on that gym floor, thinking that I may not ever see my family again. Not until shortly before this writing did the world learn how close we came to Armageddon. One solitary Russian nuclear submarine officer is the only reason that my uncle's fallout shelter eventually became a wine cellar. Vasili Alexandrovich Arkhipov disobeyed his commander's order to launch. Global thermonuclear war was averted at that last moment by one single word.

There have been other close calls and I am far from secure in my feelings about the future of nuclear safety. But, at the same time, I think it may be unprecedented in world history for a game-changing weapon to go unused for so long. Perhaps because of this weapon and the devastation of two world wars, the ability to restrain global war has been effective. Shortly before this writing, Steven Pinker published *The Better Angels of Our Nature: Why Violence Has Declined*. Instantaneous news coverage of every violent act magnifies a common misperception that violence is getting worse. To the contrary, Pinker documents that in virtually each succeeding decade since World War Two, violent death has declined everywhere on earth.

The notion that peace will only be established upon Jesus' second coming is consistent with the rest of Christian thinking. From the first page to the last page of the Bible, the basic idea is that God and all creation is involved in a cosmic battle between good and evil. If this is true, then that same drama would also have to play out on earth which is part of the cosmos. The last time there was a global scourge of warfare, Nazi Germany occupied many lands, among them Norway. Over ten thousand Norwegians lost their lives while they waited for their liberation. Rescue by the Allies' underground resistance forces was a chronically unfulfilled hope. Most Norwegians would have had no way of knowing that throughout the four long years of enemy occupation, liberation was well afoot. Allied forces had been infiltrating weapons and saboteurs, many of whom were already sacrificing their lives. The most effective efforts were the least known ones, such as Operation Grouse which destroyed the nuclear weapons heavy water production plant in Telemark.

Gradual development is not only a core of Christian thinking, but of virtually everything that is known. Not only was Rome not built in a day, but neither was the earth itself and every living thing on, in, under and above it, and all throughout the known universe.

Chapter Twenty-Two
Coming To Terms With Hell

I WAS IN SEVENTH GRADE when I read the Greek myth about Prometheus. Because he brought the gift of fire to mankind, Zeus punished him. He was chained to a boulder where some raptor would eat out his liver every day. And every day, that liver would grow back. And every supper time that same bird would return and do the same thing all over again. On and on and on and on, ad infinitum. I took away two things about that for all the years to come. First off, it was only a fictional story. And secondly, I have never stopped feeling horrible about the unimaginable agonies of a Prometheus who didn't even exist.

But my Bible says that something much worse is very real and may well be the destiny of multitudes more than just one victim. I don't like that at all. And if Hell really does exist, I frankly do not have much of a stomach for endless mass torture. Like most educated, modern people, I am tempted to simply dismiss the whole thing as way too medieval. Maybe it's no more than the superstitious boogey men that grown-ups have used to make little kids behave.

But the problem for me is that Jesus himself clearly believed in the horrible reality of Hell. Maybe only three percent of his remarks speak about it. But those sixty verses are pretty graphic. How can I trust what he says about Heaven if I can't trust what he says about Hell?

Condemned To Hell: Been There, Done That

I once was condemned to Hell by a pastor. He considered me a non-Christian because of my then-liberal Methodist understandings about Heaven. Strange how it never dawned on me until now, that a Christian pastor should condemn a young Christian to Hell because of Heaven.

When I was a junior in high school, four of us took our debate team all the way to the State Tournament. I'm less than proud to say that I single-handedly broke the tie with another team for last place. In the last sixty seconds of my emphatic closing argument, I yawned. My stress-relief reflex might have been better timed. Before I closed my mouth, the judges had sealed their ballots. And our fate. My debate partner, Alan, was a senior who would never have another shot at a state tournament. Still, he must have forgiven me, because a couple weeks later we were again riding back from another distant tournament. During the long trip, I mentioned how I also had been losing the debate in my mind with The Weed. Alan invited me to Sunday evening services with his family that evening at his church. I had never heard of Sunday evening anything at a church. At least, not at my church.

Alan and his family were members of a small, white clapboard, Southern Baptist congregation. I was relieved that by the time we entered the church, the only remaining seats were in the back. I was Methodist, after all. As the service got under way, people were being called upon to give something called testimonials. I remember the guy who testified about changing the oil in his car. He told how Jesus came and told him to use a different weight engine lubricant.

After a dozen or so of these kinds of testimonials, the pastor announced that he was going to bestow on us all a special blessing. All those who gave their life to the Lord were invited to come down to the front railing. "But first," he says, "I want us all to close our eyes and raise our right hand to the Lord Almighty in prayer." I saw this as a moment of truth for me. I had been having my struggles with religion, but I was not ready to turn my back on Jesus.

"All right then, my friends," says the preacher, "everyone who gives their lives to Jesus, just raise up your hand now."

So I did.

"Praise the Lawd," says he. "Now, whoever has raised his hand, please come to the front to be blessed."

I did not.

The preacher repeated his offer. Total silence. "Will the young man in the back please come forward?"

Nope.

"Will the young man with the white cardigan sweater in the back left row be so kind as to approach the altar of the Lord?"

I looked up and saw no other white cardigans. What I did notice was that I apparently was the only one who had raised my hand. How about all those others who had given such specific testimonies? Where were they? Well, they were looking back at me. I was told later how these people had gone through all this earlier and had gotten themselves saved. So even though we all had been asked to close our eyes, Jesus had already opened their eyes, and that's why they were looking at me. Okay then.

While I'm trying to process all of this, the preacher kind of modifies his last instruction. "Will the ushers be so kind as to help to the front our young friend back there with the white cardigan sweater?"

Oh boy. I remember not remembering the walk down the aisle. The next thing I know, the pastor is placing two heavy hands on my shoulders and he whispers that I should kneel. In a triumphant exaltation he proclaims, "Praise the Lawd that this young sinner has seen the light of Thy GLORious mercy, Lawd Jesus, and has gotten himself saved and now kneels in humble joy at the assurance that he will live for eternity in Thy heavenly kingdom, Father God!" Or something like that.

I think this may have been the moment when I discovered theology. I don't think it had ever occurred to me that I even had any theology. But there on my knees I looked up at the enraptured preacher and whispered, "But, I didn't say that."

He clears his throat and bends closer. "Ummm. What?"

"I don't know that I'm going to Heaven for sure."

He looks up and continues his proclamation, "Praise the Lawd for saving this lost soul!" Then, he bends back down to me, "You DO give your life to Jesus, don't you, son?"

"Well, sure."

"Then you are guaranteed of going to Heaven. PRAISE THE LAWD!"

"But God is the one who decides, not me," I whisper back.

The preacher's next remark is to the two ushers who had helped me forward and who had my back, as it were, the whole time. "Brothers, would you be so kind as to accompany our young friend to the parlor behind the altar where we can welcome him into the fellowship of the saved?"

Over the next hour or so, the preacher tries every which way to reason with me. Nothing he does convinces me. In God's house, I refuse to lie. We're in a room right behind the alter, for Pete's sake! So I refuse to agree that by pronouncing the sentence of accepting Jesus as my Lord and Savior, I was once and for all admitted into Heaven.

"Then, young man, I'm afraid that you are going to HELL." Capital letters intended. Every single last one of them.

At this point, I may have gotten a little defensive. "See you later," was my good-bye. And I walked out. Of the faith. For the next few years. Once again, the helping hand strikes again.

So, when I was at a tender age and trying so hard to sort out my faith, I personally experienced a representative of the Church condemning me to Hell because I did not measure up to his standard. In the years since, I have come to understand that he was defending one of the most important positions in his wing of the Church. Which I still reject. He thought that I had just called Jesus a liar because I apparently didn't believe Jesus' promise that all who believe really will be saved. If I believed, then how could I not be sure that I was going to Heaven?

In his mind, I was essentially saying that I couldn't trust Jesus at his word. But I was thinking of Jesus' other remarks, like where he said that lots of people do lots of things in his name and still go to Hell.

"Not everyone who says to me, 'Lord, Lord,' will enter the kingdom of Heaven, but the one who does the will of my Father who is in Heaven. On that day many will say to me, 'Lord, Lord, did we not prophesy in your name, and cast out demons in your name, and do many mighty works in your name?' And then will I declare to them, 'I never knew you; depart from me, you workers of lawlessness (Matthew 7:21-24).'"

In other words, simply reciting a formula of words does not cut it. Neither does self-righteous, self-delusion which Jesus said will surprise a lot of "saved" people.

I Do Not Like the Idea of Hell

But, then again, I guess that's supposed to be the whole point of it all, to be something that is not enjoyed. (However, I have known a few people who do seem to enjoy creating living hells for themselves and everyone else for as long as they can). More people these days believe in the existence of Heaven than those who believe in Hell. My guess is that most Americans these days reject the reality of Hell simply because they like Heaven a lot more than they like Hell.

The Jesus who is revered for his compassion is the same Jesus who said that most people will not get to Heaven because the road to Heaven is narrow. He's saying that beyond this temporary place, there are only two never-ending options after our last breath: a wonderful place called Heaven for relatively few souls, or an agonizing Hell for everyone else. I personally do not like that second part, especially the idea that this will be the eternal fate for most people.

But last month, a hospital bed convinced me that reality does not always seem to be affected by what I like. The previous day, I would have liked to suspend gravity, if only for me, over just one patch of ice, for only a split second. A broken shoulder, heart problems, an ambulance trip and two days in the hospital convinced me otherwise.

There are lots of things Jesus said that I don't particularly like, such as praying for my enemies, turning the other cheek, not withholding what someone wants to steal from me, and forgiving someone no less than seventy times seven times.

I also do not like the reality of black holes in outer space that destroy, not most things, but absolutely everything in their paths. The cutting edge of space sciences these days continually proves a couple things. First, despite the hopes of statistical probabilities, we still know of only one tiny blue marble in the entire universe that supports life. The second thing is that, where we are concerned, the rest of the universe does everything possible to kill us. Mind-numbing emptiness, inconceivable distances of loneliness, airlessness, asteroids, radiation, heat and freezing cold beyond comprehension are only some of the known cosmic nullifiers. Therefore, it makes total sense to me that cosmic survival really is an exceedingly rare thing.

All fancy thinking aside, I have to admit that a big part of my discomfort with the idea of Hell may simply be that I don't like it. Frankly, I am flat-out gutless when it comes to the idea of inflicting pain, even on people who have done horrible things. I can talk a good game of "hang 'em high" when I hear of an atrocious crime. But that emotional bluster routinely leads to sleep-depriving nightmares which call my bluff. When I was a little boy in the San Francisco area, we lived across the Bay from San Quentin Prison. I would stare at that fortress when the media was giving play-by-play coverage of gas chamber executions going on inside. The last one I recall was the execution of Caryl Chessman. That's when my execution nightmares started. Sometimes, I am the executioner and sometimes I am the condemned. Those nightmares have proven to me that I probably wouldn't have the stomach to methodically inflict pain on even the most despicable person.

I realize that my squeamishness is not a sufficient reason to deny ways and means to God. My problem is that God would claim such a prerogative in the first place. Hell seems so out of character with one of the most important things of Jesus Christ which is grace. That is essentially about us NOT getting what we deserve. The idea is that for people who are saved by Jesus, there is unlimited, eternal forgiveness and riches, not because it is deserved but because of grace, God's Riches At Christ's Expense. How could a loving God do something like Hell?

As I've done with several other conundrums, I try to see if there is anything which most people accept on earth that could possibly shed light on the reasonableness of God's use of Hell. I once was so impressed with an elderly member of my congregation who had asked a judge to dismiss charges against a young man who had invaded her home. Her mercy was unexpected because she had long been an outspoken, tough-talking "law and order" advocate of punishment consequences. But then she had come to know a little bit about the burglar's personal life. She couldn't let go of the idea that the burglar's life circumstances made his poor choices at least understandable. The magistrate nevertheless responded by passing sentence and sending the young man to prison. With apologies to Shakespeare, apparently there are times when the quality of mercy can indeed be strained. The judge thanked my friend for her compassion but explained that the young man had not just injured her but had injured society itself. To excuse this man's possibly understandable crime could jeopardize the orderly safety of the community and injure other victims. Likewise, might God inflict Hell to protect the well-being of His redeemed kingdom?

Early in my ministry, I took young teenagers from my church youth group to meet some refugees who had just escaped from the hills of Vietnam. The kids did not hear this next story. My host colleague directed my attention to a particular mother in this group. This poor woman had once been forced to smother her crying baby. She did this in order to save the rest of her children from being detected by enemy soldiers as they snuck across the Mekong River. The infant's fussing was totally natural and understandable. But it threatened the survival of all the other children. I have read identical stories from the Korean War and World War Two. My guess is that this particular horror has been played out many times in all wars.

Columbine

A meaningful part of my life as a small town pastor was thirty years of service as a volunteer, uniformed police chaplain. People were used to seeing me in my black clergy shirt. But when I wore the badge, I may as well have been the Angel of Death. In fact, that usually was what I was up to when I showed up in uniform. More than a few times, I was asked by school officials to make myself available to counsel staff and students when someone died, especially if it was from some sort of violence. Once I had to put out a call for all police chaplains to rush to the high school on a Friday night. A senior class boy, one hour earlier, had unexpectedly died while getting ready to meet his prom dinner date. Hundreds of students were converging at the school in various stages of shock, wailing, calm, confusion and anger. Soon, the kids were forming into small groups to head off to one home or another to simply be together. Each chaplain followed a different group and each of us stayed up all that night with the parents and the grieving students. Over the next several days I worked with school counselors to help stave off a possible sequel of suicides which too often followed these kinds of things. In this case, all proceeded well. More than once, though, at other times, I might stop into the high school in my regular clergy shirt on some routine errand. Invariably, some student I might not even know would ask, "Who died?"

Over the years, there were a couple major developments which affected how crises were handled on school campuses. The first game-changer was when most students started carrying cell phones. Whenever there was a rumor or some kind of incident, hundreds of parents would instantly receive scary alarm calls from their kids. Immediately, the school phone lines and staff would become tied up with frantic parents. Moms and dads would be racing to all the schools, causing traffic incidents and blocking first responder vehicles.

That sort of panic reaction was the result of a prior game changer that happened on April 20, 1999. That was when two high school students at Columbine High School outside of Denver, Colorado shot to death thirteen classmates and one teacher. This incident started a whole new era of mass shootings, especially in schools. Then, only two years later, international terrorists brought the whole nation to a halt by flying three hijacked airplanes full of passengers into buildings, killing over three thousand people. Americans began feeling vulnerable like never before. First responders, including chaplains, began intensive training for such things. Fortunately, that was one type of incident I never had to experience.

Out of the Columbine incident eventually came a book that was written by the mother of one of the shooters. Sue Klebold wrote *A Mother's Reckoning: Living in the Aftermath of Tragedy*. In this heart-wrenchingly honest memoir, she cracked open a sliver of light into my question of how a loving God could possibly destroy any of his children. When radio stations started broadcasting the tragedy in progress, Sue Klebold instantly realized for some reason that it might be her son who was behind the mayhem. When all other parents were praying for the safety of their children, she was praying for the death of hers before he could do more damage.

At the social level, an evil person is typically thought of as someone who does bad things to other people. But the Bible regards evil primarily as an offense against God. Cosmic stakes are eternal ones. It is clear to me that "what it's all about" is not the fleeting things which happen in the here and now, but what will be in the long-run of eternity. A consistent theme in the Christian message is the same as that of ecology, of nutrition and exercise: what we do here and now is most important because of what that leads to in the future.

As such, it makes sense to me that God would eliminate in the afterlife anything that sets itself against the integrity of his cosmic, eternal realm. Jesus showed forgiveness to all kinds of people who did bad things on Earth - prostitutes, swindling tax collectors and even a self-confessed criminal on a cross next to his. But he declared that Heaven would be forfeited by those who undermine the fabric of his eternal realm by not trusting him and by refusing mercy and compassion to the most vulnerable.

Will Everyone Who Is Not a Faithful Christian Go to Hell?

I am driven to find a biblically consistent basis for hoping that some non-Christians will be saved.

To be clear, I am not a universalist who believes that everyone will be saved, that everyone will go to Heaven, that all roads lead to God. That, right there, is where a lot of well-meaning people get off my boat, right before a lot of them try to sink it, because they think that I'm being intolerant and judgmental. The fact is that I WANT to be a universalist because I really do want everyone to go to Heaven. Well, at least the people I like (just kidding). My problem is that the only material I have the authority to quote does not say that all people will go to Heaven. In fact, it clearly says the exact opposite. Whether I like it or not.

Jesus himself really did say that no one comes to the Father but through him. Furthermore, he said that the only ones who can come to him are those who have been chosen by the Father to do so. He told others that they could not hear him because they were not among his flock to begin with. Then, to cap off things, Jesus said that relatively few will make it into heaven. Furthermore, he warned that the excluded will include many people who think they are Christians but who do not show mercy to others.

But he also warned that it is far above our pay grade to decide who is in and who is out. He said that when mortals try to pull up what they think are the weeds, we invariably wind up pulling up the good plants as well. He said to leave that work to God at the end of all things. In the fragile faith of my teenage years, that pastor tried to weed me out because it was his judgment that I did not measure up. As he tramped through the fields of the Lord, he almost trampled to death a young, emerging plant. I write this book partly for the many victims of similar helping hands.

Before my first experiences in prison ministry, I don't think I ever had a charitable thought toward prisoners. When I heard about a serious crime, my only thought about the perpetrator was that I hoped he got the book thrown at him. With the worst crimes, I can still be a bit that way. But after I had been working with these people, it kind of snuck up on me to realize that I actually found myself caring about them. No, I had no delusions about the guilt of the prisoners. Or the necessity of their sentence. In the broader scheme of things, my first concern was always for the safety and healing of their victims and potential victims. But, still I found myself caring about the inmates I was coming to know. I did not want them in torment. I wanted them to heal, and to experience forgiveness, even if they would never again see the light of day.

When I come to personally know people, I usually find myself hoping for good things in their lives. The best thing I can wish for anyone is eternal happiness. So, I look hard for any biblically defensible hope for their salvation. If even I can hope that everyone has a real chance to accept Jesus, how much more would this be desired by the Son of God, whom we believe died for them? In fact, he once said, "If you then, who are evil, know how to give good gifts …. how much more will the heavenly Father give the Holy Spirit to those who ask him (Luke 11:11-13)?"

How about those who don't ask him? I recall the time when a man who could not walk was carried by his friends to Jesus. Nothing else is said about what the sick man said or did or believed. Only the actions of his friends are recorded. But, "… when Jesus saw THEIR faith, he said to the paralytic, 'Son, your sins are forgiven.'" That story is apparently so important that it's told in three of the four Gospels. Those people who brought their friend had a tough time trying to get past everyone else. So they dragged this paralyzed guy up to the roof which was over the room where Jesus was surrounded by a crowd. Then they actually made a hole in the roof and lowered the man down, right in front of Jesus.

That is what my own instincts are about. I was called to spend the rest of my life trying to bring people to Jesus. Many of these are people who, for one reason or another, have not been able to come to Jesus on their own. I have spent my life looking for ways to open holes in the roof leading to Jesus. Those who like to build roofs are not always appreciative of the effort.

In over thirty years as a pastor, it has usually been my sense that most people who don't follow Jesus are people who have never had a decent chance to know him. Most people participate in other faiths because they were born into them, just as I was born into a Protestant Christian family. I have come to know more than a few Jews and Muslims who devoutly worship the God of Abraham. I have known non-Christian Native Americans, Hindus and Buddhists who have been devout people. Though clearly not following Jesus Christ, these are worshipers whose faiths also have been ones of sacrificial prayer, charity and humble submission to God. In my personal experience, some of these people are a lot more like Jesus than some people I have known who call themselves Christian. When Jesus was asked by a religious rule-keeper about how to get to heaven, Jesus held up as an example the charity of a Samaritan who was already considered outside the faith (The Parable of the Good Samaritan Luke 10).

Some people walk away from Jesus because of misunderstandings about him. For example, "I'm just as good as anybody else, and if that ain't good enough for him, then he ain't good enough for me." Then there are those who condemn Jesus because they understandably associate him with some so-called Christians who are grossly UNlike Jesus. More people than we will ever know have walked away because of the way they were abused in the church as children. More common in my experience have been the ones who grew up in the church and then became luke-warm "cultural Christians." Many of these people simply hopped off the wagon about the same time they were hopping off wagons on youth group hayrides. These young teens simply were goofing off in life, distracted by and attracted to the things that appeal to so many kids that age. They were children whom even our society does not regard as capable of making legal contracts. Then life moved on and both the abused and the distracted remained stuck at a thirteen-year-old level of spiritual development.

When I think of all the people who never had a real chance to know Jesus, I think of his prayer on the cross. He looked down at the ones who were actually putting him to death and he prayed, "Father, forgive them, FOR THEY KNOW NOT WHAT THEY DO." With his last breath, he was pleading for their heaven. He was asking that they be forgiven. And he was asking that they be forgiven because they did not know what they were doing.

When Jesus was crucified, two confessed criminals were also crucified, one on each side of him. One scoffed at him and the other asked Jesus to remember him in Heaven. One of the last things Jesus said was to promise that second man, "I tell you this day, you shall be with me in Paradise." Of the hundreds of people who had known this criminal, no one would have known that he had accepted Jesus, much less that he was promised Heaven, and at the absolute eleventh hour. Furthermore, the penitent prisoner is the only person mentioned to whom Jesus specifically promised Heaven.

The hopeful, pastoral side of me looks to the chief of the apostles who knew Jesus best. Peter said that, "... it is not the Lord's wish that any should perish, but that all should reach repentance (2 Peter 3:9)." More importantly, I look to Jesus himself who said that, "... I have other sheep that are not of this fold. I must bring them also, and they will listen to my voice (John 10:16)." Again, "I MUST bring them also." I grew up being constantly told by my parents that where there's a will, there's a way. The hopeful, pastoral side of me has to assume that he had to have come up with a way to, "bring them also."

In that previous statement of Jesus, I take note of two little words. First, Jesus says that sheep who cannot hear him ARE not part of his flock. Then, he switches to the future tense when he says, "They WILL listen to my voice." In other words, some sheep currently are not of his flock, but he WILL bring them also and they WILL listen to his voice. But how?

The apostle Paul wrote that, "at the name of Jesus every knee should bow, in Heaven and on Earth and under the Earth, and every tongue confess that Jesus Christ is Lord, to the glory of God the Father (Philippians 2)." This tells me that every soul will eventually know Jesus for whom he is. That does not necessarily mean that everyone will accept Jesus as Lord and Savior. The other criminal only scoffed at Jesus. History is full of true stories of captured prisoners of war who submit to their conquerors while refusing to give allegiance. It was Jesus who said that, "... the gate is narrow and the way is hard that leads to life, and those who find it are few (Matthew 7:14)." Like I said earlier, my guess is that a lot of souls will voluntarily not choose Heaven when they see that it is simply not to their liking.

When it is said that every knee shall bow, that clearly is not something that happens with most people during their time on Earth. For EVERY soul to bow and confess, this will have to be something that for most people occurs after death.

Now, it is true that Jesus himself did tell the story about a rich man who went to Hell, who had sealed his fate on Earth and was not given a chance to change his vote after death. But the way Jesus told the story is that this man had, in fact, been given a choice. Some time ago, according to Jesus, this man had already chosen to reject Moses, and the prophets. He also violated one of God's unwavering earthly demands to care for those who are vulnerable.

Everything I know about Jesus speaks to the lengths he goes in order to offer grace, second chances, grace, third chances, grace, fourth chances, grace, more chances upon chances and redemption. After all, he was the one who told us to forgive one another endlessly, even as many as seventy time seven times, if necessary.

As I wrote these words, a two-week rescue drama captured the attention of the entire world. Twelve teenage boys and their coach were successfully rescued from a watery cave system in Thailand. There were three reasons why dozens of the world's finest rescuers placed their lives on the line and one of them almost died. First of all, every trapped person was definitely going to die. Secondly, there was absolutely no way that these people could save themselves. Thirdly, rescue required others to offer up their own lives. That, right there, is how I see the predicament of every human being. Those cave rescuers tried every which way, time after time after time for more than two weeks. Nevertheless, no other way was discovered but this one route.

All thirteen of the trapped cave explorers accepted rescue. But there are multitudes of trapped people all over the world who intentionally and knowingly do not want to be rescued for all kinds of reasons. I would not be surprised if that will also be the case among many whose knees will bow and whose tongues will confess that Jesus Christ is Lord. Many will still refuse him and his rescue.

Why Would God Choose Some And Not Others?

Jesus said that, "No one can come to me unless the Father who sent me draws him (John 6:44)." Then, he tells the people who reject them that, "you do not believe because you are not among my sheep (John 10:26)." On the surface, it has always struck me as unfair that so many people don't seem to even have a chance to follow him, simply because he has not chosen them.

I have no idea why some people would have been chosen and others would not have been chosen to be sheep of his earthly pen. For that matter, I have no idea why any person is specially marked with particular talents, special circumstances, or historic roles that are denied to other people. In my own case, how come I don't get to be tall, dark and handsome? I'd settle for just one of these. Well, maybe two out of three. Especially the tall part. This has had life-long implications for me. In fact, the cosmic injustice that I was not chosen to be tall has had a lot to do with my life-long aversion to fish. I don't even like to fish.

Let it be known that I have worked at improving my relationship with finny food. I have evolved from hating fish that my folks made me eat, to tolerating fish that hosts placed before me, to actually choosing fish because my doctor strongly advises me to eat it. So, where did I wind up spending most of my ministry, but a Swedish congregation whose members loved to eat something called lutefisk. Lutefisk Christians expect their pastor to likewise love it. For those of you who are fortunate enough to not know, lutefisk is a very special type of dried cod which is loved by many Scandinavian Americans. What makes it so special is that it has been reconstituted by days of soaking in lye. This is the same lye that is also used in making soap, oven cleaners and drain openers and in digesting animal carcasses. But then the fish is baked in a soup of melted butter. It begs the question of why that first Scandinavian would ever have thought that something like that would have been safe to put in the mouth. Normally, it is enjoyed only by people who grew up on the stuff, like Germans who enjoy sauerkraut and Koreans who enjoy kimchi. I got back at my congregation by calling lutefisk "the piece of cod which passeth all understanding." Approaching seventy years old, I am just now beginning to maybe enjoy some kinds of fish. A little bit. Like gold-fish crackers. No more than once a week. And never lutefisk.

In San Francisco our folks made us eat seafood at just about every supper: shrimp, crab, abalone, sea bass, shark …. maybe even the Loch Ness Monster for all I know. I hated it all. When my science teachers taught us that humans evolved from the sea, I told my parents that I couldn't eat my ancestors. Later in life, Dad explained to me why it was, back in those early days of yesteryear, that we had no choice but to eat seafood. He said that because California was so far from the cattle farms of the Midwest, hamburger was too expensive.

But I'm not so sure about that. After all, he was the same guy who finally got me to eat seafood by telling me that he grew to be so tall because he ate shrimp. He never did explain to me why eating shrimp would make me tall, when people who were short were always called shrimps. That's what everybody already called me. Partly because I was almost a year younger than my classmates, I was always the shortest boy. The fact that my mother was only four and a half feet tall may also have played into the equation. But Dad said that if I ate shrimp like him, I could grow up to be tall just like him. To make a long story, uh, short, I made it to all of five feet, six inches. And now dropping. So, I am now a little suspicious that maybe my life-long aversion to fish may be a bit of a height vendetta. It has taken my whole life to forgive fish.

Lo and behold, it turns out that California has always been one of America's biggest beef producers, since at least the early eighteen hundreds. I'm sure Dad didn't know.

I did make my parents pay. They were the ones who constantly had to dig me out of endless anxieties, fears, jealousies, resentments, meltdowns, and perceived injustices because of the curse of being short. It wasn't fair that every other guy got to be bigger and taller and therefore more popular. I was always jealous of the athletes who just got everything handed to them because of the bodies they were given that I was denied. And to top it all off, like a daily reminder that rubbed my nose in it, Dad always towered above me.

Something else never sank in. Those people who were given better bodies and got to be the big athletes did not get a free ride. They had to endure the discipline, sacrifices and physical agonies of workouts and the pressures of public competitions that I never had to go through. Only gradually in life did I come to learn that being chosen is not always a pleasant thing.

What It Means That Only Some Are Chosen

Many of my favorite quotes are the little gripes which the Jewish papa, Tevya, sends up to God in the musical, *Fiddler on the Roof.* Tevya laments how the Jews always get picked on. "Dear God," he prays, "I know that we're your Chosen People, but next time could you please choose someone else?" I am eternally grateful that, for some reason, Jesus seems to have chosen me to be one of his sheep. But, like Tevya learned, I experience every day what Jesus promised, that being chosen can be a painful and sacrificial thing in this world. Even the great Einstein did not understand that. In what is called his "God Letter", this culturally Jewish genius said that one reason he rejected the existence of God was that he couldn't understand why God would choose the Jews who were no better than anyone else. But just as God made clear to the Jews in the Old Testament, I am painfully aware that being chosen by God for a role in this world is not meant as a reward and is certainly not because one is in any sense better or more deserving than anyone else.

In fact, being chosen or blessed in any way is something that rots into a self-destructive curse if it is not used for something greater than self. One of the books that most left an impression on me was Alex Kershaw's 2003 account of the World War Two D-Day Invasion. *The Bedford Boys* is about a small group of non-professional citizen soldiers who were chosen to be part of the first wave to assault Omaha Beach. Four years earlier, these thirty-five National Guardsmen from Bedford,

Pennsylvania had been farmers, mill workers, ditch diggers and brand new high school graduates. All but six of them would be killed helping lead that charge which was the beginning of the end of Nazi Germany and World War Two. No town in American history has ever lost more citizens in a single battle.

I believe that this is what it means for God to choose just some people for a particular role in this world. Eight hundred years before Jesus, God revealed through the prophet Isaiah, that he chose the Jews to be a light to draw the nations to God. To my way of thinking, being a sheep in Jesus' sheepfold is about a service of sacrifice.

Coming To Terms With Slavery In The Bible

I HAVE BEEN BLESSED with at least two experiences which have probably been endured by tens of thousands of others. Nevertheless, for me these moments live on in infamy.

Ice Burns

When I was in sixth grade, five of us Tenderfoot Boy Scouts were forced to endure an initiation weekend. It was a winter camp-out involving just our troop, where the senior scouts put us through our paces. We were sent on harmless, silly little errands, asking people for things like a sky hook or thirty extra feet of shore line. After supper, we were sent out on a snipe hunt, to chase down what turned out to be mythical road-runner birds that everyone could hear but no one could ever quite see. Big Terry organized us into a kind of scrimmage line to chase these things across an open field after dusk. That is, until he chased himself right into a six-strand fence of rusty barbed wire. He had to be cut out with wire cutters before being taken to the hospital for stitches and tetanus shots.

He was back in fine form by the next afternoon for the big finale. Throughout that afternoon we were prepped for a big test of some sort down at the main cabin. Big Terry's role was to prepare us mentally so that we would not be afraid of what was coming. "Some of the big guys like to get you all worked up with stories about painful things they do to you in there. Don't listen to them and you'll probably do just fine. No matter what you see when they take the blindfold off you."

Blindfold? Nobody had said anything about blindfolds. Did they?

While Big Terry kept us all together around a campfire, one of the older scouts would come by from time to time to blindfold the next one whom he led off somewhere to the initiation. Our group got smaller and smaller. That's because no one came back. Now and again we thought we could hear a scream from way off in the woods. Then it was my turn. The big escort took out the rag blindfold. He snapped it open and this revealed some smeared blood stains. When he saw my eyes bug out, Big Terry told him to fold it so as to not scare me about what was coming.

"What's the matter with you anyway?" he scolded the escort. "Mr. Larson told us not to let them see anything until we got them inside the cabin in front of the fire!" So the Scoutmaster was in on this too? Another distant scream.

After the escort put the blindfold on, Big Terry put a reassuring hand on my shoulder and said, "Don't worry. It won't last long. It'll be over before you know it."

These guys were really good.

The escort guided me carefully through the snow-covered woods and down some long, steep hill. I asked him all kinds of questions, but he never said one word. Eventually, we arrived at what must have been a cabin. My guide rapped on the door in what seemed like some kind of code pattern. I heard the door open. My guide loudly whispered, "I've got the next one." The whispering style was a really nice touch. Like a dental probe on exposed nerves.

"Wait there until we get it stoked back up."

It seemed like a long time until the door opened again. This time, two guys grabbed me and each tightly held on to my arms so that I couldn't move. They walked me across the wooden floor to the opposite side of the room until I could smell the heat and feel the glow of a crackling fireplace. They roughly removed the blindfold. As my eyes adjusted, I found myself standing beside a table full of all the parts of a first aid kit. One of the attendants said, "Where's the burn ointment? We didn't use it all up on the last one, did we?" One of them said he'd get some butter from the kitchen.

"See this?" the leader said to me. He was pointing to a red-hot coat hanger which was somehow fashioned into our troop number. It was glowing in the embers of a roaring fire.

"To be initiated into this troop, you have to wear the brand. On your back. At the campfire tonight, we report to the rest of the troop how each of you took it. Like a baby or like a scout." He lifted the glowing brand out of the fire as my two minders tied the blindfold back on. They lifted my shirt and bent me over a bench. They held me tight so that I couldn't move anything, especially my head. Someone smeared something cold and greasy over my back. But it was the radiant heat from the brand that lit my fire.

"Hold him tight!" I felt searing pain on my back as a meat-sizzling sound was followed by the whoosh of escaping steam. I screamed like I had never screamed before.

"Quick! Get the burn ointment on him! Right now!"

I was still screaming when they bent me upright, replaced my shirt, and took off the blindfold. They showed me that all they had placed on my back was a couple ice cubes. There, in a bucket, was the branding coat hanger which was still steaming in a bucket of snow. Everyone laughed, clapped me on the back and declared me an official member of the troop. I think I tried to smile. But my back still burned. It took a lot longer for the healing of my cowardly shame. I never cried again for the next twenty years. I can still count on one hand the number of times I have ever let myself cry since.

The Basics of Torture

There must be something about ice cubes and me. Years later, I awoke in a bed-sized aluminum pan, totally naked and floating in an alcohol bath of ice cubes in an Army General Hospital. Apparently, I had been in a coma for the better part of a week. For two weeks, a recurrence of pneumonia had been doubling me over day and night with muscle-pulling coughing. I finally passed out on the battlefield of war games in Basic Training. This had happened to me once before.

Two of my fellow inductees had not been so lucky. Weeks earlier, we had arrived by bus at the Reception Center around 3 AM. In our civilian clothes and uncovered shoes, we slogged our way through knee-high snow in what was a record setting blizzard. That is when we completed a couple hours of aptitude tests in our snow-soaked feet. Then we were led a couple blocks through the driving blizzard to an old World War Two barracks. We were ordered to grab an hour or two of shut-eye before morning chow. The next thing I knew, all the bare-bulb barrack ceiling lights snapped on. Two military policemen stormed in, banging garbage can lids and ordering everyone to stand at attention. Flashing emergency lights on all kinds of vehicles next door were lighting up the dawn. We were told that a recruit next door had just died from some disease. So began a two week medical quarantine which interrupted Basic Training before it ever began. We were ordered to report to Sick Call if we noticed the early symptoms of some suspected highly contagious disease. The signs of spinal meningitis were essentially the same as those of a common cold. By mid-day, every guy was sure he had it.

The next night was a replay of death, two barracks over. For the next two weeks we were only allowed the clothes on our backs without even a change of clean underwear. Each of us was issued what the Army would refer to as "Poncho, rubber, green, olive, one each." We had nothing to do but sit around all day, every day, playing cards, writing letters home, and trying to wash out our underwear amidst bursting water pipes. By the time we were released to begin training, all of us really were sick, coughing out our lungs and retching out our guts. But no one wanted to report to Sick Call, because missing any training could get you "recycled." Every last one of us would rather have died than start Basic Training all over again. Two others in our battalion did just that.

Three months later, the ice bath was an effort to bring down my fever. A nurse told me that at one point I had briefly spiked at one hundred and seven degrees. For the next two days, I was taken in and out of ice needle showers and was forced to drink pitcher after pitcher after pitcher of ice cold cherry Kool-Aid. My single room had no windows or even a wall clock. I was totally disoriented to time, not even knowing if it was night or day. I worried that no one back home would ever know what had happened to me. I had no visitors until days later when my First Sergeant showed up. He told me that if I didn't pass the rifle marksman tests today, I would have to be recycled. I am not exaggerating to say that, for me, this would have been a fate far worse than death. He explained that the doctors didn't think I was healthy enough to be released but that I could discharge myself against medical advice. That is exactly what I did. In my bathrobe, pajamas and dress shoes, I crawled aboard the sergeant's open jeep just a split second before he gunned it for the firing range.

Miles later, I was virtually sun-blind by the time we arrived at the firing range. My near-blindness probably didn't matter all that much since I could hardly hit the broad side of a barn in the best of circumstances. I was the only shooter on the range that late afternoon. Sarge brought over a whole box of loaded ammunition magazines. He told me to switch the rifle to full automatic like a machine gun. I shredded just about everything in sight and he called that good enough.

My guess is that my Basic Training experience was pretty much the same as what countless others have gone through. But from what I gather by talking to others, ours set some kind of records in brutality. These were the days soon after American troops had been savaged in the Tet Offensive of Vietnam (which official American military history records as an American victory). Our training area had a big billboard which showed a cartooned battlefield of American corpses. The Grim Reaper stood among the dead. The caption read, "Let no man say, 'Had I been better trained.'" Many of the training cadre were badly messed up survivors of Tet. A lot of them were not professionally trained drill sergeants but were short-timers pulling temporary duty until their enlistments ran out. As we were belly-crawling through graveled mud, we were constantly yelled at about the training failures that cost them all their friends "in Tet." I had a couple buddies who were able to dismiss all this as just a game. I never could. I lived virtually every day in terror. The death of those first two recruits, my own near-death in the hospital, and a couple suicides all proved to me that this was not just a game. When I returned from the hospital to my unit, I found out that fully seventy-five percent of the guys had also landed in the hospital. Some of the sergeants and officers had been replaced. I still have flashbacks.

Some people go through these kinds of things and then want to inflict it on others down the line. That's why a lot of people like to belittle newcomers. Like the old adage says, "Hurt people hurt people hurt people hurt people." I went the other way. These so-called rites of passage made me identify with victims. That is why I have come to think of these experiences as a blessing. Admittedly, what I endured was nothing at all compared to the victims of historic and criminal torture. By no means could I ever say that I know what such victims felt. Nevertheless, my terrors may be the closest that a typical, modern, middle class, American white boy might ever get to experiencing torture. Even so, I can hardly begin to imagine what a Jewish child might have felt like under Hitler's terror. Or what an African slave child might have felt like on an American plantation. Or what a Cherokee child might have felt on the Trail of Tears.

Even though I love history, I have little interest in how people lived, or the battle maneuvers they executed or the weapons they used or the clothing they wore. It is the personal stories that draw me. "How could they have pulled THAT off?" "What in the world were they thinking when they did THAT?" "Imagine how they must have felt. " I can no longer bear to go to another Holocaust Museum, another slavery exhibit, another re-telling of the Trail of Tears or the Wounded Knee Massacre, or reenactments of Jesus' crucifixion. I can never escape the knowledge that such things really happened to real people who had real feelings. These things actually cause me physical pain and can send me into several hours of depression. But, when I avoid going to such things, I then feel like ten of the remaining eleven apostles who couldn't even bring themselves to be with Jesus at his crucifixion. I have always had this odd sense that I owe these people at least a token of personal sacrifice, at least to not look away, to try at some puny level to feel pain in their name.

This is part of the reason why I have always been nauseated by America's history with slavery. It was one of the absolutely most horrible things perpetuated and tolerated by my nation and my church. I say "slavery was" somewhat loosely because I know that the infections of slavery still continue in countless, more "civilized" ways in our society. At the same time, as the least of those who ever stood up at all, I feel pretentious to bemoan the continuing injustices and maltreatment of my cousins of color. And I actually do have cousins of color.

Freedom For Me, But What For Thee?

Nevertheless, I am becoming increasingly embarrassed by my own hypocrisy every time I ignore the full story of our founding fathers' fight for liberty. On the one hand, the men and women who fashioned this nation out of the American Revolution deserve every bit of honor accorded to them. They and what they accomplished are so inconceivably phenomenal, that I have long suspected the direct inspiration and intervention of God. But, like Israel's greatest kings, David and Solomon, these inspired patriots also displayed phenomenal sinfulness. To remedy what they considered to be their own bondage, they declared independence by saying that one of the self-evident truths was that all men are created equal. Underscore "men." Then, they brought God into the very next phrase by declaring that these equally created men are, "... endowed by their Creator with certain unalienable Rights." Of the innumerable cache of rights, our founding fathers listed Life, Liberty and the Pursuit of Happiness. But when they went home to their wives and children, Washington, Jefferson and Madison were among twenty-five of fifty-six signers who also went home to hundreds of slaves they owned. When our fathers reconvened eleven years later in Philadelphia to write the Constitution, the debate on slavery was so intense that it almost scuttled the new nation at the very start. Fully half the signers, strangely including even some of the slaveholders, considered slavery to be morally intolerable. It was a strategic compromise which decided that only three out of every five slaves would even be counted as people for purposes of determining the number of each state's allotted representatives. It would take another seventy-seven years and the bloodiest war in American history to finally outlaw slavery.

But to this day, one of the "books" the church still reveres in the New Testament is a letter called Philemon. In this short letter, the apostle Paul is returning a runaway slave to the master and owner named Philemon. This poor slave had actually run to Paul for refuge! Paul uses this letter to ask Philemon to treat this slave with grace and compassion as a brother in Christ. Nevertheless, this letter is seized upon as proof that even Jesus' chief evangelist supported slavery. This has always been a thorny problem for me. It begs the question of how we can trust the Bible if it seems to makes mistakes like that of supporting slavery.

I have a voice in the back of my head that warns me about the temptation of self-serving rationalization in the following thoughts. Nevertheless, the best professional scholarship I can bring to the matter suggests that the Bible does not, in fact, support what we usually think of as slavery. Everything in the Bible actually prohibits the kind of slavery that was practiced in pre-Civil War America.

In the King James Version, which was the Bible most commonly used by Christians during the Civil War, it does not call Onesimus a slave but rather a "servant." The actual Greek word that Paul used was "doulos" which was a bond servant. In early America, this would have been more like an indentured servant. These were people who more typically had chosen voluntary servitude for a specified period of time to improve their meager fortune in a contractual labor agreement.

Accordingly, in the same King James Version of the Gospel of Mark (10:41-45), Jesus himself calls for each of his followers to actually become a doulos. In that passage, he is rebuking his apostles for getting into a childish squabble over which of them was the greatest and would get the best place in Heaven. In the King James Version it reads, "But Jesus called them to him, and saith unto them, 'Ye know that they which are accounted to rule over the Gentiles exercise lordship over them; and their great ones exercise authority upon them. But so shall it not be among you: but whosoever will be great among you, shall be your minister: And whosoever of you will be the chiefest, shall be servant of all. For even the Son of Man came not to be ministered unto, but to minister, and to give his life a ransom for many.'"

Some other English versions of this same passage do have Jesus calling his followers to be slaves. However, synonyms in that same passage used by other versions are words like servants or bond-servants. Clearly, the slavery that the New Testament condones is not the slavery of so many founding fathers or of the Civil War South. What is commended by the New Testament is a voluntary, respectful, non-abusive, self-less servitude that is actually commanded of all Christians. In fact, that is precisely what the apostle Paul is writing to tell Philemon.

I am increasingly convinced that fewer people are bothered by mistaken notions about Paul calling Onesimus a slave than the fact that Jesus calls us all to be bond-servants of one another.

Chapter Twenty-Four

Coming To Terms With God's Role In The Agonies Of Children

I THINK THAT MY BIGGEST FAITH QUANDARIES occur when I am slammed into the suffering of children. I was a traumatized child who grew up to become a therapist for severely handicapped and often abused preschool children in the inner city. I then served thirty years as a parish pastor and police chaplain. I am the father to two daughters and two grandsons. I believe that there is nothing more precious on this Earth than little children. Anyone who knows me knows that. The flip side of that coin is that there is nothing that causes me more pain than the suffering and the death of little ones. Nothing threatens my faith more than the fact that God allows this to happen.

But as I point my finger at God, I can't help but wonder what the other fingers are pointing back to in myself. Am I judging God by comparing him to things that are other than God? When people place things before God such as statues and golden calves and money and forbidden sexual behaviors, the Bible calls this idolatry. But except in thriller books, certain types of psychpaths and movies, I am not sure that I've seen a whole lot of people choosing what they think of as bad things to place in the center their lives. My guess is that most often, people place in the center of their worlds things which they think of as good. Therefore, idolatry would usually be a matter of placing what people think of as good things ahead of God. Most people in the world believe that from the very beginning of all human existence, bad things happened when people strove for what they thought were good things. And since these are regarded as good things, people typically do not have to be forced. This happens through enchantment.

In the Garden of Eden story, the first people were enticed by desiring not an ugly, terrifying thing, but rather a beautiful, pleasant-tasting fruit. The tree from which it came was not a tree of ignorance but rather a tree of knowledge. It was not knowledge about trivial things but knowledge of good and evil, with the promise that their eyes would be opened. And it wasn't so that they could become the evil masters of a diabolical crime organization, but so that they would be like God. Most people to this day would see these as good things to be desired.

That is precisely what I see happening these days, with people desiring ostensibly good things to take center stage in their worlds. Again, if I point my finger at others doing this, my other three fingers point back at myself. It occurs to me that maybe this kind of attractive idolatry is where I myself have been having issues with God. Am I doing this with children? Am I placing children at the center, ahead of the Creator, whose first principle was that nothing else was to come before him?

When I worked with little children, some of their disabilities would just make me want to cry. I keep a gallery of pictures on the mantel of my mind. One six-year-old little girl would never again walk, talk, comprehend, move in any way, or even move her eyes on purpose. She had been a wonderfully happy six-year-old who was the best big sister in the world. That's why she rushed into traffic to push her little sister out of the way of an oncoming car.

Next to her was a four-year-old little girl who was in the same shape. Until a year ago, she also had been a normal, happy child until she fell off her swing onto a thick cushion of grass. Nevertheless, her neck broke in the almost worst way it could. That's because she survived.

So often, parents would anguish over why these things happened. What did they do to cause it, or what could they have done to prevent it? It turns out that Christian scripture actually has addressed this issue.

"As Jesus went along, he saw a man blind from birth. His disciples asked him, "Rabbi, who sinned, this man or his parents, that he was born blind?"

"Neither this man nor his parents sinned," said Jesus, "but this happened so that the works of God might be displayed in him (John 9:1)."

In other words, the fact that the man had been born blind and had to struggle all his life had nothing at all to do with the man or his parents. It had to do with what

God was accomplishing for an eternal impact on multitudes of the human race. I am not at all sure that this explanation would have made me feel a whole lot better if I had been that man or his parents. At least not in the emergency room of my heart. But whether or not I like something has nothing to do with reality. The fact that I do not like natural disasters does not make them untrue. Throughout history, many parents have forfeited their children for things much less than God, such as the nation.

Jesus said and did much the same thing when he deliberately refused to attend to his gravely ill friend, Lazarus. The man's sisters were understandably upset that Jesus did not come when they had sent for him. In fact, he deliberately postponed travels until he received word that Lazarus had died. His apostles were bewildered as to why Jesus waited until it was clearly too late. He said to them "For your sake I am glad I was not there, so that you may believe (John 11)." Once again, Lazarus' course of dying and Jesus' role in Lazarus' suffering was not about Lazarus at all: it was about something much bigger than Lazarus. This all happened in order to develop the faith of the apostles who were to bring the hope of life after death to all future generations. I cannot think of too many mortals whose death is more remembered than that of Lazarus.

Some skeptics claim that Jesus would never have said such insensitive things. A pastor these days would be viciously denounced for even suggesting things like Jesus did. Some suggest that writers must have put these words in his mouth. But why would someone make up stories like this that would portray Jesus in such a seemingly heartless light? But, like it or not, this is what, how and why Jesus did what he did. And it has never been forgotten.

Coming To Terms With God
ALLOWING Children To SUFFER

How can there be a God at all, much less one who is powerful and loving, who can allow children to suffer and die? The key word here is "allow." I point my finger at God and say that whether or not God actually made something horrendous happen, God at the very least allowed it.

Finger-pointing again leads me to the Principal Principle to consider how such an unreasonable thing could in any way be reasonable. Where are those other three fingers pointing? First of all, is there any similar thing I have experienced in my own life which makes sense as to why a loving parent would allow a child to suffer? Well, in point of fact, there is. Our first child was born with a couple tiny little pieces of skin attached outside one of her ears. The fact that she was our first born is significant because this was our first run as parents. Everything we were experiencing was for the first time. At least in my case, the newness was the source of no little amount of anxiety when things got tough from time to time.

The ear tabs themselves were about as minor a thing as you could imagine. It just meant a quick trip and snip. My wife, the nurse, asked me if I could be the one to go into the procedure room. I got to hold our precious little doll and cuddle her and play with her .... while the nurse stuck her with a needle of Novocain. Precious Little Doll looked at me like I had just betrayed her. She said as much in her way. Then the fun began. I couldn't watch. It looked like a much bigger deal than it really was. I wondered if my daughter would ever trust me again. My guess is that she doesn't even remember this. I do. And it was just the first of many times like this to come.

Loving and responsible parents take their tiny children for painful medical procedures all the time. How does that come across to a twelve month old who has such limited ability to understand any explanation? If the child were capable of putting things into words, she might demand to know why Mommy and Daddy are letting that bad person hurt her. And then, when that same child is a little bit older and can understand just a little more, it's time to do a booster shot. Through her screaming she hears, "Oh sweetie, Mommy loves you." Do you think that would make any sense at all to that child's mind? And when yet another shot is needed a year later, she can understand the words but still cannot comprehend Daddy saying that the shot is good for her. Volumes of poetry, music and literature reflect the experience of so many people who have testified how the best things in life have directly come from the most painful times. Anybody who has been coached or trained knows this.

It occurs to me that I am no more capable of understanding God's actions than a child is of understanding grown-ups who can make scary and hurting things stop, but who don't. I have to conclude that if doctors, nurses, dentists, parents, teachers and probably dozens of other people can be said to justifiably and necessarily inflict suffering on uncomprehending little children, then why cannot that be true of God?

Coming To Terms With God
ALLOWING A Child To DIE

Skin tabs are one thing. But, sometimes God allows much tougher things. Johnny was two years old and his family was ecstatic when his cancer treatment team found no remaining traces of cancer. Five days later I held his little, white-socked foot as he took his last breath on his shattered mother's lap. She was asking the so-called man of God one word: "Why?" I was asking God the same question. My question was a little more specific: "Why did God allow this? Why did God not stop this?"

A couple years later, on a blazing hot summer afternoon, I was the police chaplain who escorted a devastated father down a long, dirt country road toward a body bag. That dark blue, zippered vinyl package held the crushed remains of his four-year-old little boy. The child had just been accidentally backed over by his mommy who had done absolutely nothing wrong. Daddy insisted on looking. I, as the support escort, was supposed to be the one to unzip the body bag. Every one of my steps was a desperate plea to God to stop this. But God had not stopped the accident. Just ten steps from the bag, the father collapsed into the arms of his own big brother and relented. I had never known a boy with a first name like his. Twelve years later, I held my first grandson who had the same name.

At funerals of children, a pastor will often say that he or she has no answers except to know that, "God cries with us." When I hear that, I myself want to cry out, "Well, isn't that nice, as far as it goes?" For me, that actually doesn't really go too far. Every helpless mortal at that funeral is already crying. We could use something more than a Chief Crier. Yes, Jesus did cry at the death of his friend Lazarus. But then he followed his crying by asking

Lazarus's sister if she remembered about the resurrection. Her answer is essentially, "Well, yeah. Eventually." That is when he brings Lazarus back to life. Right then, right there. He did it once. Why not now?

I would tell the congregation that now more than ever, we needed to trust that "Jesus loves the little children;" that God himself came to Earth as a baby and personally experienced every one of the years of childhood; that when the Son of God grew up, he would tell even his apostles to not interfere with children who are trying to get to him; how he would hold little children on his knee and say that to such as these the Kingdom of Heaven belongs; that unless we have a faith like a child, we ourselves would not inherit the Kingdom.

But sooner or later on some Sunday, the officially assigned scripture would come around where I would have to preach about Jesus healing a child. As I would plan my remarks, I knew that there would be several parents in those pews whose children had not been healed. Every time those Bible stories came around, I would invariably be up late into Saturday night, scrambling to come up with some way to save these poor parents from God's slap in their faces. As I prepared my thoughts, I could hear these parents weeping, "He saved someone else's child, but he wouldn't save mine?"

More than once I went to the office late at night to rewrite, copy and fold hundreds of newly designed bulletins in order to shift the whole worship service to a different theme altogether: different scripture passages, different prayers, different children's sermon, and by all means replacements for hymns like "Children of the Heavenly Father" which says, "Though He giveth and He taketh ......"

How could a terrified parent trust a God who could allow her child to die? That kind of grief could overwhelm me to the point of spiritual amnesia. Time and again, I would actually forget what had been revealed to me the several times our own baby was fighting for her life. Our second baby had to undergo many massive cardiac procedures in the early days of pediatric cardiology surgery. Among other firsts, she was the first toddler to receive an adult pacemaker. Heart transplants were rare and usually only for much stronger adults. My wife was a college nursing professor and I remember asking her if she thought we might soon have to consider a heart transplant. Her answer stunned me.

"I would not be in favor of that," she said.

As I relive that moment, I remember being totally unable to find words to express my shock. I must have found some words at that time because she explained her reasoning to me. At that point in time, all organ transplants, especially heart transplants, were extremely difficult for people to survive and thrive. Organ transplants meant endless heavy medication battles against organ rejection. "Success" offered a tragically short life extension. "Are we wanting to put her through this? For her? Or is it for us?"

Fortunately, we never had to cross that bridge. But others did, when their only temporary option was a grizzly medical course. As a friend and later as a pastor, I accompanied other parents as they chose to let their children die sooner rather than later. Loving parents every day allow their children to die as the best option. Unlike God, they make these decisions because they cannot do the impossible. But these parents nevertheless do allow their children to die for reasons that do make sense. Why, then, is it not plausible that God would let children die because of reasons unknown or unfathomable to us, but worthy nonetheless? Especially if this were to more quickly usher such a child into joyful life that never ends?

In our child's first four years, her fragile heart and lungs were trying to strengthen as she struggled to gain weight and build natural immunities. We had to be so careful to try to minimize her exposure to colds and other infections. Friends and family eventually learned to automatically reschedule visits if any of them had an illness or had even been exposed to a contagious person. Well-meaning acquaintances who did not know the rules provided for us a constant exercise of awkward vigilance. Even though she was in a state of chronic but managed heart failure, the time eventually came for her to play her way into the world. We had to struggle to risk letting her go to preschool where kids were constantly passing around colds. She caught everything, and everything was a threat to her lungs and thereby risked worsening her heart failure. Every cold took forever to clear. Then came grade school and decisions about what to allow in physical education. And then field trips. And then camps.

And then came her college senior year-abroad opportunity. She could have chosen some place like England. Or France. So, naturally, she chose Bangladesh. Of course it would have to be a third world setting with poor medical resources and a nationally compromised blood supply. As always, she and we took the question to the cardiologist who had been our guardian angel. I was hoping that he would play the heavy. Well, he did. But not in the way I wanted or expected. Here is what he said: "Mom and Dad, we have not put her through everything, only to encase her in a crystal bubble."

In other words, we had to come to terms with living. And maybe her dying. As we have to accept with each of us, every minute of every day. We had to plan a dozen things to minimize risks and invent plans to deal with problems if complications should arise. As it turned out, three weeks before her planned departure, she contracted mononucleosis and had to replace that trip with another opportunity. We had to work really hard to not reveal our grateful ecstasy for the wonderful gift of infectious mononucleosis. Any other time, that illness would have scared us out of our protective minds. Even in her crushing disappointment, she had the mature grace to not let on that she had our number.

But how many loving, responsible parents around the world on that same day, every single day, lost children to medical conditions, car accidents, who fell off swings, drowned in lakes, who were abducted, etc.? The only thing they could have done to prevent any possibility of such things would have been to chain their beloved children to a wall inside the house for their entire lives. Some people have actually done that and these have become the stuff of horror crimes. Likewise, it occurs to me that God could have made us like rocks or brute animals or pets or robots or permanently imprisoned people who would not have the freedom or capability to get into lethal situations.

Every day, all parents deliberately allow their children to do all kinds of things with the full knowledge of potential lethal consequences. So why is it not reasonable to imagine that God might have some loving reason, unfathomable to us, to also watch children die when he could have prevented it?

Coming To Terms With God Actually CAUSING Children To Die

God allowing children to die is one thing, but the idea of God actually causing children to die is something else. I have never experienced a situation where I knew that God has done that. But I have had to teach and preach about a number of places in the Bible which says that God has done exactly that. The most famous example was when God himself sent the angel of death to kill every first-born male of every age in Egypt, hardly any of whom would have had any awareness of or responsibility for what was going on. I just heard a pastor try to split the difference by saying that technically it was the Angel of Death, not God who did the deed. A court of law, however, would give the harshest sentence to the one who actually ordered the hit. Again, when King David enticed Bathsheba into adultery and had her husband killed, "the Lord afflicted the CHILD that Uriah's wife bore to David, and he became sick ... on the seventh day the child died" (2Samuel 12:15-18).

As a police chaplain I have been on the scene with grandparents who were babysitting their two-year-old who fell out their fifth story apartment, grandparents who were babysitting when their two-year-old wandered out and drowned in their pool, a mother who had backed over her four-year-old, and countless parents who were at home when their teenager committed suicide in one way or another. Especially at the death of a young person, people often need to find someone or something to blame. The most convenient target is themselves, whether or not there is any clear connection. As painful as that is, blaming oneself can sometimes offer a false promise of making some sense, providing some order to the chaos.

But some of the toughest people to help have been those who have known enough of the Bible to be dangerous to themselves. When these biblically literate people have been prone to target themselves as the cause of the child's death, they have often believed that God was punishing them for something they had done or not done. They know that, according to the Bible, God really has done that sort of thing. This has not been the only time that I could have wished that people had not read the entire Bible.

These days, in order to comfort people, most pastors are sorely tempted to say, "Oh, God would never do something like that." I myself have never been able to say that, not because I think God actually caused this or that particular death, but because according to the Bible, God has done exactly this kind of thing in the past. Again, I have a hard time not pointing my finger at God. Where, then, are my other three fingers pointing? I ask where in this world has it ever been thought reasonable for people to have killed children? Unhappily, I do find examples where this has been thought reasonable, albeit with some important disclaimers. I so deeply grieve the examples that I'm about to describe that I actually experience sharp physical pain whenever I think of them. Secondly, the cases that I am about to describe are wildly extreme. Thirdly, though I myself do not find some of these examples to be reasonable, my larger point is that many Americans have and still do acquiesce to the acceptability of doing these things.

More than once, fellow veterans of the Vietnam War era have trembled to tell of their deliberate shootings of small children. This would invariably happen when a child, with an unpinned hand grenade, would be walking toward a group of brother soldiers. In each case, the child was about to die anyway and failing to shoot would cost many other lives. I have heard that same story from soldiers in current conflicts. When I was a soldier preparing for the eventuality of combat, I practiced that scenario again and again in my mind. I am aghast that I found myself capable of imagining having to do that.

As precious as children are, many people agree that there are things that supersede even a child's physical existence. Why then would such a thing be inconceivable or unacceptable for God to do, whom the Bible says is in cosmic warfare, where eternal existence always trumps temporary physical existence?

When God killed children in the Bible, the only thing that makes sense to me is the principle of long term perspective. In these horrendous heartbreaks, the fact is that these children were instantly taken away from the life-scarring memory of the destruction of their families. They were spared a life-time of revenge. They were exempted from a slow death of starvation, disease and climate. If almost all of our existence is in eternity, maybe these children really are the ones who were awarded a Home run.

PART V

WHEN I DON'T HAVE A CLUE

Chapter Twenty-Five

Not If, But When

My Hunt For A Missing Teen

IN 1999 IN CENTRAL MINNESOTA, a nineteen- year-old named Katie Poirer went missing from a rural convenience gas station. Three weeks or so after the disappearance, she still had not been found and this led the news everyday. I was a police chaplain and felt compelled to drive two hours to the town and volunteer to help search. A couple weeks earlier, the main party had searched a forested area, and I was asked if I would be willing to walk it one more time. Alone. I was told that I was roughly the same age, appearance and body structure as a person of interest. The idea was for me to search the area as though I myself were carrying a dead or struggling person the size of Katie. Specifically, I was asked to focus on areas where I would try to take such a victim. I was told what kinds of clues to look for, such as the brand of cigarettes and the brand of beer that might have been discarded by the person of interest. I was not to disturb anything I saw, but rather to tie off a red plastic ribbon at the spot. That way, my mark would stand off from the yellow ribbons of the previous search party.

I arrived at the designated area probably around one o'clock on this early June afternoon. Yellow ribbons of previous searchers fluttered on bushes and branches, confirming that I must be in the right area. The sky was cloudless and the day was bright. But the forest was as dim as eight o'clock at night. I walked alone. I heard nothing but my loud foot crunches. In fact, the forest was totally devoid of any sounds of squirrels, birds or insects. The nearby highway traffic could not be heard. There were no overhead airplanes. Over the next two hours, the darkening and silent wildwood felt like some kind of sinister sanctuary where maybe something terrible this way had passed not long ago. Here and there I would tie off a red ribbon at another "promising" spot.

The deepening gloom closed in and something dawned on me: I'm supposedly wanting to find something. What if I DO find something? After weeks of her missing, what is it that I would be likely to find? Just as I realized that I really didn't want to succeed, I found something where no yellow ribbon had been placed. Off the trail, near a small rise of terrain, there was some kind of tamped down depression, like where deer might have bedded down. I discovered a couple crumpled up packs of the brand of cigarettes I had been told about. Strewn about were also several crushed beer cans of the suspect brand. None of the trash had been here long. I tied off lots of red ribbons and sketched a map. When I gazed at the trash on the ground, I could feel the inescapable fact that some kind of person had obviously been here. And then a light went on in my mind: I had not yet heard of anyone having yet been arrested. I knew that some predators, including murderers, haunt the site of their buried kills.

What if one was still in the area? I decided that I had been in there long enough.

I walked out of that forest rather briskly, looking over my shoulder the whole way. Once again, I had to keep a tight leash on my imagination. I reminded myself of the first time in basic training that I had patrolled something or other, walking picket all by myself with my M14 automatic assault rifle. They gave us each one bullet. Imagine that, a whole bullet. The next closest sentry used his on me from half a mile out when something my direction spooked him. Fortunately, I have no idea where that round went. But he got to explain it.

At the search headquarters, Katie's grandfather thanked me for the information and said that investigators would probably check it out the next day. On the six o'clock television news that next day, the lead story was that possible remains may have been discovered. The news video showed investigators working at a site which looked just like the spot I had reported. Days later, remains were identified as charred bone and tooth fragments of Katie Poirer. The next month, Donald Blom was arrested and he eventually was sentenced to life without parole. He was a year older than I and could have looked like my brother.

When I was tramping around that forest, I was asking myself where Katie was, where the predator was and hoping that I would stumble across neither. I was also asking myself where God was and this time hoping that I would find out. Not a clue.

To Search Does Not Always Mean To Find

Anyone who follows the news has heard emergency officials announce that a search and rescue mission has turned into a recovery operation. Not even the smartest, most experienced, well equipped and most motivated searchers always find what they're seeking.

That is also true in my faith searches. My guess is that most people of even great faith have mountains or even a range of mountains of one kind or another which their reasoning simply cannot climb. Though not an issue for me, some people think that if God makes homosexuals, it is illogical that he would forbid them to be sexual in that way. With other people, it is just as illogical that God would forbid inappropriate use of the gift of alcohol in a person whom he made with the appetite and vulnerabilities to alcohol and who harms no one else. The insurmountable faith mountain for other people is why God allows genocides or slavery.

The all-time greatest mountain challenging my faith is the centuries God has allowed children to be sexually abused by representatives of Jesus Christ. All throughout both the Old and New Testaments, God repeatedly demonstrated his willingness to remove people who angered him. So why does God allow legions of pedophiles to remain as officials in the Church? The only thing which makes any sense to me is that God is once again allowing the hideous sinfulness of his religious leaders to bring down the entire institutional house of cards.

According to the Bible itself, God has done this very thing many times at the level of nations and worship institutions. What comes to mind is an incident in the Gospels where,

"As Jesus was leaving the temple, one of his disciples said to him, 'Look, Teacher! What massive stones! What magnificent buildings!'

'Do you see all these great buildings?' replied Jesus. 'Not one stone here will be left on another; every one will be thrown down (Mark 13:1-3).'"

I am not at all sure that the institutional church will or should survive these kinds of pervasive scandals, but I am certain that he will. I am not the least bit worried about the survival of Jesus and his message. If his survival after crucifixion is true, then he already has survived the very worst man can do and he did it through human sinfulness. If he was not actually resurrected to rise above humanity's evil, then it is a moot issue whether he outlasts the Church's evil. But I believe he did and he will.

Chapter Twenty-Six

How I Deal With Insurmountables

IN RETROSPECT, THERE SEEM TO BE FOUR ways that I cope with God-quandaries when I don't have the beginning of a clue.

L.O.P.

I have simply come to the point of accepting that everything has a limit beyond which the human mind cannot go.

Whether or not one accepts things as literally true in the Bible, it is a consistent theme throughout both testaments that there are places where humans are not to go. After humans were cast out of the Garden of Eden, it was an agent of God that prevented them from returning. When Moses climbed up Mt. Sinai to receive the ten commandments, no one else was allowed to even approach the base of that mountain. Jesus told his apostles that where he was ascending, they could not follow for now. The apostle Paul wrote that now we can only see things dimly until, eventually, we will know things completely. Parents routinely tell children that only someday will they understand certain things. Soldiers are routinely admonished that some things are simply beyond their pay grade.

There are so many places where my ability to figure out God-questions is like a rubber band that gets stretched to the absolute breaking point. Rubber bands have always had a dear place in my life. When I was a kid, my mother was adamant that I should never play with guns. But she was also the one who liked to tell me that where there's a will, there's a way. So, I specialized in flashlights that had buttons which I pressed. My ray gun could hit targets anywhere in the house. Eventually, I graduated to rubber bands. Soon I became family-renowned for my ability to shoot down houseflies in mid-air. That was something that Mom actually appreciated. The years went by until that infamous day when I apparently mistook my new bride in a bathing suit as some kind of target of opportunity. I scored a direct hit that revealed a new side of her. As it were. Our tender marriage may well have been saved by The Treaty of the Broken Arrow. This was a sacred agreement of eternal disarmament which was written on parchment. The offending twenty-gauge rubber band was deliberately stretched beyond its breaking point into two neutralized pieces.

The ability to figure things out reaches breaking points in every field of human endeavor. My rubber band technique resembled that of an archer. I would pull the rubber band from the tip of my right pointer finger, along the top of my extended right arm, all the way back to my right cheekbone. I learned early and often that there is a whole world of hurt between stretching a rubber band TO its breaking point and stretching it beyond its breaking point. It might have been helpful if something on the rubber band had a warning that said, "This far and no further." Then again, that might have been too many words to squeeze on to the stretchy weapon. Maybe an acronym would have worked better. Something like LOP: Limit-Of-Possibility.

Just about everything we try to figure out in life seems to have a point of LOP. Every year, I would attend an annual Nobel Science Conference which each year would focus on a different single topic. One year, the subject was human longevity. There was only one point of unanimous agreement among the world-class experts. They were of one mind that science would probably never be able to extend the maximum human life span much beyond a hundred and twenty years or so. Now, the history of science is littered with all kinds of claims that something will never happen, only to be proven wrong. The limit of human longevity might also be breached someday. Nevertheless, the fact remains that there are many Nobel-level scientists who are perfectly comfortable with the notion that there are limits to where human endeavor can go.

Medicine can do increasingly wonderful things to aid the body and postpone death - up to the point of creating life and curing death, where it meets its LOP: Limit-Of-Possibility. Social sciences and human services can impact crime, up to the point of actually eliminating crime and evil where it meets its LOP: Limit-Of-Possibility. Governments can avoid and mitigate international conflicts and injustices, up to the point of actually eliminating war itself, where they meet the LOP:

Limit-Of-Possibility. Even the everyday understandings of gravity break down at the ultra-extremely tiny world of quantum mechanics.

In *The Language of God*, Francis Collins, the head of the Human Genome Project and later the National Institutes of Health, talks about the limits of the greatest scientific discoveries. At the time of this writing, there is widespread scientific consensus on how The Big Bang did its work all the way back to one tenth of a millionth of a millionth of a millionth of a millionth of a millionth of a millionth of a millionth of the first second. That is really, really, really, really, really, really, really impressive! But, after saying that, Collins says, "The existence of the Big Bang begs the question of what came before that, and who or what was responsible. It certainly demonstrates the limits of science as no other phenomenon has done." In other words, LOP.

The fact that all rubber bands break does not cause me to disbelieve in the elasticity of rubber bands or fail to rely upon them. But at the same time, where the most important relationships are involved, I am reluctant to break the band.

Sometimes my faith itself seems like a rubber band at its breaking point. But those struggles are no more intense for me than that breakfast conversation was for my nine-year-old grandson when he expected his grandpa to keep him from getting killed by his little brother. I explained to my enraged little man that he had been in no danger of getting killed. I told him that one of my responsibilities was helping him learn to figure out things for himself. I also said that sometimes I do that by staying out of the way. This had never occurred to him and I'm not entirely sure that my explanation completely did the trick. I am not suggesting that my explanation of my reason has anything to do with God's reasons. My point is that our righteous little guy was absolutely and totally outraged by an utterly inconceivable apparent breach of faith. The gap between my field of view and God's perspective certainly would have to be infinitely greater.

Knowing The Do-er

I bank on what I have consistently known about God.

Like many pastors, my first role was as a youth pastor. One teenager was particularly well-liked by his peers and by me. Jim not only was funny, but he usually had quite a mature common sense. If I had to be away from the group for a few minutes, Jim was the one I could count on to keep an eye on things. So, I was totally surprised when I returned to find him taking part in some disaster in the making. Curiously, I have no recollection of what exactly was going on.

But I do remember saying something like, "Jim, I leave you in charge for just five minutes and you go and do something stupid like this. That's not like you. Somebody could have gotten killed. What in the world were you thinking?"

He looked down and kind of shuffled his feet. "Well, Billy said it would be cool."

"So," I continued, "if Billy told you to jump off the Empire State Building, I suppose you'd go and jump off the Empire State Building!"

He gave me a quizzical look. "Well not again."

I almost asphyxiated trying not to laugh out loud. I knew right away that Jim must have had a totally legitimate explanation, for three reasons: it was totally in the open, and Jim not only showed no defensiveness but could even tease both of us. Most importantly, I knew Jim's track record of reliability.

When I have personally known and respected somebody up close for a long time, and I think I see something that does not make sense, I have learned to place my bets with what I've long known about this person. In such situations, I try to believe that there must be a compelling explanation that would suspend my criticism, if I only knew all the relevant facts. This principle has rarely failed me. There are relatively few people who fall into that category, but Jesus is one of them. I have never studied anybody as closely for so long. Sometimes his words can be confusing to me. But his actions were consistently clear, especially when children and other vulnerable people were involved. He would take children on his knees and rebuke even his apostles, no less, when his minders tried to get in the way of little ones. His harshest condemnation was for anyone who would lead a child astray. There was never a hurting child brought to him whom he did not heal. Most importantly, he had actually been a child himself.

That is why it was so shockingly out of character when he insulted a crying mother who begged him to heal her demon-possessed daughter. He didn't say a single word. Then he tells this desperate woman that he was sent only to help Hebrew people. To say that I'm appalled by this is an understatement. When she persists, he insults her again and tells her, "It is not right to take the children's bread and throw it to the dogs." No matter how many times I read this, my guts twist inside me. She continues to plead and he finally relents by saying, "'O woman, great is your faith! Be it done for you as you desire.' And her daughter was healed instantly (Matthew 15)." This is not one of my favorite stories, even though I like the way it ends. More importantly, like many of the things which Jesus said and did, this story has given multitudes of discouraged people the justified hope to persist in prayer, no matter how worthless they may feel.

If Jesus seems to do anything out of character, his otherwise consistent actions provide ample reason to give him the benefit of the doubt. If God seems to do or allow anything out of character, I think of Abraham at the foot of Mount Moriah. I myself have literally climbed that actual mountain more than once. It is here where a city would be built with the name "Place of Peace." Most people call it Jerusalem.

Looking for the Promise

When there are apparent actions or statements from or about God which baffle me, I try to understand them within the context of all the promises which he has made.

The most gut-wrenching mystery for me in the entire Bible is when God commanded Abraham to sacrifice his son. He came within a dagger thrust of doing so. Down through the ages, more than one thinker has probably noticed something that had long gone right over my head. When Abraham and his group got to the foot of Mount Moriah, "Then Abraham said to his young men, 'Stay here with the donkey; I and the boy will go over there and worship and come again to you (Genesis 22:5).'" Abraham could have had no clue how this would come to be. Nevertheless, his expectation was that both of them would somehow come back down. How could he have possibly bet his son's life on this?

In the Middle Ages, Martin Luther wrestled with this incident. He concluded that when things about God do not seem to add up, our only hope is to focus on the things that are promised. Then we need to place our focus on whatever was promised. In this case, despite the horrible command, what Abraham had first heard a long time ago from this same God, was a promise (Genesis 12). The promise from God was that a nation of heirs would spring forth from Abraham and Sarah's son (Genesis 15). It was an inconceivable (pun intended) promise of descendants to two childless geriatrics. They had even laughed at the idea. But it was God who got the last laugh. When Abraham and Sarah eventually saw the promise kept, God had them name that son Isaac, which meant "laughter."

By the time of the test at Mount Moria, Abraham had known God up close for a long time. He had seen the most impossible of promises kept. Therefore, he would have had reason to expect that this same God would keep another impossible promise about the same son. Abraham and Sarah had only that one son. For God's promise of descendants to hold true, Isaac would somehow have to come back down that mountain. Abraham was able to trust Isaac's life to the profound fact that this first Hebrew knew the one in question.

Developing Spiritual Muscles

I look to see how the baffling things about God serve to strengthen my spiritual muscles.

Even though Abraham trusted in God's overarching promises, the yeahbutologist in me still kicks into high gear. Why would God have commanded the sacrifice of the still childless Isaac when, from the beginning, he had promised heirs specifically through Isaac? I start once again to read the story to see if there is something else I had missed. Sure enough, there it is in the first line of the story. "After these things God tested Abraham ...." This was a test of some kind. It makes sense: a lot would come to rest on Abraham. His character would have to be known. Again, the yeahbutologist: but God knew what he had in Abraham. After all, he chose Abraham decades earlier. What was left for God to know?

Several thinkers have suggested that it was not God who needed to know. It was Abraham who needed to know what he himself would and wouldn't do. It is common wisdom that until you've been in a particular situation, you don't really know what you'll do. Once again, I go back to one of the hardest, most frightening shapers of my own character which was the military crucibles of basic infantry training and Officers' Candidate School. We were being tested all the time. I always thought that it was the Army trying to find out what I could do. But I realize now that it was at least as much about me finding out what I could do. It was there that I learned the truth of what the philosopher Nietzche meant when he said, "That which doesn't kill you outright will probably make you stronger in the long run." Learning that I could survive under the worst and most terrifying circumstances has sustained me a thousand times since.

The file drawer of my childhood memory has a different folder for each of the many places I briefly lived and each of the thirteen schools I briefly attended. The file drawer of my adult years is organized into folders for each of my careers: soldier, hotel night auditor, speech and language pathologist, pastor. The people files in one folder almost never touch those in another folder. They did once.

Mary Ellen and I had taught together for years in two preschool special education nurseries. Many years after I left the schools to enter the ministry, she looked me up to introduce me to her special friend. His name was Russ. He had just been told that he only had a few weeks to live with cancer. Because I was a pastor and he had no church connection, they wondered if I would be willing to see him out and do his funeral. Russ and I took to each other like old friends who hadn't missed a beat. Seems like we had known each other forever. I really hope that gets to be true. He was one of the nicest, most genuine guys I had ever known. Never thought I would ever feel that way about a drill sergeant. But then again, he's the first one I ever got to personally know. We had served at about the same time. That just happened to be a brief period in my life when I actually fantasized about burying drill sergeants. Now I was sorry that my dream was coming true. Of all the tough things I experienced in basic training, what I most struggled with was all the yelling, the emotional battering, the threats, the punishments, the humiliations at the hands of these professional bullies. Why did they have to treat us like that? I hated that and I hated them with every cell in my body.

One of them pretended (I think) to chamber a round in his .45 pistol and point it at my head when I dozed off for the third time in class. I do have to say that I never saw one of these sergeants ever hurt anyone physically. I also never saw one of them disrespect a person because of skin color, heritage, or religion. Come to think of it, I remember noticing even then that these otherwise nasty excuses for human beings never used any profanity. But they caused us a lot of pain. And they did scare the stuffing out of almost all of us, every waking second of our miserable lives. Russ told me that it was, in fact, all an act. But a serious one. This was during the Vietnam War. The harassment was deliberately meant to stimulate and then teach us to control things like fear and anger.

Could it be the same with God? Jesus' follower who suffered the most said, "…. we rejoice in our sufferings, knowing that suffering produces endurance, and endurance produces character, and character produces hope, and hope does not put us to shame (Romans 5:3-5)." The point of it all was to develop hope.

Until my teenage years, we moved just about every year. I was always the new kid in school. I was always the one who was enrolled after the school year started. I was always the kid who had to walk into every class late, interrupting the teacher, and right in front of all the others who were settled in. I would have to display my incompetence and explain that I couldn't get my locker open, or that I got lost in the hallways, or that I got confused about which class I was supposed to be in this hour. The students bullied the "stupid" kid between classes and the teachers bullied the "stupid" kid in the classes. Every year. Every single blessed year.

"It's nice of you to join us. Find your desk. You only have three minutes now to finish the quiz."

"Open your books to page fifty-eight. Mister Garlic, come to the front and read the first paragraph. Why didn't you bring the right book?"

In my late sixties, I still have nightmares of those classrooms. I can still smell those halls. I can still hear the bell tolling my doom that class had started without me. Again. Even as I write these words, my breathing has picked up and I'm still feeling the pain all over again. Though there were dramatic exceptions, my parents usually refused to intervene with teachers who were difficult. They said many times that school was not just about developing skills of reading, writing and arithmetic. Just as importantly, they said, school was for learning social skills, like how to deal with difficult people, especially those in authority. They got that right.

In this world, we need to develop all kinds of muscles. And not just physical ones. In front of Jesus, that mother did more than simply ask for his help. She persisted when no answer seemed forthcoming. Some of the most difficult things to understand about God result in developing our spiritual muscles to live in this world and, more importantly, to live in the next one. For reasons that are yet well beyond my horizon, the spiritual muscles include things like persistence and faith and hope and love and forgiveness and obedience and selflessness and charity and prayer and dependence on God, and peace and fellowship. I have come to believe that vulnerable people and our personal trials are the schools which develop such spiritual muscles.

PART VI

THE REAL REASON

Chapter Twenty-Seven
I Grew Up In It

WHEN I WAS IN SEMINARY, WE OLDER "RETREADS" were told that the most frequent question we would get was why each of us decided to become a pastor. One professor said that his answer was that he liked potlucks a lot. I recently told someone that I became a pastor because I wanted better pay, better hours and weekends off. She returned the serve, "You weren't all that smart back then either!"

What I know for sure is that I did not decide to become a pastor in order to attend committee meetings. In fact, I was known to say that God so loved the world that he didn't send a committee. When I retired, the only promise I made to myself about retirement was that I would never again serve on a committee. But there is another old adage which says, "Man proposes, but GOD disposes." And, once again, I am proof that he has a sense of humor. It wasn't even a year after I recovered from cancer that I found myself elected to the board of directors of our homeowner association. I soon found myself at the helm, helping manage six million dollars of construction projects. Fortunately, we were blessed with the wisdom and experience of a number of people who guided us in how to analyze, evaluate, choose and supervise a labyrinth of competing contractors and technical options. Complications were expected and we were not disappointed. I would then calm myself with the assurance that we had made the best decisions after having exhaustively looked at all conceivable options.

That is not how I became a Christian and a Lutheran pastor.

The reason I'm a Christian is not because I carefully studied all the alternatives and selected the religion that most appealed to me. Neither did I choose my wife that way. It has never been about which religion or group I think is more effective in one regard or another. It's not because it makes the most sense to me. It's certainly not because Christians are the people I like the most.

Same thing applies to how I wound up in my family of origin, or the family I now am in. Or the readers I wound up with, for that matter. (Oh, hi there!)

Some people come to a family by being born into it. Others grow up in the family to which they were somehow brought. Very few of us had any say in the assignment. Mom and Dad took us to protestant churches. If they had taken us to Catholic churches, I probably would be a Catholic. If they had taken us to synagogue, I would probably be Jewish and if they had taken us to mosque, I would probably be Muslim.

I became a Lutheran pastor pretty much the same way. When the notion entered my head to maybe consider the ministry, we were worshipping in a Lutheran congregation. That's because my parents had taken me to a Lutheran church when I was a teenager. That is how I came to meet the girlfriend who would become my wife. That is how she and I came to be worshiping in a Lutheran congregation. Finally, this is why it never occurred to me to consider anything other than a Lutheran seminary.

Usually, this whole chain of events is why cynics, or some inner accuser within me says, "You're only Christian because that's what you grew up in." That dismissal has typically stimulated a defensive rebuttal in me which tries to explain why that isn't true. But, at the mechanical level of things, it IS true. There is always debate on how much of a person is the result of genetics and how much is from environment. In my case, it's kind of an unnecessary distinction, because I had nothing to do with either. My physical appearance, my personality, my name, my speech and language all have been because I was born into it. I had nothing to do with being born a free, white, upper middle class male in current day America. That totally unearned and undeserved advantage unfairly gets me at least a giant scissor step toward all kinds of opportunities. I'm now at the point of thinking that my faith in Jesus also has a lot to do with where I grew up. But even so, I'm not at all sure that all this was simply an accident of circumstance.

Chapter Twenty-Eight
Home

My Hobo Home

WHEN I WAS A LITTLE BOY, my dad and I walked a lot of miles in parades. We dressed up as hobo clowns, with little me as an identical, tiny version of my six-foot-one-inch hobo daddy. When I was an adult, I came across a poster in a store that was a close-up of a little boy hobo clown. His red, ping-pong nose had fallen off at the end of a long, long parade. Dad recognized the photo, because he was the one who always applied my make-up, which showed his unique signature. Three-year-old little me had been totally played out at the end of some long football bowl parade in California. Dad recalled that moment when a professional photographer had asked his permission to take my photo. Apparently, the man had won some big international award for it. Under the photo of the exhausted little clown was a caption: "Happiness is not always measured in smiles." Dad and I continued the gig maybe another ten years from Minnesota to California to North Dakota and back to Minnesota. Decades later after I had been ordained, Dad and I resurrected the act as a Christian clown ministry called "The Father and the Son." When my youngest daughter was in grade school, he made her up as a little girl hobo clown. Their act was called "Buddy and Babe." The last time she saw him, he lay dying of a brain tumor. She dressed up as Babe and rubbed his nose with her little red, ping-pong nose.

But once upon a time, I really was a little hobo. For maybe a half hour. In Hayward, California. Apparently, I was unhappy because my mean parents wouldn't let me do something that my friend's parents let him do. It was a second grader's version of one of the world's greatest-ever injustices. My folks said that I lived in the Garwick family and not the Finkenbinder's family. I may have escalated the conversation by saying something like they were the worst parents in the whole wide world and that I wished I could go live with the Finkenbinders. It's entirely possible that I may have said something like this before, because they seemed ready for this. They called my bluff. Both of them agreed that they totally understood and that they would help me move out. Right now, in fact. They packed Mom's little cosmetic suitcase with underwear, one shirt and one pair of pants. Then they made a little lunch for me, wrapped it in a red bandana, tied it up on the end of a broom stick and walked me to the front door. They each gave me a hug and a kiss, wished me well in my new life and handed me a nickel with the reminder to write. They closed the front door and I started my trek down the sidewalk into the big, wide world. I carried my suitcase in one hand and my hobo stick over my other shoulder. I got as far as the corner before I realized that I didn't know our address to send a letter. But I did know where my home was.

My Fernweh Home

One way or another, everybody comes into some sort of family home. One way or another, most people move away from that family of origin and establish a home of their own. Both of those homes are temporary.

Some people are also drawn to some additional place. I have always been drawn to the Emerald Isles. I've never been there, but every time I see photos or movies which take place in England, Ireland, Scotland or Wales, I feel like I belong there, like maybe I've come from there. Somehow, those lands have always called to me. Apparently, many people have these kinds of feelings about one place or another, and strangely enough it is often about those same Isles. The German language has a word for this sensation which apparently does not translate easily into English. "Fernweh" (pronounced fawn VEIGH) means something like yearning for a place to which one has never been.

I have no idea why, but my earthly fernweh seems to be the Emerald Isles. Imagine my delighted surprise when I discovered Garwick Bay on the Isle of Man, right across from Ireland! Ours is not a name that you often stumble across. In the United States alone, you're more likely to see more than 77,000 other names that are more common. At some level, it really does feel that in some way or other, I have been there. It really calls to me, almost like a homing instinct of some kind. I really do understand why reincarnation appeals to so many people. But, as with all things, the fact that something makes sense to me does not necessarily make it true.

Our families of origin, the homes we move on to, and even the fernwehs people talk about are passing, earthly things. It seems reasonable to me that these temporary homes could well be shadows of a permanent home. I suspect that Jesus Christ is my actual Fernweh. I think I must be one of his sheep. Plain and simple. There are other shepherds. Other voices do sometimes turn my head. But his voice is the only one to which I keep coming back. My guess is that I do this for the same reason that a lost child in a crowd will only recognize and walk toward the voice of her parent.

Our second grade grandson was proud to show me what he had written in school. The title on the paper was, Why I Like My Grandpa. "1. He is funny 2. He brings us toys 3. He makes pancakes 4. He takes us fun places." I cherish that paper. But I also know that these are not the real reasons he loves me. With both of "my boys", we bonded immediately. It was love at first sight. I personally have never met a little person whom I haven't thought is cute as a bug's ear. I would rush into the street to save any child. But no child will ever be the same to me as our two daughters or our two grandsons, and no woman will ever have the same place in my heart as my wife. But, beyond the fact that we are each others', I am no more capable than my second grader of objectively and really explaining our love for one another. Why this one and no other? All mushiness aside, the more we mature, the more we know that none of us is the best at anything. We learn soon enough that even the ones we love the most are far from perfect. There is always someone who is more …. whatever. Nevertheless, the mutual love among us in our family is deeper and more intense than for anyone else on Earth. Go figure.

But I'm not at all sure that the love within our family goes far enough to explain the reason for my faith in

Jesus Christ. After all, I obviously do not say that everybody else should have that same relationship with my wife that I do! It would be ludicrous to suggest that such a relationship with my wife would be the only way that somebody could acquire citizenship. But as a traditional Christian, I do say precisely those things about Jesus, that he is the only one who is able to save every soul on Earth.

My guess is that whoever is seeking a reason to believe in Jesus is someone who possibly has always been a sheep of his fold. It sometimes seems to me that when a person cannot ignore Jesus, it may be because she recognizes the voice of her shepherd. When I see someone continually attack Christianity, I hear Queen Gertrude in Hamlet whisper, "The lady doth protest too much, methinks." Such people strike me as candidates for eventually returning home. I suspect that the person who is not currently one of his sheep would more likely hear the voice of Jesus and not have the slightest interest in wasting any time or energy on the issue.

Perhaps I am writing this memoir simply because I am a sheep of the Great Shepherd. Could also be why one or two readers may have waded through all of this.

Hope to see you later.